Managing change in organizations

Third edition

....

Managing change in organizations

Third edition

....

Colin A. Carnall

An imprint of **Pearson Education**

Harlow, England · London · New York · Reading, Massachusetts · San Francisco
Toronto · Don Mills, Ontario · Sydney · Tokyo · Singapore · Hong Kong · Seoul
Taipei · Cape Town · Madrid · Mexico City · Amsterdam · Munich · Paris · Milan

Pearson Education Limited
Edinburgh Gate
Harlow
Essex CM20 2JE
England

and Associated Companies throughout the world

Visit us on the World Wide Web at:
http://www.pearsoneduc.com

Typeset in 9.5 on 12 pt Stone Serif
by Mathematical Composition Setters Ltd, Salisbury, Wiltshire, England

Printed and bound in Great Britain by
Bell & Bain Ltd., Glasgow

Library of Congress Cataloging-in-Publication Data

Available from the publisher

British Library Cataloguing in Publication Data

A catalogue record for this book is available from
the British Library

ISBN 0-13-916297-6

10 9 8 7 6 5 4
06 05 04 03 02

Contents

....

Preface to the 3rd Edition

·············

This edition represents a significant step forward in my thinking about change in organizations. Over the past 10 years or so a significant number of organizational innovations have emerged. So much so that the organizations we now create are fundamentally different. Where once the focus was upon command and control, now the focus is upon value added for customers and for other stake-holders.

I have retained the practitioner style of previous editions. Nevertheless I continue to belive that the practitioner seeks the guidance that useful theory can povide to direct practical work. Theory into practice remains the key focus of the book.

This edition includes new material on the organization of the future, learning organization, a value added workbook to help readers rethink their own organization and a new ending which seeks to draw out the conceptual links which run through the book.

As before I must acknowledge the advice, help and co-operation of many people in organizations around the world as we have worked on these problems. Our purpose has always been to create the future organization. Certainly I have learned much from these efforts. I have also valued the feedback from many readers who have taken value from earlier editions and taken the trouble to feed that back.

Business transformation

CHAPTER 1

The transformation perspective

Introduction

For 15 years I have engaged in teaching, writing, researching and consulting in the field of organizational change. Throughout that time I have taken the view that the implementation of change is difficult, time consuming and often requires 'mind-set', culture and value change. I have also believed that the route to such changes lies in behaviour: put people in new settings within which they have to behave differently and, if properly trained, supported and rewarded, their behaviour will change. If successful this will lead to mind-set change and ultimately will impact upon the culture of the organization.

I have viewed the strategic change literature with a degree of scepticism in at least one respect. Much of the literature at least implies that the strategy bit is easy. This view holds that it is only when we get to implementation that the fun starts. This is natural enough. Corporate history is full of organizations which proved unable to implement strategy. Hamel (1996) convincingly argues that strategy is only easy when the process of strategy formulation limits the scope of discovery, the breadth of involvement and the intellectual effort expended. If the focus is upon planning to convert market research into next year's budget then strategy is about programme, not about the future of the organization longer term. And yet many organizations are changing the 'rules of the game' within which they operate. The boundaries of industries are shifting. New entrants are revolutionizing industries. When computer companies enter education they bring an impetus towards revolutionary change. When retailers act as banks by offering cash at the checkout they do the same. When consumers can get a credit card from General Motors or where insurance is sold by telephone, we are looking at fundamental reconfigurations of industries. Thus it is that a book on how to change organizations must look at how organizations themselves have been and are being transformed. Part of the focus of this book is to examine the new forms of organization now emerging which are fundamentally different to the traditional hierarchical model. We seek to understand how and why they are emerging and how change can be handled within and through these new organizational models.

New 'rules for the organizational game'

To explore this theme let us turn to two case studies.

CASE STUDY

Ford and the Global Car

Under the label Ford 2000 the company seeks to transform itself into a global corporation deploying a new 'philosophy' of doing business (see Parry-Jones (1996) for more detail).

By 1993, despite being profitable, the world's second-largest automotive producer engaged on a major programme of development. Ford also recognized itself as part of a complex and intensively competitive sector, not least with issues of oversupply in various markets. The existing business philosophy emphasized the production of cars in the regions where they were to be sold. Yet Ford was engaged in separate development processes in different regions of the world for what were essentially similar products. Moreover, whilst Ford was well positioned in the USA and Europe, it was less well placed in those areas where growth in demand is likely.

Moreover, customers are more sophisticated, more demanding and more aware of what is available around the world. The market is increasingly global. The company has merged its semi-autonomous regional operations into a single world-wide business. Product development will focus globally.

Change of this type had been attempted earlier in Ford's history. The Escort development had been shared by teams in Europe and North America but differentiation resulted. Amalgamations within Europe were achieved in the late 1960s. The Escort experience lead Ford to realize that a world car development needed single leadership to achieve the needed integration – easy to say but not easy to achieve. The Mondeo development was a further stage in the process. Lead from Europe, this work was facilitated by a communications infrastructure allowing the sharing and analysis of data and decision making across borders. The communications infrastructure supports a world-wide engineering release system, a world-wide purchasing system and a global conferencing facility. Are these infrastructure developments not as important as the concept of single leadership in enabling the company to overcome the problems of national pride and narrow perception that limited the past attempts?

In turn the Mondeo development lead Ford to learn vital lessons, in particular

▶▶

'simultaneous engineering'. Achieved via 'vertically integrated teams', it contrasts with the former sequential process with its attendant possibilities for conflict between those who design and those who manufacture the product. In early 1994 a 'study team' of 27 managers from a variety of functions and countries began a 10 week programme looking at how to learn the lessons of the past and achieve genuine globalization. It was decided to merge the existing operations in Europe and North America. Ford established five vehicle centres to take lifetime responsibility for the development of all vehicles of a given class produced and sold anywhere in the world. In addition Ford has created a single global unit for technology development. All employees with Automotive Operations have been deployed within this world-wide 'matrix'. The vehicle centre is responsible for developing and launching new vehicles and has lifetime responsibility for quality, serviceability, profitability and overall programme management. Formerly the development team's work ended at launch.

The focus therefore is upon *horizontal integration*. Not least of the advantages is that decisions can be made closer to the action. With the introduction of an integrated global cycle plan for product launch, major product changes are planned to be achieved in half the time. The matrix combines vertical integration with horizontal integration and raises fundamental questions about the role of senior management in devising strategy, ensuring that the needed capabilities are in place and so on.

We point to two themes relevant to this book, as follows:

1. Ford has begun the process of rethinking itself as a business. Specifically it seeks to emphasize the horizontal process of creating value for customers, not least because doing so provides opportunities to exploit economies across the horizontal value stream.

2. Whether or not you deem Ford to be a 'learning organization' it is clear that Ford has learnt a number of lessons, each of which allowed it to create a new part of the 'platform' from which it now seeks to globalize.

As we shall see throughout this book, these two themes reoccur frequently when looking at leading-edge practice in strategic change.

CASE STUDY

'Changing Childbirth'

In 1993 the UK Department of Health published a report entitled 'Changing Childbirth'. By the early 1980s evidence of dissatisfaction as a result of fragmented care and obstetrician-led

▶▶

services was apparent. Continuity of care was emerging alongside the perception that women desired choice of care and place of delivery and the right of control over their own bodies at all stages of pregnancy and birth.

Whilst the research, evidence and analysis underpinning and providing the context for 'Changing Childbirth' is complex and not short of controversy, for our purposes the focus of the report for maternity practice is best summarized by quoting the report's indicators of success (within 5 years, i.e. by 1998):

- Every woman should know one midwife who ensures continuity of her midwifery care – the named midwife.

- At least 30 per cent of women should have the midwife as their lead professional.

- At least 75 per cent of women should know the person who cares for them during their delivery.

- At least 30 per cent of women delivered in a maternity unit should be admitted under the management of the midwife.

Often measures designed to achieve these success indicators were being devised in the context of another development, integrated patient care (IPC).

IPC is an example of a general rethinking of patient care brought in from the USA in the early 1990s. It focuses upon aspects of care such as continuity of care, improved documentation, physical redesign of buildings, locating facilities close to patients, staff role reviews, etc. Sometimes known as patient-focused care (PFC), this philosophy places the patient at the centre, seeks active involvement of the patient, continuity of care, decentralization, multi-skilling of care staff and streamlined documentation. Finally a further concept is the *pathway of care*, which in essence is the time sequence of events, tests, assessments, experiences and outcomes associated with the patient's care process. If the objective is to seek high-quality 'seamless' care for individual patients across the boundaries of department, directorate and discipline into which hospitals have been fashioned by history, then *horizontal focus* is a key issue.

At Brighton Health Care NHS Trust these concepts have been implemented along with team midwifery within the community. Three teams of six full-time equivalent midwives based in different geographical locations aimed to provide 24 hour care for 250–350 women. The service encompassed all aspects of midwifery care including home assessment of labour and care continuity. An early evaluation concluded that team midwifery enabled Brighton to provide a more patient-centred care at the same high standard of care (avoiding a perceived risk of the team approach) with no evidence of decreased satisfaction for the women involved (there has been a very high reported satisfaction) or for midwives (again a concern which did not appear to materialize).

The early research (see Hart, 1997) indicates significant progress towards 'Changing Childbirth' success indicators. Whilst some evidence of tension emerged between team midwives and their labour-ward colleagues, it was also clear that there were many perceived advantages. Moreover, many of the negative points emerging appeared to be linked to other factors, i.e. workloads in general, problems of working conditions, problems over grading within the reward arrangements. Clearly continuity of care was seen as linked

▶▶

positively to job satisfaction. The general practitioners interviewed were satisfied both with the service overall and with team midwifery but this was not without perceived problems, some related to the adequacy of resourcing and GP involvement (which may lessen given continuity of team-based care?).

Interestingly enough, recommendations for further development place much emphasis upon developing relationships, partnerships and care protocols (which define the parameters within which care professionals practise). Care protocols are clearly intended as a means of ensuring clear definition of roles and thereby to create a platform for improved partnerships. Overall the case study powerfully reinforces the horizontal focus of strategic change, applied not principally to reduce costs but rather to create improved care. That said, we do not suggest that cost effectiveness is not a key driver behind innovations of this kind, albeit given the apparently infinite demand for health care this is probably more about securing higher volume of activity within existing budgets, i.e. about reducing cost per case. The other crucial point here is the essential role of *partnership*. Partnership between professional groups both within the hospital and in the community is essential and represents a complex challenge in the health care environment for the latter part of this century.

Thus from these two case studies we see evidence of new thinking in three areas as follows:

1. Rethinking the organization in terms of a horizontal stream of value-added activities focused upon customers/clients.

2. The learning organization and how to achieve that state.

3. The vital role of partnerships.

Thus it is clear that the world of major change is no longer simply a world concerned with 'resistance to change'. Indeed I have often wondered why 'resistance to change' loomed so large in discussions about change. Many argue that people are motivated by challenging jobs, discretion, autonomy, etc. These same people also pointed to the prevalence of 'resistance to change' without posing the obvious question. Change seems likely to create the very conditions which people are supposed to find motivating. Therefore why are we so concerned about 'resistance to change'?

Changing organizations

Many offered an easy answer. Change was being driven by new technology. New technology destroyed jobs and, some said, diminished many of the jobs which remained. At the time some commentators obviously felt that there was a finite amount of work to do. If technology destroyed jobs then either there would be fewer jobs around or working weeks would need to be reduced, the retirement age reduced and other innovations such as job shares would be needed.

Without suggesting that the economic problems of the modern world had been 'solved' and taking account of the point that the structure of employment had changed dramatically (e.g. more part-time work), even a cursory glance at employment statistics in the western world suggests that much of this 'lump of work' or 'finite limits of work' argument is nonsense. Throughout the 1980s more people have entered employment despite the fact that technology and other changes have increased productivity, often quite quickly. Again I recall being impressed by talk of 3–4 per cent p.a. improvements in productivity in the 1960s. Now 6–8 per cent p.a. can be commonplace, particularly when recession or competition stimulates corporate restructuring. Moreover, in case after case improvements of 50 per cent or more are commonplace now. And yet this is not the only change since 1971. The power of 'vested' interests is now by no means as strong. Whether you believe that this is due to 'Thatcherism' or to long-term social and economic changes is unimportant. It is nevertheless the case that collectivist ideas have given way to a focus on the individual. Indeed the moral challenge we now face is whether 'possessive' individualism is to be the order of the day (Macpherson, 1962).

Thus various changes have gone forward across much of the world. In particular public sector organizations have been privatized; market mechanisms have been introduced; large organizations have been broken up; and others have been 'flattened'. Decentralization has created corporate structures focused on 'strategic business units'. People talk about 'networked organizations', 'federal' organizations and empowerment.

It is obvious that all of this has placed greater demands on the capabilities of managers. But these changes have also transformed the nature of what some call the 'psychological contract between the employing organization and the employee'. If 'jobs for life' cannot be guaranteed, then people have to apply for their 'own' jobs on reorganization; where flattened structures mean empowerment for some but redundancy for others, you would expect that to happen. Where organizations use early retirement or voluntary retirement as an essential part of policy and where some organizations emphasize the benefits to organization and employee of subcontracting, maintaining a stable core of permanent employees and a periphery of subcontractors, they are reflecting a significant change.

Once upon a time managers and professionals and, for that matter, other employees, particularly skilled employees, expected to stay on one career path and in one organization throughout their careers. Now people *expect* careers to include periods in more than one organization and expect to have more than one career in a working life.

It would defy common sense to suggest that social changes of this extent would have no impact on the nature of the relationship between employer and employee. One depiction of this change was published in the *Harvard Business Review* 'Global Management Survey, 1990'. Every 10 years HBR surveys chief executives throughout the developed world. Roughly 6500 CEOs responded in 1990. In Figure 1.1 we reproduce the results for one question in which CEOs were asked to describe managers, either senior or 'all others'.

From the figure we can see that CEOs at least view managers as better educated, more creative, more ambitious, but less loyal. Indeed the survey suggests that this is true in each of the countries surveyed, even in Japan, although the relative position, particularly on loyalty, is different. I have discussed this figure with hundreds of man-

Global Management Survey				
	Well educated	Creative	Ambitious	Loyalty
Senior managers 1980 1990	36 66	23 48	25 58	49 37
Others 1980 1990	22 52	18 37	16 37	48 32

Figure 1.1 Global Management Survey

agement audiences throughout Europe. All agree that the change is real. All suggest that this change is a consequence of various social, economic and technological changes. But all emphasize that loyalty is a two-way process and that organizations demonstrate less loyalty to their managers, mainly as a consequence of de-layering and other major changes which have lead to the 'redundant executive' capturing as much if not more of our attention than the redundant unskilled or semi-skilled worker.

All of this suggests that the statement so often articulated, 'the most important resource of this business is its people', is increasingly meaningful not merely as rhetoric but also in practice. If we depend more and more on fewer people and if the loyalty of those people, particularly managers, can no longer be assumed but rather must be earned and retained, then clearly we need to be concerned about how we utilize them, develop them and resource them and about the opportunities for rewards, promotion and success which we provide. If changes depend upon the people who implement them then one must be concerned to ensure that those people possess the necessary skills. If those same people are motivated by challenge and opportunity then we must provide that as well. But if the latter will only follow if changes are successful then the introduction of changes which our people view as being credible, as likely to succeed, becomes a paramount issue.

Does this not then mean that the task of developing, implementing and managing major strategic changes becomes a key management challenge of the modern world? Some say that it must begin with the articulation of strategic vision. You need to be able to conceive of what the organization might become in 3 or 5 or more year's time. To do this managers must combine analysis and intuition, knowing and doing, thinking and feeling. Visualizing strategic change is not merely a matter of analysis, it requires the ability to think about, to conceptualize, the future, the willingness to experiment and learn, to see what might happen, to estimate how the organization might respond, and much more.

But all of this relates to individual behaviour which will take place in teams, whether boards of directors, management teams, working parties or whatever. Thus we need a range of inputs into the discussion and debate on strategy if we are to understand the social, political, economic and technological trends with which we must deal, and so we need many inputs perhaps both from inside and outside the organization. However, if we are to bring these people together effectively then we must adopt managerial styles conducive to learning, to development, to creating and to articulating/communicating vision. In part it demands that we understand the processes of innovation, adaptation and change – what hinders change at individual, group, unit and corporate level and what can be done about these 'blockages'. Processes such as these are often referred to under the rubric 'culture change'.

Here we simply wish to make the point that successful strategic change seems to demand a combination of cognitive/analytical skills and knowledge alongside a range of behavioural or process skills and knowledge. In Figure 1.2 we set out a 'map' of the cognitive/analytical components which appear to be needed. Here we suggest that successful strategic change requires knowledge and techniques for corporate diagnosis, in the culture change area and in putting together programmes of change. All of this is not enough, however, without the necessary process skills needed to encourage learning and change.

In a world in which the ability to change is a key 'engine of success' the shift from strategy into capability demands leadership, action planning, the ability to cope with pressure and uncertainty and a willingness to learn. More analysis helps us in that it aids our understanding of where we are and how we came to get there – but analysis alone will not create the future.

From Figure 1.2 we see that strategic diagnosis is driven by and/or formed by ideas formulated about the future of the organization leading to a 'vision of the future'.

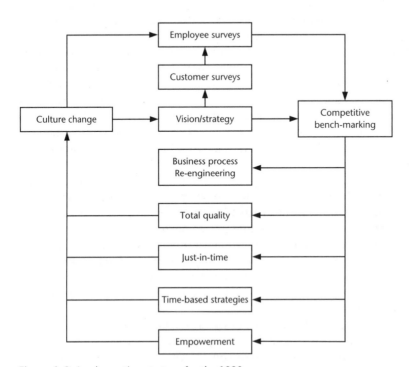

Figure 1.2 Implementing strategy for the 1990s

There are techniques available for vision/strategy formulation, employee surveys, customer surveys and competitive bench-marking and so on, but it is important to focus initially on what we are doing in the diagnosis process. We are not merely attempting to collect symptomatic evidence but to *understand* what has happened. Thus falling sales or increasing costs are problems which demand some form of change, but it is impossible to say what without understanding *why*. So much is obvious enough but rarely do we really attempt to understand what has happened as part of a preparatory diagnosis of what and how to change an organization.

Miller (1990) provides us with an impressive treatment of the dynamics of corporate success, decline and renewal. This is important both because it extends the ideas of how the seeds of success and failure can be understood and because it provides us with a better understanding of the corporate dynamics within which we are enmeshed and attempt to transform and introduce changes. In turn this is vital simply because much treatment of change is too narrowly focused.

What does this mean? Basically most studies of change are narrowly focused on what is being changed and are treated in rather a static way. Thus we see that an organization is deemed to need improved quality and the discussion focuses upon the implementation of a total quality management programme and the associated culture changes needed for it to be successful. Rarely is any attempt made to carry out a longitudinal study (there are a few rare exceptions to this) but even less often is there any real attempt to examine the dynamics which created the need for a total quality management programme in the first place. Thus it is that we often cannot judge whether or not the programme will succeed.

Why is it that people are often managed inappropriately in a period of change? There are two main reasons. Managers managing change are under pressure. This pressure undermines their own performance. Also, organizations often do not possess managers who are sufficiently skilful in handling change. Kotter (1988), for example, suggests one 'syndrome' associated with inadequate leadership, which we might similarly associate with inadequate change management. In summary, the argument is that successful organizations can carry the seeds of their own later decline, unless managers learn to be both successful and adaptable. The syndrome is set out in Figure 1.3. The tensions created by declining performance create performance problems.

Thus the argument combines the success of a few key people, a period of early success and growing organizational complexity followed by declining performance creating pressures towards short-termism and an inward focus. All of this can lead to a lack of credibility amongst top management combined with a 'fear of failure' throughout the organization.

Particularly interesting is the point about 'fear of failure'; the pressures are dual in nature. On the one hand the short-term approach combined with a functional or departmental orientation, centralization and autocratic management styles creates a powerful tendency to limit risk taking. On the other, managers moving rapidly through careers and not having to face up to their mistakes do not learn the interpersonal skills needed to do so. They find facing up to performance issues difficult. Therefore, when forced to do so by those same short-term pressures, they often do so inadequately and in a volatile, even primitive, fashion. This further reduces risk taking, over time creating an organization within which the 'fear of failure' is very high

Stage 1: the firm is in a strong position, with little competition. It develops systems, man-
          agement practices and a culture which depend on a few capable leaders. The
          management style is a combination of autocratic, directive and paternalistic

Stage 2: the firm grows and becomes more complex. Competition increases and new
          technology emerges. The firm now needs strong and capable leadership but
          does not have enough people with these skills. Many people with good leader-
          ship potential left because of the frustrations created in stage 1. However, the
          firm's performance does not deteriorate dramatically. It remains well placed in its
          established markets. It 'lives' off its reputation.

Stage 3: declining performance leads to a focus on short-term results. Internal tensions
          lead to conflict which cannot be handled constructively. Senior managers seem
          incapable of facing these tensions. Functional rather than corporate policies
          prevail. The firm lacks a co-ordinated strategy. This, in turn, undermines efforts
          to improve the quality of management.

Figure 1.3 Syndrome of ineffective leadership and change management (after Kotter, 1988)

indeed. There is a powerful 'vicious circle' in place continually reinforcing any tendency to underperformance.

Kotter (1988) identifies a number of the 'characteristics needed, to provide effective leadership', overcoming the problems identified in the syndrome outlined above. To be effective, leaders need a range of knowledge of industry, business functions and the firm. Also needed are a broad range of contacts and good working relationships in the firm and the industry. Linked to this will be a good track record in a relatively broad set of activities. Kotter also refers to 'keen minds' (whatever that means), strong interpersonal skills, high integrity, seeing value in people, and a strong desire to lead.

All of this points us towards the new strategy paradigm proposed by Hamel and Prahalad (1994). For them, competing for the future means lifting our sights. Re-engineering internal processes is not enough, we must regenerate strategies. Transforming the organization is essential but the winners (such as CNN) transform their industry. Having strategic plans focuses attention internally; what is needed is a new strategic architecture. The essential point is that it may be necessary to re-engineer our processes to reduce cost and improve service but that is insufficient to gain competitive advantage because our competitors can do the same. To be successful we must create new strategies aimed at transforming our industry – whether it is food, medicine, education, entertainment or whatever. In the modern world renewal demands that we do more than identify how to do more, better and for less. We must also regenerate what we do.

Kay (1995) attempts to identify the origins of corporate success from distinctive structures of relationships between the corporation and employees, customers and suppliers. Continuity and stability in these relationships allow for a flexible and co-operative response to change. At the core of his analysis lies the concept of added value. This, he argues, derives from the architecture of the firm (basically the structure of relationships referred to above) and the application of distinctive capabilities in particular markets. Continuity and stability provide for the development of organizational knowledge (of its identity, vision, distinctive capabilities and invisible assets (Itami, 1987)), the free exchange of information, and a readiness to respond quickly and flexibly to changes in the world.

In turn the distinctive capabilities which provide the basis of competitive advantage are architecture, innovation, reputation and strategic assets. Architecture is both internal (the corporate structure and management processes) and external (networks of relationships with suppliers and other organizations – joint ventures, strategic alliances, etc.). Strategic assets are the inherent advantages a corporation may possess (e.g. licences, access to scarce factors) which cannot easily be copied.

'Strategic bench-marking' has taken up a vital role in organizational diagnosis for change. This adds an important idea to the concept of diagnosis. The vital point is to compare your own organization with the world's best. Thus we identify where we are, the causes of our present situation *and* (through bench-marking) we identify the potential for improvement and ideas for change. Bench-marking as a technique has evolved (at least in principle and concept) from first-generation bench-marking in which the focus would be on bench-marking a particular product or system, through competitive bench-marking, process bench-marking, strategic bench-marking to 'global bench-marking'. Thus the ambitions of its proponents are nothing short of being world class.

Most importantly bench-marking represents a learning technique. Essentially cognitive in orientation, it applies rational analysis based on comparisons to the process of diagnosis. It is also (like all diagnosis) an intervention in the system and must be understood as such.

Similarly, business process re-engineering has attracted wide attention and many adherents (and cynics). Admittedly more than a technique for diagnosing what needs to be changed, it nevertheless incorporates techniques for diagnosis. Most importantly, proponents of this approach conceive it as a technology for breakthrough or 'discontinuous leaps in performance'. The focus is upon the 'business architecture' – locations, structure, technology and skills. Alongside the analysis of the business architecture conceived in terms of value added is risk assessment looking at change and organizational issues. Our contention is that in techniques such as bench-marking and business process re-engineering we see a combination of the soft organizational development approaches of the 1970s and the socio-technical systems school, but now operationalized because of the opportunities provided by new information infrastructures. Thus diagnosis has become more thorough and broader in scope.

Transforming the organization

Managing major changes successfully requires us to take an organization-wide approach. Change creates stress and strain both for those who support change (through overwork, the challenge of leading change in an uncertain world, the pressure of dealing with other, often anxious, people, the inherent uncertainties all are subject to in some degree and so on) and for those who are either indifferent, opposed or fearful of change.

Organizational learning is a vital component of effective change. Following the work of Quinn (see in particular Quinn, 1992) organizational restructuring and strategic change should be based upon effective diagnosis and bench-marking, information and incentive systems. A key point, however, in achieving strategic change amidst organizational circumstances looking less and less like traditional hierarchical structures is that 'managed incrementalism' is a strategy for change implementation explicitly designed to manage risk. However, this does not need to imply that change is slow, random or gradual.

All of this assumes that change implementation requires the following:

● that we build an awareness of the need for change;

● that the case for changes is made convincingly and credibly;

● that the process of change is a learning process – you don't get everything right initially;

● that dramatic changes can feel chaotic and uncertain as people seek to come to terms with new skills etc.;

● that attention must be given to broadening and mobilizing support for change, whether through task forces and project teams, through the use of incentive systems and training, through pilot schemes and so on;

● crystallizing the vision and focus for the organization but not necessarily – at the outset, indeed initially, the vision may be very broad, and much has to be learned before an *emerging* strategic vision can be articulated;

● that the focus is on people and on the process of change.

Alexander (1988) provides a review of the implementation literature. He supports the idea of Pressman and Wildavsky (1973) that 'Policies are continuously transformed by implementation actions that simultaneously alter resources and objectives'. Thus strategy (or policy) and implementation interact and emerge. Alexander also notes that implementors are, or should be, concerned both with preventing failure (by avoiding the common implementation problems) and promoting success.

There are three learning modes which are of relevance to managers concerned by change, as follows:

1. *Learning by doing*: this is an internal process. We learn by experimentation, by trial and error, by pilot trials and so on.

2. *Learning by use*: this is essentially learning from the external world. We learn about how to improve our own product/services by gaining feedback from customers and by competitive bench-marking. Thus we gain from the customer's experience of using our products/services and through comparing ourselves with competitor organizations.

3. *Learning from failure*: which speaks for itself but which, to be available to us, demands that we accept that failure will happen from time to time.

Our argument is that concepts such as transformational leadership, entrepreneurship and the learning organization each embrace these ideas. Beyond this we recognize that major changes are typically implemented as major programmes organized around simple themes (e.g. 'right first time' for total quality programmes or 'next steps programme' for major programmes of culture change).

A good current example is that of 'time-based competition'. The key idea is that the way we manage time – whether in production, in new product development, in sales and distribution – represents a powerful source of competitive advantage. This idea has spawned another, that of 'business process re-engineering'. At the core of both is a strategy for change utilizing analytical techniques to analyze the organization, seeking continuous improvements to work and information flows and to the use of time. The emphasis is upon the organization doing the work itself, utilizing its own people, empowering people at all levels to achieve change. Bench-marking is a key analytical technique utilized in such programmes as are techniques such as 'pilots' and 'break-through teams'. According to Stalk and Hout (1990) breakthrough teams should be given radical goals such as reducing time in half in order that assumptions will be challenged. Bottlenecks, breakdowns, failures, unmet customer needs all become opportunities to learn. All of this implies radically new ways of thinking about the organization.

Finally Argyris (1993) explains something of the constraints to achieving effective learning in organizations by pointing to the distinction between what he calls single-loop and double-loop learning. At the core of his explanation are two key points about professionals (managers and a growing proportion of employees are professionals or quasi-professionals of one sort or another), as follows:

1. Essentially the life experience of most professionals through schooling, university and early career is characterized by success, not failure. Because they have rarely failed they have never learned how to learn from failure. Thus when things go wrong for them they become defensive, screen out criticism and put the 'blame' on others. Ironically their ability to learn shuts down just as they need it most.

2. In common with our opening remarks for this book, Argyris takes the view that organizations assume that learning is a problem of motivation. Thus create the right structures of communication, rewards and authority and accountability – designed to create motivated and committed employees – and learning and development will follow. Sadly Argyris tells us, this is fatally flawed. People learn through how they think – through the cognitive rules or reasoning they use to design and implement their action.

For Argyris organizations can learn how to encourage learning, how to resolve these learning dilemmas. At the root of his solution is to find ways of constructively questioning the rationale or reasoning behind someone's actions.

Let me give you an example from my own experience. The day before I came to write these lines I was acting as chairman of the audit committee of the board of directors of an organization in which I am a non-executive director. The organization had, last year, subcontracted its internal audit work to an outside firm. We were discussing the report from the internal audit for the last year and considering the plan for the current financial year. We had noticed that the budget for last year had included 25 days for 'management and planning'. The out-turn had been 30 days and the budget for the current year was 32 days. In our view 25 days (which represented 10 per cent of the internal audit budget) was high. No explanation was given for the 30 days out-turn nor to justify a budget of 32 days this year. We raised a series of questions. What activities were included in management and planning'? What was the value of those days? We also noted that overruns on various audit projects undertaken by the firm during the last year had been due to problems of getting information – was this a sign of good planning? Or of the need for more planning? The director of the internal audit firm was defensive. He referred to industry norms of up to 20 per cent for planning audit work. We acknowledged that but pointed out that the audit needed for our organization was relatively straightforward. Eventually he said, 'Well I had hoped that we could develop a co-operative approach and engage in a free and frank discussion'. To which our reply was: 'That's what we are doing!' There is little doubt in my mind that the criticism had placed him on the defensive, automatically. Whilst he recognized that he sought an open relationship he felt drawn to defend the number of days ascribed to 'management and planning'. More importantly he felt constrained from explaining that the reason for the high number of actual days was that there had been so many problems during the previous year (in which the organization, and, therefore, the finance function, had been founded) that he and other senior colleagues had been forced to spend time on site problem solving in order to get things done. To say so would be to be critical of the finance director – or at least apparently so!

Argyris argues that people can be taught to reason in ways which reduce and overcome organizational defences. To quote from the extract:

> they will discover that the kind of reasoning necessary to reduce and overcome organizational defenses is the same kind of 'tough reasoning' that underlies the effective use of ideas in strategy, finance, marketing, manufacturing and other management disciplines ... it depends on collecting valid data, analyzing it carefully, and constantly testing inferences drawn from the data .... Good strategists make sure that their conclusions can withstand all kinds of critical questioning.

At its basics, then, 'productive reasoning'.

The value-added organization

As I write this chapter I have just completed the review of an MBA dissertation draft. The author works for a global telecommunications business. His company is concerned that they are not achieving the rate of change required of world-class companies in that sector. I was struck by part of his diagnosis which reads as follows:

> Current change methodologies are employed within functional silos and the informal way in which strategy is cascaded through various differentiated groups and departments dilutes the value of the strategy ... [which] should be focused on understanding how the business processes deliver overall enterprise value ... needs to develop a process for implementing strategic improvement ideas in those value streams.

This quote captures two or three 'big' ideas about change. Firstly, that many change programmes fail because they are implemented within a part of the organization – there is an absence of an integrated approach as between divisions, departments and the like. Secondly, that successful change may best be achieved by focusing change efforts horizontally, i.e. along the customer value stream rather than vertically up or down the structure. This idea does not negate all the notions of bottom-up, top-down and cascading change programmes which you will have read about, experienced and/or managed, but it does provide a different perspective when thinking about change.

Another 'big' idea is that of organizational learning, whether in the context of strategy, management development, organizational development or major change. Many practitioners and consultants/researchers point to the vital role of organizational learning in a period of change. In so far as major change involves implementing new organizational arrangements to deal with new conditions (whether in external markets or internally within the organization) it is obvious that change requires and leads to learning. It requires learning if the need for change is to be accepted. It involves learning particularly because our initial attempt to resolve the change problem needs to be evolved with experience.

However, the circumstances within which we seek to engender change are now fundamentally different. We are each of us aware of the fundamental changes going on: globalization, deregulation of markets, new technology, privatization, fundamental rethinking about the nature and role of the state, and so on. Moreover, we are each of us dealing with the organizational consequences, including downsizing, flattening of structures, empowerment, outsourcing, strategic focus, the 'lean' organization, acquisitions and mergers, joint ventures and strategic alliances, multi-functional team working and much more. Many now conclude that the 'mind-set' through which senior managers view the world has changed in consequence.

Therefore, the characteristic model of the successful organization has changed. Once we sought economies of scale via horizontal and vertical integration. Eventually we discovered that these economies of scale were often illusory. Some of the 'costs' of scale were increasingly alienated and demotivated employees but, in particular, inflexible and inwardly focused organizations. Observers concerned with these problems noted two linked points:

1. What appeared to be a growing alienation of many within modern society coalesced around attitudes to bureaucracy – whether public or private. Organizations which could give genuine priority to delivering value to customers would begin to break down the alienation many felt about these large bureaucracies.
2. Whatever else we could say about large, multi-level bureaucracies it is obvious that they are expensive, but much less obvious that they deliver value for money.

And so many began to seek means of encouraging flexibility and entrepreneurship. This led to a fundamental shift in our thinking about how to change organizations.

Traditionally, we have sought to change the organization within its existing boundary. We have not sought to ask whether or not the boundaries themselves should be changed. The one exception is a change strategy adopted throughout this century – that of acquisitions and mergers. It is not our purpose here to discuss this topic. Here we merely point out that such a change strategy involves rethinking the boundary of the organizations as pieces (companies, divisions, etc.) are added or subtracted.

This tendency to rethink the boundary of the organization has accelerated as part of the changing mind-set we refer to above – and indeed may have caused that change in the first place. Throughout most of this century the large, integrated and centralized organization was excellent at co-ordination and control – and may have been good at settling conflict (although personally I doubt it, though it may have been good at reducing the level of manifest conflict). Conversely, in order to seek higher levels of innovation, organizations first decentralized via the multi-divisional form. But faced with the continued problems and the inability to develop every new technology/capability internally, organizations increasingly decentralized through joint ventures, alliances and ultimately 'the virtual company'.

Here, however, we note something which is becoming a standard of management practice when the focus is upon the supply chain. Firstly, a company needs to build strong ties with its suppliers in order to secure its ability to pursue innovation, improvement and enhanced value. Secondly, a company needs to develop critical technologies *internally* if it is to secure its position on the value chain. Here we see the argument that strategic networks can be very effective as a means of acquiring particular capabilities and of creating high-powered incentives towards improvement, change and enhanced value. Our concern here is not to evaluate the argument, but merely to emphasize the new style of thinking involved in even raising the question.

Most importantly for our present purpose we have seen a tendency to replace planned, organizational change with market-induced change. Sometimes the market mechanisms are internal – and there is a long history of the development of such mechanisms – e.g. performance-related pay schemes, the emergence of strategic business units, the development of competence-based models for performance management, share option schemes and so on. Increasingly we see the tendency to use market mechanisms to secure change. Strategic alliances, networks, outsourcing, deregulation are all attempts to introduce or encourage market-based incentives. The idea of purchasing being separated from provision has influenced companies and governments. In the UK and elsewhere in the world, government departments have been converted to free-standing agencies. The UK health service has been reorganized into large-scale purchasing authorities and self-governing trusts providing hospital and other services alongside general practitioners providing primary care. Similarly, a global business such as Glaxo has reconfigured itself from having regional sales operatives supplied by regional factories to a situation in which the sales business is free to source from the best available supplier. Here the certainties of allocated budgets are replaced by the pressures, disciplines and incentives of competition.

But is this sufficient? At the same time we all of us point to our present anxieties and uncertainties. Some argue that this is a consequence of downsizing and a consequential higher risk of unemployment. Others point to the growth in part-time employment. Critics of this kind of thinking point out that unemployment has not changed in the world's leading economies over the last 20 years, although the level fluctuates, inevitably. You can counter this by arguing the view that the big change is that for the first time it is middle-class employees experiencing job insecurity. They are more vocal and we are experiencing the consequences. Perhaps also the shift in organizational mind-set referred to above is relevant. Where the focus of activity is the horizontal value chain it may be that people who once understood to whom they report must now report to more than one individual and meet multiple and sometimes even conflicting (certainly ambiguous) performance objectives.

One formulation of how to achieve economic success in the midst of these ambiguities relates to the concept of 'trust' or social capital. The most influential recent work is that of Fukuyama (1995). For him one solution to the problem of scale lies in the emergence of networks such as businesses held together by family ties, cross-ownership, long experience of joint work and so on. In particular, he points to the advantages of establishing long-term relationships between members of a network. All of this is now known to us as supply chain management. He argues that networks based upon reciprocal obligation enable scale to be achieved without the problems of size and alienation referred to above. These networks appear to have emerged in societies with cultures which encourage high levels of trust (e.g. Japan, South Korea, Germany, northern Italy). In 'low-trust' societies stable networks can be created via cross-ownership but will certainly be more difficult to sustain.

Increasingly, major corporates begin to work on the briefing of 'social capital' via value-added strategies. Here the organization is defined as a horizontal value stream supported by other activities (e.g. marketing development, senior management, finance). Each part of the organization has performance parameters defined in terms of value to its customers. Organizations use competence models and assessment, 360° feedback techniques and the balanced scorecard as a means of putting this into effect. The objective is to identify what each activity contributes by way of value to its customers, measure that and feed that information openly to the people involved in the activity, their customers and senior management. Part of the role of management is to help each activity to drive its performance forward in terms of these parameters.

A longer-term task of senior management is to identify and access the capabilities needed for the future. There are few organizations which have developed a coherent system of the type outlined here but there are many examples (in telecommunications, financial services, health care, manufacturing, utilities) of organizations working on such approaches.

The implications of the above can be sketched out graphically by looking at how we depict organizations. Traditionally, we depict organizations as structures of hierarchical authority whether we describe an organization of tastes which is functional or divisional (see below for more detail). Thus we typically construct the pyramid as shown in Figure 1.4.

Rarely were organizations as simple as that. Rarely would the above describe behaviour within organizations, which is why sociologists created the distinction between 'formal' and 'informal' organization, where the latter describes how people work with, through and around the formal organization in pursuit of various objectives, their own as well as the organization's.

Increasingly, managers recognized the problems referred to above, and, in particular, problems of change. This lead many to complement 'top-down' models of change with 'bottom-up' models seen by some as particularly relevant in the field of implementation.

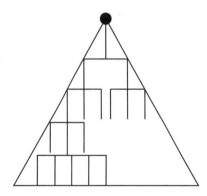

Figure 1.4 Traditional depiction of organization

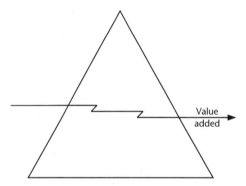

Figure 1.5 Value added

But both are 'vertical' models, i.e. the focus is upon how the organization arranges its internal affairs, how authority is used, how information is transmitted.

If the concern is to create change designed to ensure value added for customers and clients the pyramid needs to be rethought because value added for customers flows horizontally (see Figure 1.5).

This led many to ask how it was that we could think through the management of change without thinking horizontally. From this some immediately reject the inverted pyramid shown in Figure 1.6 in favour of depictions such as those set out in Figure 1.7.

In both of these depictions the focus is upon how or whether value is added either to internal or external 'customers'.

Many now conclude that we are in the midst of a paradigm or mind-set change regarding views on how to organize economic activity. New forms of organization are increasingly discussed and/or applied. Networks, virtual organizations and homeworking are each variants which attract continuing attention. For our purposes there are two points to note:

1. Increasingly we see two approaches to change in use, a planned approach to change and a market-based approach. In the former we decide the direction, objectives, stages, milestones, change methods and so on. In the latter we seek to motivate

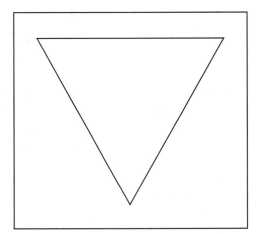

Figure 1.6 Bottom-up change management

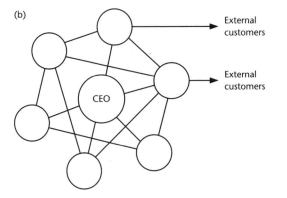

Figure 1.7 Depictions of organization: (a) horizontal management; (b) cluster organization

people in pursuit of a particular direction, desired objectives, preferred patterns of behaviour, but we are less concerned about milestones etc. This is a topic to which we will return, but the basic argument is that too much attention to targets and milestones creates expectations which can lead to fewer results than were achievable. In the latter we establish market mechanisms as a means of motivating changed behaviour. So long as we also provide adequate resources, information and support this often leads to dramatic changes in behaviour.

2. It appears that innovations such as the virtual organization, networks, alliances or homeworking create the potential for isolation. Thus cohesion becomes a crucial issue. New forms or sources of cohesion are needed if the traditional sources of department and structure are no longer present. More generally, economists now argue that *social capital* is essential to success. Social capital can be seen as the extent of social cohesion and is firmly linked to a sense of social solidarity, shared values and common commitment. If these are high then we have a high level of social capital. In an increasingly fragmented organizational world social capital becomes a crucial determinant of success.

Taking this second point further, the defining characteristics of the virtual organization are emerging as follows:

● They have a shared vision and goal and/or a common protocol of co-operation.

● They cluster activities around their core competencies.

● They work jointly in teams of core-competence groups to implement their activities throughout the value chain.

● They process and distribute information in real time throughout the value chain.

● They tend to delegate from the bottom up wherever economies of scale can be achieved or when new conditions arise.

These characteristics require and/or facilitate trust relations. This is social capital. It is interesting to note that these characteristics are also generally deemed valuable in other circumstances: mergers demand them and lean production requires them. In reality the changed focus of those concerned with organization from vertical concerns over control and co-ordination to a horizontal concern for value added creates the circumstances in which trust is essential to success. Fukuyama (1995) puts it thus:

> it is possible to argue that in the future the optimal form of industrial organisation will be neither small companies nor large ones but network structures that share the advantages of scale economies while avoiding the overhead and (other) costs of large, centralised organisations. If this will in fact be the case, then societies with a high degree of social trust will have a natural advantage. Networks can save on transaction costs substantially if their members follow an informal set of rules that require little or no overhead to negotiate, adjudicate, and enforce. The moment that trust breaks down among members of a business network, relations have to be spelled out in detail. (At this point the network resembles either a market or a hierarchical organization – author's note.)

In fact, managing networks, managing professional practices, managing alliances and joint ventures, managing virtual organizations and managing lean production all share these characteristics.

Castells (1996) comes to a similar conclusion. For him 'the main shift can be characterized by the shift from vertical bureaucracies to the horizontal corporation'. This shift is characterized by seven main trends, as follows:

1. Organization around process, not task.
2. A flat hierarchy.
3. Team management.
4. Performance management based upon customer satisfaction.
5. Rewards based upon team performance.
6. Maximization of contacts with suppliers and customers.
7. Information, training and retraining of employees at all levels.

These developments derive from a recognition of the limits both of the original functional, hierarchical model and attempts to modify this model via the Toyota lean production model or later equivalents such as business process re-engineering.

Ernst (1994) identifies five types of networks, as follows:

1. Supplier networks
2. Producer networks
3. Customer networks
4. Coalitions
5. Technology co-operation networks.

The network does not replace multinational corporations but rather offers the means through which MNCs now operate. Indeed national companies, public sector organizations and even voluntary organizations operate within networks; hence the current interest in supply chain management and interagency working. Networks provide the means through which we deal with increased complexity and/or global scope.

In addition to the trends identified by Castells (1996), here are some other approaches to developing the future organization:

● Activity-based costing combined with customer analysis. This latter approach identifies key processes in terms of importance and customer satisfaction (see Gouillart and Kelly, 1995). The focus is upon internal and external customers.
● Models of managerial competence.
● The 360° appraisal, a process in which managers are appraised by boss, peers and subordinates thus focusing attention on the value they add.
● Business process analysis.

Taken together these approaches represent an emerging value-added strategy to design and manage the new organization.

In the above we have tried to identify the nature of new thinking and practice which is leading managers to radically rethink organizations. We have looked at some of the consequences and implications of this work – although for a critique see Rifkin (1995) for projections regarding the end of work. Finally, we identify some practical method-ologies used by practitioners as they rethink and reconfigure their own organizations. The next session deals at length with business process re-engineering, one of the key methodologies to which we have referred.

Clearly issues related to cohesion, sociability and mind-set are vitally important to an understanding of how to manage these new organizational forms. Thus corporate culture comes to centre-stage (see Goffey and Jones, 1996).

CASE STUDY

British Petroleum Engineering

Quinn Mills (1991) suggests that a cluster organization makes the boxes and lines of a typical organization chart irrelevant. They are replaced by circles each representing a semi-autonomous cluster (Figure 1.8).

In essence, at the heart of the structure there are 16 clusters of engineers through which BPE meets client needs. The outer circle comprises three hierarchically organized activities,

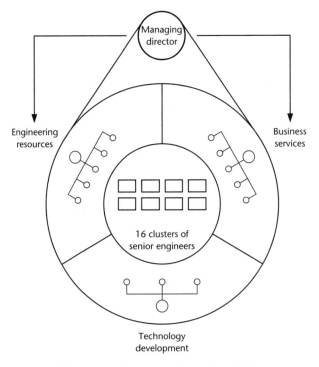

Figure 1.8 BPE organization (after Quinn Mills, 1991)

▶▶

namely engineering resources, business services and technology development. These units work to ensure that BPE has the necessary engineering resources, technology and that it meets client needs. Thus for example business services seeks to fit client needs to the cluster's outputs securing an agreed programme measuring performance as the programme unfolds. Business services therefore acts as an account manager. The managing director and the three general managers (of engineering resources, business services and technology development) form a core team. The hierarchical relationship is between that core team and the resources in the cluster. The focus of the organization is on how those resources can be configured to meet varying client needs, rather than on who is reporting to whom!

Another interesting point to note is that the role of the three 'departments' is configuring resources to meet either customer needs or development (i.e. acquiring the right profile of engineering resources and developing the right technologies). Does this focus represent a recognition of the need to develop learning (the learning organization), intellectual capital or invisible assets? It is now commonplace to argue that intellectual capital (i.e. the intangible assets of the organization) comprises renewal and development, customer knowledge and loyalty and process knowledge. They argue that Skandia, one of Sweden's leading insurance and financial services organizations, defines intellectual capital that way. It is interesting to note the similarity of themes looking at the BPE situation.

The network organization

A logical extension of the cluster organization model, the network model adds partnerships across the boundary raising the fundamental question of where the boundary of an organization lies. This can be depicted as shown in Figure 1.9, and one should note that the key aspect of a network organization is that it seeks to add the pursuit of flexible specialization to the advantages of the cluster organization (see Barnatt, 1995).

In principle a network can be a combination of a number of organizations each of which can take any form. In Europe, Airbus Industrie comprises French, German, Spanish and British aerospace companies each of which is organized hierarchically at least to some significant extent.

Lipnack and Stamps (1994) identify five organizing principles for networks:

1. *Unifying purpose*: the glue holding it together. Shared ideas, values and goals.

2. *Independence*: each member should be able to stand on its own while benefiting from being part of the network as a whole.

3. *Voluntary links*: characterized by multiple links as a means of attracting needed skills, resources, access to markets, etc.

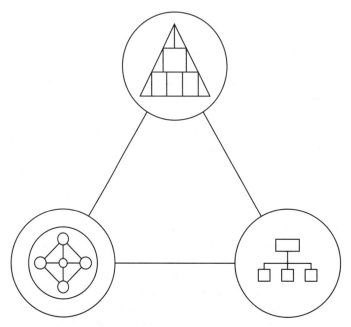

Figure 1.9 The network organization

4. *Multiple leaders*: networks comprise people, groups, companies, each of which has something unique to contribute.

5. *Integrated levels*: multi-level, not flat, because to survive networks need a tendency to action. Thus hierarchy remains a feature of this organizational form but not a documentary feature.

Clearly therefore the literature on strategic alliances has much to tell us about how these forms of organization can be sustained and we will return to that in a later chapter. For now suffice it to say that the key principle missing in the above is reciprocity.

Following Williamson (1975) the network is an organizational form through which resource allocation decisions are made, *not* simply through hierarchy but more extensively through market mechanisms. A network will only continue if each 'member' believes that the net result is of advantage and that all 'members' contribute positively. Increasingly the issue of relative contribution is crucial to the longer-term cohesion of our organizations.

In fact regardless of the use of hierarchical, matrix, cluster or network organization models, the concept of *value added* provides the psychological and organizational 'glue' from which to create cohesion. We will develop this view in the next chapter, but in essence here two sets of principles may operate. Organizationally the work of each of us is aided through understanding and seeking to maximize the value of work of others whose input is needed for our work. This supply chain management is based upon a process view of organization. Ultimately cohesion arises out of a shared sense of purpose. This is achieved from the perception that each contributes to the achievement of those purposes, i.e. that we all will the ends and will the means. We know that this is real only by understanding the contribution of all – thus the focus upon value added throughout the organization. There was the practical and psychological consequence in terms of consistent behaviour and cohesion.

If some are deemed not to contribute then this leads to disruption, a sense of 'unfairness' to tension and conflict. This implies evaluative criteria linking rewards to effort based upon ideas such as reciprocity, contribution (or performance), capacity, need or the fulfilment of commitments. Often evaluative criteria will be based upon a complex mix of such ideas. The important point here is to note that ultimately cohesion in an organization arises out of perceptions and we argue that a primary focus of perceptions of an organization relates to issues of value (see Carnall (1986) for a fuller treatment of these issues).

Conclusion

In this chapter we have suggested that various 'drivers' for change have created a critical mass of organizational change. This appears to have lead to a fundamental shift in the way we configure and manage organizations. Moreover, the mechanisms we use to achieve change are also changing. Where once planned approaches held the field, now increasingly market mechanisms play a vital part. New forms of organization have emerged based upon a horizontal and value-added metaphor (as compared with a vertical or command and control metaphor). These create new management concerns and challenges not least that of how to achieve integration.

Exercises

1. Can you think of examples of market-induced change in your own organization? Have such changes under- or overperformed in terms of the achievement of objectives? Has their introduction been easy or has it raised new issues and anxieties for the people involved?

2. Is your organization beginning to think about horizontal value chains? Does this lead to a rethinking of the role of senior management? How?

3. Can you identify examples of cluster or network structures in your own or any other organization? How well do they work?

CHAPTER 2

Management structures and management in action

Introduction

Organization structures allow us to organize and deploy resources. They allow us to define job activities, responsibilities and accountabilities. They provide for decision making and information flows. They help to establish the power structure for the organization. They influence the identity and corporate image of the organization. They establish people's attitudes, at least in part.

The weekend before writing this chapter for the first edition of this book I was running a management development workshop for a large investment bank. The bank had made losses but to no greater extent than other, competing, institutions. Yet the financial press had been critical of it and not of others. Moreover, its parent institution (a large bank which wholly owned the investment bank) had replaced a number of key senior managers and was engaged in a review of the investment bank. Meanwhile, the attitudes of staff, middle and senior managers were very problematic, not surprisingly.

Why was that? Well, there had been the stock market fall in autumn 1987. But the bank's competitors had experienced the same fall. Much discussion and debate at the workshop was concluded with the view that the strategy and structure developed by the investment bank when it was founded was unclear. Many grand statements of objectives had been made but it was much less clear whether the structure established provided the right balance of information, power and resources to support the various activities within the organization in achieving those objectives. Moreover, it was felt that the main deficiency had been in the professional management. There had been overreliance on 'market makers'. Such people may well be able to exploit market opportunities but had they the skill to create and sustain a large investment bank? Some of their main competitors had been managed more closely by parent organizations, they argued, giving them the advantages of both professional management and 'market makers'; a better balance had been struck between control from the 'parent' and autonomy of the subsidiary.

Was the structure of the investment bank appropriate to the tasks and opportunities it faced? Was the relationship and structure between it and the 'parent' appropriate? To what extent had the weaknesses in organizational structure left it vulnerable to the 'autumn crash'? To what extent had weaknesses of strategy, structure and control, the impact of the 'crash', and subsequent losses undermined the confidence of employees, including senior management? To what extent had its corporate image been 'dented', leaving it open to the attention of the financial press? Well, we cannot answer all these questions here, much as the managers in the workshop could only debate them without drawing final conclusions. However, one thing is clear. Organizational structures can be an influential element in whether or not an organization can be effective.

Management structures and management in action

It is conventional to establish and describe various management structures. Broadly speaking there are the six following alternative 'model' structures:

1. The simple or entrepreneurial structure
2. The functional structure
3. The product structure
4. The divisional structure
5. The matrix structure
6. The federal structure.

However, we shall see that it is not as simple as that; nevertheless let us quickly review these six structures.

The entrepreneurial structure

This is the simplest of these model structures. Everything typically depends on the entrepreneur or owner of the business. They make the decisions. They undertake much of the work. Other employees are taken on to carry out specific tasks. Little or no identifiable departmental structuring exists. These are flexible organizations. Trading companies are often structured in this flexible way. Partnerships are typically a variant of this structure.

Growth and geographical dispersion, and the need for outside investment, can create pressures to change from this structure. For example, in the property industry many estate agency partnerships have either been acquired by financial institutions or, having generated internal growth, have established divisional structures. Increased competition and, more importantly, business opportunity are creating the pressure for change. The managing director of a holding company now owning some 300 estate agency outlets, organized into geographical divisions, recently made two compelling points about this industry. Firstly, for every £1 profit he could make selling property in the domestic market he could make £7 if he could sell an endowment policy linked to a mortgage. This opportunity was attracting financial institutions into the market. Secondly, the public image of estate agents was low. Organizing the industry could help to improve the service it provided, by improved information provision to clients. It might also allow the industry to improve its image by developing and enforcing codes of practice. Whatever the truth of these predictions, the pressures for change are self-evident.

The functional structure

Growth often leads to the development of a functional structure. Here similar activities are grouped into departments: personnel, marketing, finance, operations and so on. Co-ordination is achieved through a board of directors or management committee, overseen by a managing director or general manager. If the organization is not too large the functional structure provides the following three main advantages:

1. It allows for the development of particular kinds of expertise, engineering, technology, finance, personnel, etc.
2. It provides career paths for professional staff who work with and then manage people from a similar background.
3. It provides for the effective utilization of personnel across various departments.

However, further growth, geographical dispersion or product/service diversification can create pressures on this form of organizational structure.

The product structure

Managers operating within a functional structure are unlikely to devote the necessary time and commitment to each of a range of products/services or markets. It will be difficult to establish criteria by which priorities are to be established. Individuals need to be accountable for products/services, or markets, if they are to attract appropriate resources. The functional structure provides us with a good basis for achieving internal efficiency of functions and co-ordination. It does not provide us with a good basis for product/service/market growth in a competitive environment. In practice, it turns out to be difficult to allocate resources to the different products/services on any rational basis.

In the product structure, activity is grouped around products/services/markets. Each group will have its own specialists, at least from disciplines which are best organized at product level (say, for example, engineering and marketing). Typically, finance and personnel may remain functionally organized, reporting directly to the management committee or board, alongside the product groups. This structure brings with it the two following key advantages:

1. The product groups are better equipped to respond to market demands for growth or change to products/services. They do not need to compete for resources unless the rate of growth is such that the resources allocated to them must be expanded.

2. The work of the various specialists (engineers, marketing) becomes directly related to the market. The likelihood is that in this structure people can and will become 'closer to the customer'.

However, growth or decline in a product/service can be difficult to handle. The former leads to a demand for more resources, the latter for the reassignment of staff between product groups.

The divisional structure

Further growth can create pressure on senior management, who will become 'swamped' by day-to-day matters. This means that either senior management tend to ignore broader matters and corporate planning *or* they tend to ignore the operational matters, creating a managerial 'vacuum' within which co-ordination may become difficult. Divisionalization involves breaking the organization down into relatively autonomous units, called divisions. Each division might serve a particular product, or a particular market; each will have its own divisional chief executive and management committee or board; each might be organized on functional, product or even matrix lines (see below); each may have a different structure.

This structure creates the following four advantages:

1. Cost and profit performance are matters for the divisional managers. The group chief executive need not be concerned with these issues ordinarily.

2. The main functions of a group are overall financial planning and management, strategic planning, business development and management development. However, clearly, divisional managers need to be involved and much care needs to be given to establishing the involvement of the divisions. Various options are feasible.

3. Each division is free to respond to the demands of its own markets within a framework created by overall strategic plans and budgets.

4. This structure allows accountability to be 'pushed' down the organization, providing a balance between corporate development and control and local, market autonomy. However, striking the balance can be difficult in practice.

The matrix structure

The various structures we have described are attempts to combine market and functional focus to organizational work. The matrix structure is one in which both foci are given importance throughout the organizational structure. Indeed, the structure gives each equal importance. However, beware: as we shall see, structure is not everything! Matrix structures are often found on large construction, aerospace or computer software development projects. Where an organization deals with more than one complex project there is a need both to co-ordinate and develop project and various specialist activities. As the demand for various specialist inputs is variable over the life of a product we need a structure which promotes both effective deployment on a project when needed and adaptability over time so that resources can be easily switched between projects. The matrix structure identifies project management structures, accountable for the project, and functional structures, accountable for each discipline, say engineering, operations and so on.

Matrix structures have the following three advantages:

1. They allow for the development of cohesive and effective teams of specialists working towards the objectives of a key project.

2. They provide for the professional and career development of specialist staff.

3. They provide for the flexible use of specialist staff.

However, the difficulty of handling a matrix structure can lie in the problem of reconciling the need for flexibility with the need for project co-ordination and control. This reconciliation implies good working relationships between project and functional management which may, in practice, be difficult to establish.

The federal structure

This structure carries the decentralization of the divisional structure a stage further. The group establishes strategic business units for each product market and controls them from the centre without an intervening divisional structure. This reflects the fact that, in practice, further growth often means that divisions operate more than one unit, firm or plant.

Accountability could readily become confused between group, division and firm levels. The three advantages of the federal structure are as follows:

1. Accountability is clear and defined at unit level.

2. Resources are not expended at divisional level.

3. Groups can achieve growth or divestment quickly to suit corporate strategies.

However, the emergence of the 'federal structure' can recreate the pressures on senior management which the divisional structure once removed. Effective reporting systems, information systems and decentralization are three keys to the solution of this problem.

Management in action

In practice, organizations implement variants of the above structures. Many large organizations in both the public and private sectors operate divisional structures alongside some element of matrix management. Thus an international oil company and a large hospital group I know are both organized into divisions; both have a finance function separate from the divisions (divisional directors and the finance director both being on the executive committee or board) but both assign finance staff to each division.

At local level, people interpret the demands of the tasks in hand, alongside ideas of good financial management practice and standing orders, rules and regulations, in ways which allow them to get on with their work, as they see it. In practice, the task of senior management is to establish priorities and to achieve both control and adaptability. The reality is that, at all levels of management, there is considerable discretion on a day-to-day basis. Top management attempts to exert complete control are generally counterproductive. They discourage initiative and encourage ritual or even ineffective behaviour and take time and money to exert!

People have long distinguished the formal from the informal structure of organizations. The formal structure is that defined by organizational charts, job descriptions and so on. The informal structure is that which emerges from and around the formal structure.

> For centuries observers and leaders have remarked on the distinctions between expected and unexpected behaviour in organizations. The fact that the distinctions continue to be made under various names points to an apparently universal condition. From at least the time of Augustus Caesar, these dissimilarities were recognized and incorporated in the terms de jure (by right) and de facto (in fact), which are roughly equivalent to legal or official, and actual but unofficial. In industry and business today one repeatedly hears the same general meaning phrased as 'administration versus politics', 'theory versus practice', 'red tape versus working relations'.
>
> (Dalton, 1959, p. 219)

Dalton defines formal or official as 'that which is planned and agreed upon' and informal or unofficial as 'the spontaneous and flexible ties among members, guided by feelings and personal interests indispensable for the operation of the formal, but too fluid to be entirely contained by it'. Thus the informal system is a system of mutual help and adjustment. For example, a piece-work system may require that a supervisor only issue a new job to an operator when the previously issued job is finished, exchanging the old job card for the new card. The operators might wish to accumulate a number of cards because this provides them with a reserve of 'time' that they may use should problems hinder the completion of a job. In such a situation the accumulated time may be booked in and average bonus maintained. Supervisors and operatives must work together and both may ignore the formal requirements of the system, the supervisor being prepared to issue a new job without demanding the previous job card, the operators 'accumulating' cards to use in the event of problems, and so on.

Informal communication may arise from work-related or social reasons. Most work just cannot be done without some informal communication. Many studies show that managers of all kinds prefer informal and verbal communication to documents and that they spend around 45 per cent of their time communicating outside the formal authority structure. Regular channels are often slow and unreliable. The information that a manager obtains from outside the formal system is often qualitative but it is rich with meaning. A manager walking through a department 'sensing' an uneasy or tense atmosphere would be short-sighted to prefer the formal evidence that this is an efficient department. Will it continue to be efficient? Should changes in work patterns or methods need to be introduced; can this be achieved effectively? In fact most managers bypass the formal systems of communication (now increasingly known as the management information system, MIS) and build their own networks of informal contacts (Mintzberg, 1973).

The second reason for the existence of informal communication in organizations is social. People need to relate to each other. Moreover, people may bypass the formal system in order to advance their own personal ambitions or needs. They 'leak' sensitive information to outsiders, or they hold information back. It is worth noting that informal communication can be vital to the success of an organization, particularly where employees work in a hostile or unsafe environment.

The importance of informal systems has been shown in many studies, notably by Strauss (1963) in studies of purchasing departments. He found that the most effective and high-status purchasing officers favoured mutual adjustment over direct supervision and standardization. To resolve conflict with other departments (e.g. engineering departments), they were reluctant to appeal to the purchasing manager, to rely on the rules or to require written agreements; rather, they relied on friendships, the exchange of favours, and their own informal political power. They tended to 'oil the wheels' of the formal system. If we are to understand behaviour in organizations we must understand both the formal and the informal.

Authority and communication are facilitating processes for the two basic flow processes: work flow and decision making. Decisions include much else besides what we normally understand as objectivity, rationality and purpose. When making decisions people are constrained by past decisions and by the culture of the organization. Many individual and group inputs are made in a decision process, and the outcome may be a decision that nobody particularly supports or feels committed to.

Decisions are often based on inadequate, and even conflicting, information. Moreover, decisions are sequential, rather than once and for all processes. Commitment and support for the implementation of a decision are crucial factors. Decisions are not complete until the necessary resources are applied in the appropriate manner. Delay or scaling down of resources may change a decision subsequent to the meeting where the decision was 'apparently taken'. These are issues to which we shall be returning in a later chapter.

The dilemmas of organization

For all these reasons, too much concentration on the management structure itself can be misleading. Managers are often designing and redesigning the management structure, assigning different responsibilities and resources to divisions and departments. Decisions about the management structure pose a number of dilemmas which must be resolved if organizations are to be managed effectively. But by 'resolved', we do not mean once and for all. We mean resolved in the internal and external circumstances of the organization at any point in time (see Chapter 5 for more detail). There are six main sets of dilemmas, as follows:

1. Centralization vs. decentralization
2. Global vs. local
3. Efficiency vs. effectiveness
4. Professional vs. management
5. Control vs. commitment
6. Change vs. stability.

Centralization versus decentralization

Once upon a time it was not relevant to ask managers 'Is your organization centralized or decentralized?' but, rather, 'In what direction is it going this year?' There seemed to be a cyclical process at work. In good times when markets were growing, organizations decentralized to encourage local initiative in what might be varied local markets and circumstances. In tougher periods when markets were 'tight' and income generation a problem, organizations centralized in order to gain greater control over expenditure, employment policies and so forth. However, the picture is complicated by the growth of organizations. Growth from the small entrepreneurial business to the large and diversified conglomerate seems to impose patterns of organizational design. There seem to be distinct phases in the growth of an organization, each with its own tensions and its own distinctive organizational solution, albeit not necessarily applied in pure form in any particular case. We have already examined these in the various management structures considered earlier in this chapter, each discussed in the context of the growth of organizations. And we said there that, currently, in many organizations, managers are creating structures which both centralize and decentralize; namely, to centralize key issues such as finance, business development, acquisition, corporate strategy and management development, but to decentralize operational/profit accountability to the unit, whether a business unit or some other unit (a school, hospital, police force, etc.).

As will be clear already, there are arguments for and against centralization and these depend upon the circumstances. These issues are addressed at length by Brooke (1984) and are summarized by Child (1984) as follows.

For centralization

1. Co-ordination is more straightforward if decisions are made at clearly recognized points within the organizational structure.

2. Senior management have a broader perspective on developments within the organization and maintain conformity with established policies. They are more likely to keep up to date with recent developments, throughout the industrial service.

3. Centralization of control and procedures provides a way of assisting the various functional areas in the organization – research and development, production, personnel, finance and administration – to maintain an appropriate balance. This occurs by centralizing decisions on resource allocation, functional policies, targets and human resource matters.

4. Centralization can allow rationalization of managerial overheads by avoiding duplication of activities or resources where similar activities are being carried out independently in divisions or subunits.

5. Top managers are seen to have proved themselves by the time they reach a senior position. Although a point in favour of centralization, there is a danger that management can adopt the attitude that purely because they are at the top, they are right.

6. Crises often require strong leadership to cope with external and internal pressures.

Centralization of power and control of procedures focus on a key person or group. Thus arises the opportunity for speedy decision making and control over communication and co-ordination.

For decentralization

1. Delegation can reduce the amount of stress and overload experienced by senior management, especially when operating in large-scale, complex organizations. When senior management become overloaded, the exercise of control is diminished. Delegation can remove some of the burden from senior management, allowing them to spend more time on policy issues and long-term planning.

2. Many believe that the motivation of employees will increase with the higher degree of discretion and control that they can apply to their work. The opportunity to make decisions and be involved can help to provide personal satisfaction and commitment for the individual. It is assumed that individual goals will broadly be in line with those of the corporate organization. In situations of delegated power, the matching of personal goals and corporate goals is more likely to be possible, but delegation can be severely tested in situations where people work independently of each other. The problem here is to motivate people sufficiently to co-ordinate their activities without too much central direction.

3. Large or growing organizations need managers who are able to cope with uncertainty because of the volume of complex tasks that have to be performed. It is impossible for one person or small groups of people to supervise such complex activities simultaneously. Delegation can therefore assist management development by widening the on-the-job skills of managers and hence provide a number of people who are capable of undertaking senior management positions.

4. Delegation generally allows for greater flexibility by providing for less rigid response to problems at the operative levels in the organization. Decisions do not have to be referred up the hierarchy.

5. By establishing relatively independent subunits within an organization, where middle management are held responsible for operations, delegation can result in improved controls and performance measurements. Accountability can be identified.

Decisions on the level of centralization and decentralization are neither simple nor final. They depend on the circumstances and may need reviewing as circumstances change. Criteria to be considered over and above the points made above are as follows:

● The objectives, strategy and technology of the organization.

● The ability of senior management to develop and implement a new management structure.

● Timing, particularly taking account of other changes in the environment or within the organization (see Chapter 8 for more detail).

● The skills and attitudes of employees and their commitment to the organization.

● The size of the organization, including size of divisions and/or units.

- The geographic dispersion of the organization.
- Time scales and decision making. Technological, safety or other reasons can mean that some decisions must be made quickly, and locally, although organizations can still establish procedures, policies and guidelines to provide a decision framework.
- Relevant external issues such as legislation or central/local government requirements.

Thus it is that in practice these are complex criteria but are central to the question of how responsive and adaptable organizations can become.

Global versus local

This is a variant of the centralization vs. decentralization dilemma but in a sense more important because of the scale factor. Once a company has begun to operate internationally, establishing manufacturing, marketing and/or distribution/after-sales support operations around the world, it faces this dilemma of how to balance the need to motivate managers to operate successfully within a given local market with its particular demands and characteristics against the demand for global development and coherence. Thus we may need to develop and leverage a particular technology across the globe, in the way that drug companies such as Novartis are so skilled at doing. Additionally concern to develop an integrated capability, coherence in culture and an integrated logistics chain can create pressures on local needs.

Efficiency versus effectiveness

The third dilemma is that between efficiency and effectiveness. This dilemma will be examined more thoroughly in the next chapter but for the moment suffice it to say that efficiency may be defined as achieving stated goals (say the manufacture, sale and distribution of a given product or service) within given resource constraints. Effectiveness includes efficiency *and* adaptability to future circumstances. The effective organization balances immediate efficiency with the ability to deploy new products and services for the future. The dilemma emerges in all sorts of practical ways. When cuts in budgets are needed it may seem relatively easy to cut training and research and development (R&D). Both may incur cost but not generate income and seem, therefore, to be more likely candidates for cuts than are operational activities. Yet both might be important to the future of the organization.

It should, however, be noted that both training and R&D are services which can be sold externally, thus generating income. Thus the dilemma is not between today's figures and activities which focus on the future but create cost in today's 'bottom line'; rather, it is between adopting an *internal* or an *external focus* to our activities.

The efficient organization focuses on internal efficiency and control. The effective organization constantly strives to ensure that all its activities pass externally imposed criteria. These may be the ability to generate income by sales, or income by grant-aid (e.g. by obtaining research contracts), or by other external reference points. To be effective an organization must adapt to changing external circumstances.

There are various practical ways of overcoming this dilemma between efficiency and effectiveness. They all depend on achieving a better understanding of the necessity for change and adaptability. This may be achieved in the following variety of ways:

● Job rotation can be utilized to give people a broader perspective of the organization's work.

● Following the first point, selection and training of people can emphasize a broader background.

● Intensive use may be made of all available media of communication in order to create a better degree of shared understanding of the organization's tasks, resources, opportunities, etc.

● An organizational climate can be created which supports experiment and risk taking (see below).

● Participation may be increased in planning, both generally and by specific approaches such as quality circles.

● Innovation should always be on agendas for strategic planning, management development activities and workshops/conferences.

● Project groups can be established to resolve specific tasks and problems. Such groups should be recruited from all the departments involved, creating broader perspectives and quicker acceptance of new ideas.

● Product champions should be identified, along with organizational champions whose task is to create resources and time for new activities to be proved and to integrate the emerging new products/services or systems with existing corporate strategy.

In various ways these ideas are designed to open up the way in which we think about our organization. They aim at helping people to take a broader and more flexible look at what they do, and at what they might do. Adaptability and innovation are reinforced by making them an explicit part of the work people do. Of course it is not easy to do these things. Moreover, we need to act within a coherent framework of management strategy. For the moment we leave these ideas as a starting point. We return to them later in the book and within a broader strategy for change.

Professionals versus line management

The fourth dilemma is the extent to which organizations rely on professional expertise or the 'street-wise' approach of the line manager. The professional brings the technical input and ideas which have been applied in other situations. The line manager has knowledge of the specific local circumstances. With the ever-increasing specialization within occupations, combined with the growth of organizations, we often either employ specialists and/or contract for their services with outside organizations (e.g. management consulting firms, universities, etc.).

Take information technology as an example. Can or should development be in the hands of professional information technology staff or of line managers? The former understand the technology, the latter understand the business and local needs. This is a simplification, of course, but the plain fact is that many large organizations appear to have gone through at least three phases of development, partly to do with this dilemma and partly to do with technological factors. The first phase saw the introduction of computers under the control of data processing specialists. Systems development took time and often users found the results were elaborate, unwieldy and not particularly helpful. The development of smaller computers (desktops, personal computers, etc.) led many users to develop their own local systems. These often proved to be useful locally but were incapable of integration into broader organization-wide systems and databases. Thus information technology specialists attempt to re-establish their influence by providing advice and support to users. In the third phase, projects are explicitly project managed, often by users and not specialists.

Such problems are common throughout the various professions. Achieving the right balance often turns out to be a question of creating the right systems within which to manage the professionals (be they engineers, accountants, lawyers, doctors, or whatever).

Professionals have a knowledge base and a set of values which distinguish them from other groups of employees. This knowledge base comprises the skills and techniques which their training has equipped them to deploy. It is worth noting that many people question attempts by professions to monopolize the application of specific knowledge and techniques. Nevertheless, we know that organizations use professionals – engineers, accountants and lawyers – as well as what we might call quasi-professionals – personnel specialists, marketing specialists, and so on (quasi-professional only because the relevant professional bodies have yet to gain the status and control of the profession achieved by, say, the accounting institutions). Our purpose here is not to define professional but, rather, to examine how organizations seem to manage professionals. Increasingly, organizations manage professionals on the following principles:

● *Emphasize decentralization*: managers depend on the contribution, effort and skills of the professional employee. Thus motivation and control are sensitive issues and too much direction can be counterproductive. Managers tend to share responsibility and the professional has to learn to take responsibility for management decisions and how to communicate with management. Examples include the growing input into management of doctors in the health care field and of data processing specialists and marketing specialists in corporate management.

● *Depend less on 'rational' controls*: too much concern and reliance on quantitative measures can lead to unintended consequences (see Chapter 9). That does not mean that less monitoring and planning is needed. Quite the opposite! However, performance review is carried out with, rather than on, professionals. Involvement is important because judgement in handling a range of quantitative and qualitative measures becomes important.

● *Place greater emphasis on intrinsic motivation*: in particular, career development seems to be of great importance, and attention must therefore be paid to delegation, challenge, training and development as well as to motivators such as pay, status, etc.

● *Place greater emphasis on team working*: different professional groups will hold and argue strongly for their own diverse views. Thus professional organizations must handle conflict. People skills and team-building skills are therefore of great importance.

● *Place more emphasis on conflict management*: the conflict referred to above needs to be managed. Uncertainty and complex tasks create the conditions for conflict, along with the previous point above. Management need to keep in close touch with the various professional groups, and use team building and involvement to communicate decisions quickly and effectively. All these are means of handling conflict constructively.

● *Use matrix management and project structures*: there is a real need to create structures which place primary emphasis on the work to be done and on how to provide for the contribution of different professional groups to that work. These structures emphasize task or team cultures. The various professional groups will be inter-dependent, thus emphasizing the need for matrix or project (taskforce) approaches to planning and to management.

● *Place more emphasis on trust*: trust is difficult to establish. Managers, other employ-ees and clients place trust in professionals. This creates great pressure for consis-tency and fairness in the management of organizations; without it some stakeholders may become dissatisfied. There will still be organizational politics but for these to be constructively managed they need to be surrounded by a reasonable degree of openness.

● *Place more emphasis on values and ethics*: top management devote considerable time and energy to articulating the organization's mission, values and ethics. They cannot control professionals directly and thus codes of behaviour conducive to trusting relationships are very important. This should be a joint management and professional task. Often it is neglected because it does not solve everyday issues and problems. Nevertheless, longer-run success seems to depend on greater self-regulation within professional organizations.

From control to commitment

The improvement of organizational effectiveness involved depends on our ability to diagnose the organization's problems, to identify solutions, and to adopt and adapt these solutions to organizational life. One approach to these various challenges has been described by Walton (1985). This approach is based on the assumption that man-agers have generally relied on inadequate models for managing their employees. They expect and accept much less from employees than is potentially available. Management has failed to motivate employees or to develop their latent capacities (and thus has failed to develop 'invisible assets' – see Chapter 9).

Walton refers to this traditional model as the control model. In this model, work is divided up into specialized tasks. Performance expectations are defined as 'standards' that define the minimum acceptable performance. Both expectations and standards are the lowest common denominators. No attempt is made to establish maximum or potential performance.

Two developments prompted movement away from this model. Changing employee attitudes and expectations meant that attempts to gain control created a dissatisfied and low-performing workforce which, in turn, meant that control and efficiency was undermined. Intensified competition was a second development. The control model seems to produce reliable but not outstanding performance. Since the 1970s it has been clear that this is not enough. Competitive advantage can be created out of high performance. High performance requires high levels of commitment.

In the commitment model, jobs are designed to be broader and teams, rather than individuals, are the units that are held accountable for performance. Performance expectations are set relatively high. Continuous improvement is expected and encouraged. The management structure tends to be flatter. People rely on shared goals for co-ordination; influence is based on expertise and information, not on position. In Table 2.1 we set out, in somewhat modified form, the control model and the commitment model,

Table 2.1 ● Management models

	Control model	Transitional model	Commitment model
1. Job design principles	Individual attention limited to performing individual job	Scope of individual responsibility extended to upgrading system performance, via participative problem solving groups in QWL, 'right first time' and quality circle programmes	Individual responsibility extended to upgrading system performance
	Job design deskills and fragments work and thinking	No change in traditional job design or accountability	Job design enhances content of work, emphasizes whole and separates doing and task, and combines doing and thinking
	Accountability focused on the individual		Frequent use of teams as the basic accountable unit
	Fixed job definition		Flexible definition of duties, contingent on changing conditions
2. Performance expectations	Measured standards define minimum performance. Stability seen as desirable		Emphasis placed on higher 'stretch objectives', which tend to be dynamic and orientated to the marketplace

(continued)

Table 2.1 ● *Continued*

	Control model	**Transitional model**	**Commitment model**
3. Management organization: structure, systems and style	Structure tends to be layered with top-down controls	(No basic changes in approaches to structure, control or authority)	Flat organizational structure with mutual influence systems
	Co-ordination and control rely on rules and procedures		Co-ordination and control based more on shared goals, values and traditions
	More emphasis on prerogatives and positional authority		Management emphasis on problem solving and relevant information and expertise
	Status symbols distributed to reinforce hierarchy	Some change, e.g. existence of participation councils	Minimum status differentials to de-emphasize inherent hierarchy
4. Reward policies	Variable pay where feasible to provide individual 'incentive'	Typically no basic changes in reward concepts	Performance-related rewards to create equity and to reinforce group achievements, e.g. profit sharing
	Individual pay geared to job evaluation		Individual pay linked to skills, performance
	In downturn, cuts concentrated on hourly payroll	'Equality of contribution' among employee groups	Equality of commitment and result
5. Employment assurances	Employees regarded as variable costs	Assurances that participation will not result in job loss. Extra effort to avoid redundancies	High commitment to avoid or assist in re-employment. Priority for training and retaining existing workforce

Table 2.1 ● *Continued*

	Control model	Transitional model	Commitment model
6. 'Open-door' policies	Employee views allowed on relatively narrow agenda. Employees see risks associated with stating views too openly. Methods include open-door policy, attitude surveys, grievance procedures, and collective bargaining in some organizations	Addition of limited, *ad hoc* consultation mechanisms. No change in corporate governance	Employee participation encouraged on wide range of issues. Attendant benefits emphasized. New concepts of corporate governance
	Business information distributed on strictly defined 'need to know' basis	Additional sharing of information	Business data shared widely
7. Employee–management relations	Adversarial employee relations; emphasis on interest conflict	Thawing of adversarial attitudes; joint sponsorship of QWL or emphasis on common objectives and purposes or change programme	Mutually in employee relations; joint planning and problem solving on expanded agenda. Unions, managements and workers redefine their respective roles
8. Management acknowledge philosophy	Management's philosophy emphasizes management prerogatives and obligations to shareholders	*Ad hoc* shifts in stated priorities	Management's philosophy accepts multiple stakeholders– owners, employees, customers and public

following Walton (1985). We also identify the transitional mechanisms needed to move from one model or organization to the other. Does this mean that all accountability in the commitment model is through teams? Walton (1985) does not make that clear. However, the view taken here is that modern thinking emphasizes a duality. The individual manager is accountable for the performance of his or her team, at all levels. However, in order to engage high-level performance the manager needs to develop strong team working. Only then will people's ideas, talents and commitment be harnessed.

Change versus stability

In a changing world the organization must change to survive and prosper. However, must everything change? Moreover, while we are changing we must still deploy people to produce goods and services as normal, even if we are demanding extra effort from them as they experience change. The final dilemma is that of balancing change with stability. In a real sense this book is about this final organizational dilemma. We thus propose merely to 'signal' the dilemma now. Throughout the book we shall deal with this dilemma.

Leadership and 'excellence'

O'er structures of government let fools contend.
Whate'er is best administered, is best.

(Alexander Pope)

These words, written long ago, direct our attention to the quality of leadership and to managerial performance. An appropriate organizational structure will not enable people to work effectively unless they are appropriately managed. Moreover, in many circumstances different organizational structures can be equally effective as long as management is practised to good effect. We often refer to the 'organizational choice' available to those concerned in the design of an organizational structure (see Trist *et al.*, 1963), by which we mean that the various technological, economic, social and political pressures on organizations do not require unique solutions. In reality, variations of the basic structure are not just possible but are often found in practice. In any event, the informal structure is much more important than the formal structure when trying to understand an organization. Moreover, the structure alone does not define an organization's solutions to the organizational dilemmas discussed above. Rather, corporate policies and management practice do so. Finally, therefore, understanding managerial performance is important if we are to assess whether or not an organization's structure is appropriate in practice.

This suggests that we must look at more than the organizational structure if we are to assess an organization properly. Much attention is now devoted to 'corporate culture'. A number of authors have attempted to define the corporate cultures they see as emerging in 'excellent' companies.

A number of books reviewing the characteristics of excellent companies have been published, notably *In Search of Excellence* by Peters and Waterman (1982) and, more recently, *A Passion for Excellence* by Peters and Austin (1985). Other books include Rosabeth Kanter's *The Change Masters* (1983). These books suggest that effectiveness is more likely to emerge from organizational cultures which encourage the following:

- *Accountability*: this word is being used more and more when discussing management problems and practices. Where once we meant the fiduciary accountability of the board of directors to the shareholders, we now refer to something quite different. We now refer to direct and personal accountability for performance. The stress is upon the individual manager and the performance of the unit or team. Clearer accountability and tighter central control of finance and strategy have gone hand in hand with decentralization of activities and resources to unit level. If the 1960s and 1970s were the eras of involvement in management books, the 1980s was the era of the individual. If we are now seeing the 'failure of collectivism' as both moral philosophy and organizing principle we are also experiencing the re-emergence of individualism. In the 1990s and beyond the issue is whether economic individualism can become transformed to moral or socially responsible individualism.

- *Synergy*: this is the capacity to obtain co-operation and collaboration. People increasingly question instructions. Professionals expect to have a say in what they do. In consequence, effectiveness cannot be ensured by 'fiat'. Coercion may well generate compliance, but will fail to produce effort or creativity. Thus it is that the task of management includes the skills of achieving co-operation and collaboration. Moreover, much work demands the efforts of people drawn from varying technical disciplines, such as engineering, chemistry, metallurgy, marketing, accounting and so on. In practice getting things done normally involves gaining co-operation.

- *Cross-cultural skills*: in all organizations we work with people from a diversity of backgrounds. Whether we are looking at a large public service organization in an urban environment or the various facilities of a multinational corporation, we deal with cultural diversity. Management development involves developing what managers do. Thus, building the cross-cultural skills for handling this diversity is important. We shall see that these skills emerge from developing the skill of empathy, but more of that later.

- *Managing interfaces*: management involves the skills of co-ordinating the deployment of people, information, resources and technology in order that work can be carried out effectively. Managers in manufacturing, the public services, in charities and in schools are all exhorted to this end in books, journals, newspaper articles and television programmes. Yet managers spend most of their time engaged in fragmented and, often, problem-solving activities (see Stewart, 1982; Mintzberg, 1973). The nature of management work seems to comprise the resolution of problems arising from lack of co-ordination rather than the planned and systematic pursuit of co-ordination. Our knowledge of the circumstances of work is fragmented and incomplete. And thus interface problems are common. Thus people concerned to carry out a task can find that the necessary resources, information or equipment are not available.

- *Financial realism*: when I worked as an engineering designer I often made design choices on technical but not commercial or economic grounds. The cost implications of decisions were not considered during the design process. In an increasingly competitive world this approach has become recognized as outmoded. Finance is a crucial input to any organization – not the only one, or even the most important, but one which must be confronted in decision making. Effective or 'excellent' organizations appear to be characterized by managers taking financial issues properly into account alongside other issues such as technical or marketing factors.

If these are some of the characteristics of 'excellent' organizations, how can managers encourage them to emerge? To understand this it is necessary to understand how managers work.

Strategy and structure

Many argue that there is a definite link between strategy and structure. Chandler's (1962) classic study argued that to be successful organizational structure had to be consistent with strategy. It is certainly widely accepted that a number of factors will have an important impact upon success, including the following:

1. The degree of uncertainty in the environment within which the organization operates.
2. The extent of diversity in products and markets, with larger firms in many markets often operating a divisional structure, based on products, or geographic regions, or even combinations of both.
3. Size, larger firms tending to adopt professional management approaches, more formalized procedures, etc. (but see below).
4. Technology, in the broad sense of both the physical infrastructure (machines, computers, factories, offices, etc.) and the 'software' (e.g. the organization of work, product knowledge, information flows, work flows, etc.).
5. Culture, in that there seem to be national differences in appropriate forms of work organization and management style; in some countries team work seems to be more strongly emphasized, in others managers rely less (or more) on formal authority. Quite a lot of research has been undertaken in this area since the landmark study by Hofstede (1968). Some argue that you can identify regional influences (e.g. 'European managers', 'Asia–Pacific' managers), whilst others suggest that either diversity within regions – even within countries – is too great for this to be meaningful, whilst others suggest that the advent of global corporations, information technology, integrated management training and development is creating some convergence. Be that as it may, there are differences which, at the least, must be understood.

There are many research studies of the above (see below). A classic study on the growth of organizations (Greiner, 1972) suggests that they experience periods of evolution and revolution. Both size and age (of organizations) are important variables: the former can lead to problems of co-ordination and control, the latter to inflexibility as attitudes become fixed over time. The main message here is that as each period of revolutionary change creates a new form of organization, then new management styles, control systems, reward systems and structures are introduced.

Classic shifts in organizational structure include the emergence of the multi-divisional structure. Large corporations diversified into a variety of markets often geographically widely dispersed. Problems of control and co-ordination, the need to achieve focus of management effort, allocation of R&D expenditure, etc., led firms to create divisions which then operated relatively autonomously (although in reality the true extent of the autonomy was often questionable and in many firms seemed to vary with the economic cycle – the centre tightening control in the downswing of the cycle).

Of course there are many other factors to take into account. For example, divisionalized organizations may find it difficult to capitalize on efficiencies which may be derived from sharing certain resources (e.g. manufacturing capacity, R&D, sales and distribution outlets/resources, etc.). In addition many organizations face rapidly changing markets and customers wishing to buy changing configurations of products or services. Sometimes it is difficult to sell where a product from various divisions is required. In some cases (e.g. a classic case are computer companies such as Bull in France) some products compete. In any event the purchaser may wish to complete a single deal through a single point of contact. Divisionalized organizations can find this difficult to achieve. One solution to these problems was the strategic business unit concept (Barnett and Wilstead, 1988). Here the focus was on the product market, with a strategic business unit making sense where one could define a clear set of customers and a distinct set of competitors, for which it was possible to create a separate functioning business with an identifiable strategy and in which financial performance could be measured.

In recent times, however, a rapidly changing market, technological and other pressures have led firms to create more adaptability and also to seek to focus on core competencies in which they are likely to achieve excellence. This has led to dramatic changes. Firms are 'de-layering'. For example, at a recent conference I attended, a senior executive from the North American computer industry claimed that large organizations had removed between 1 and 1.5 layers of management *on average* in the last 5 years. In consequence there are, in those organizations, many fewer managers, carrying more responsibility and more demanding jobs than formerly. Information technology, through making access to data easier, is supporting team-based approaches to management. The need to respond quickly to market pressures is leading many organizations to push responsibility down the organization, whether under slogans such as 'empowerment' or through customer service or total quality programmes. For these and other reasons connected with shareholder value, many large businesses have 'de-merged'. In many countries the public service is being reformed along similar lines. Public sector organizations which were once very hierarchical have been either privatized or taken out of the public service as independent agencies. We can see developments like this in North America, the UK, New Zealand and elsewhere. Health care reform in Thailand is proceeding apace on the basis of pushing responsibility down to providers (local hospitals and clinics) rather than managing them directly from the centre (in the capital city).

Over and above all of this, companies outsource, engage in joint ventures and strategic alliances, in order that each element of the 'value chain' (see Porter, 1985) is delivered in a high value-added way. This development is having a powerful impact, creating what some call the 'networked' organization and others are now calling the 'virtual' organization.

Let us look at this trend in rather more detail (the discussion here derives from various sources, including Hastings (1993) and recent work by a colleague, Professor Bill Weinstein, of Henley). Basically there has been a shift from a belief in the advantages of size to the advantages of adaptability. Thirty years ago many organizations set out to achieve integration from raw materials to final customer service, owning and controlling all functions in the value chain with only marginal subcontracting. That way one could control costs, create certainty of delivery, project innovation and limit transaction costs (here we refer to the avoidance of the costs associated with, for example, having to purchase supplies in the open market as opposed to simply ordering from one's own wholly owned supplier).

Increasingly some top managers are asking whether these larger groups are 'manageable'. The risks and problems of inertia are greater. Product development becomes a major problem. 'Time to market' grows with size. I well remember hearing an IBM Europe senior executive (in the late 1980s) complain that any new product proposal had to have seven different senior executives sign it off before it could proceed, including people located locally at the Paris headquarters and elsewhere. The possibility for delay is all too obvious. There is a growing literature on this time-to-market issue (see, for example, Clark and Fujimoto, 1991; Stalk and Hout, 1990) and no one is suggesting that size is the only problem, but the latter study shows that time to market can be reduced significantly by moving from a hierarchical to an 'entrepreneurial' structure, and even further if a 'time-based management' approach is adopted.

Thus we can see countless organizations focusing on their core competencies (Prahalad and Hamel, 1990), dealing with 'preferred' suppliers with whom they develop strong links, delayering, downsizing and focusing upon 'invisible assets' like product market knowledge, competitor intelligence and the like as a source of added value (see Itami, 1987). The practical consequences of these trends are that organizations are now much more likely to be engaged in strategic alliances, joint ventures, outsourcing, networking, joint development projects and so on. This implies a new context for managers.

In the new organization the manager is much more concerned with managing across boundaries (often as well as across borders). There is more dependence on 'outsiders' and less reliance on 'insiders'. Any part of the organization can be 'outsourced'. In the public sector the process is 'market testing'. It creates new pressures. It also means that achieving added value is more a matter of external networking and possessing relevant knowledge about the outside world than formerly. Increasingly managers find that rather than utilizing hierarchy and command and control they are managing exchange relations. Co-operation and negotiation are more relevant. Effective communication becomes vital, but this places greater emphasis on the need to develop internal managerial and technological skills. Without doing so the organization risks being excluded because it brings no added value.

All of this implies that empathy, the ability to seek gains for all partners, flexibility and learning all become vital skills in the new organization. As we shall see, they are also vital skills for those managing major change. Hastings (1993) talks about organizational networking in terms of the need to break down organizational boundaries, create successful partnerships, connect computers and connect people. This implies a new set of priorities for management in this new organization. New management roles that Hastings thinks may be emerging include those of mentor (long talked about, increasingly practised), broker (connecting people, ideas and resources) and what he calls the counterpart. This he describes as a vital role for the success of joint ventures and strategic alliances, but it can be extended into project teams and other internal networks. The role is about providing explicit liaison between links (e.g. joint venture partners) over and above the informal linkages. Looking at cultural change at BP, he reported the company view of the old and the new culture (the latter being one intended to encourage networking) as in Figure 2.1.

Not least of the characteristics of effective people in the new culture is that of *personal impact* – influencing others through example and recognition of their needs. But to conclude, the new thinking about organizations emphasizes the need for new thinking about careers and career development as well as moves to develop what has been called 'the self-reliant' manager (Bones, 1994).

The other source of pressure for change to which we have briefly referred is that of internationalization. Doz and Prahalad (1991) identify characteristics of the diversified internationally operating company as follows:

● Organizational solutions based simply on either centralization or decentralization will not meet the complexity of the modern environment.

● Processes and structure need to allow differentiation to meet the needs of various products, functions and countries.

● Integrative processes are needed if diverse interests are to be balanced – that is, we must work at maintaining interfaces, networks, etc.

● Effective information flows throughout the business are a vital source of added value.

Old culture

- Hierarchies
- Boundaries
- Internal focus

- Paternalistic
- Second guessing
- Controlling

- Analysis
- Risk aversion

New culture

- Teams
- Connections
- External focus

- Empowerment
- Trusting
- Supportive

- Action
- Calculated risk taking or innovation

Figure 2.1 The new and old organizational cultures (after Hastings, 1993)

- Flexibility in structure and process and the capability of including external partners are important.
- There needs to be stability and consistency of purpose – a leadership task.

So once again the demands arising out of internationalization lead to the need to create and operate networks (see Bartlett and Ghoshal (1989) for an analysis of NV Philips as an international network).

It is important to realize that the issues we have referred to are not simply personal issues for which the solutions lie within the 'people skills' area; they are business issues demanding business skills – indeed the management skills required combine business and personal skills. Gould and Campbell (1987) articulate this idea through identifying three corporate styles which you can observe in large, diversified groups, as follows:

1. *Strategic planning style*: strong central management involvement in strategy development through an extensive planning review process and powerful initiatives to secure development of the business arising from the centre. Focus on creating shared vision leads to flexibility in performance targets, with performance being viewed in the context of longer-term objectives.

2. *Strategic control*: emphasis on planning at the business unit level, with the centre concerned primarily with the exercise of tight controls.

3. *Financial control*: the annual budget becomes the key control mechanism, focusing attention on short-term targets.

For Gould and Campbell, where the prime orientation of senior management is characterized by the belief in short-term results, the financial control style will emerge. Where the orientation is on longer-term competitive advantage seen as arising out of more than only financial success which can be developed, in whole or in part, from the centre, then one of the other two styles will predominate. In the former it is not necessarily the case that senior management do not accept that competitive advantage emerges out of factors other than financial performance, but rather they disbelieve the notion that centrally driven initiatives are the best source of competitive advantage.

They then link these styles to a number of factors, including the shape, size and diversity of the product/service portfolio, stability in the environment, the personality of the chief executive, the financial condition of the business and so on. From all of this we can begin to see that over the last 20 or 30 years changes within the global economy have created new management problems demanding solutions both more complex and more demanding of management skills than traditional hierarchies. We now turn to what managers do.

ABB (Asea Brown Boveri), known as the European company the giants of Asia feared, is an interesting example of how these dilemmas of organization are faced e.g. the global–local dilemma in particular. As a company it operates in 60 or more countries through over 1300 separate legal entities. It operates in a range of electrical and power engineering activities, often engaged in major capital schemes for governments in the developing world. Thus the local imperative is a strong one. How is the business held together globally? The CEO spends much of his time visiting subsidiaries articulating the group strategy and seeking to understand local needs. The group has a well-developed information system for financial and management control. Much attention is given to identifying and then developing the careers of a cadre of 'high fliers' seen as the future senior managers of the business. Thus considerable effort is devoted to integrating diversity. The approach is not simply about organizing for co-ordination and control. The group appears to organize around local needs and then wraps those local operations within arrangements designed to pursue integration across the world. Key technologies are managed by a senior executive with a global remit to maximize the leverage of that technology for the group.

Managerial performance

Managerial performance is a combination of knowledge and skill applied in practice. Management is about 'getting things done', about action. Managerial work is surrounded by circumstances which create problems including uncertainty, incomplete information, change in the environment or elsewhere in the organization and conflict. Mintzberg (1973) has developed a comprehensive empirical picture of the nature of managerial work through observing and recording what managers actually do. He describes the managerial job in terms of roles (see Table 2.2).

From his empirical work Mintzberg characterizes managerial jobs as follows:

- They are remarkably similar and can be described in 10 roles (see Table 2.2) and six sets of working characteristics.

- Much managerial work is challenging and non-routine, but every manager has some routine and regular ordinary duties.

- A manager is both a generalist and a specialist.

- Information is an important part of the manager's power.

- The major pitfall for the manager is having to be superficial because the workload is too high.

- Management science has little effect on how the manager works because when under work pressure he or she fragments activity and uses verbal communication, making it difficult for management scientists to help.

- The management scientist can only break this 'vicious circle' with real understanding of the manager's job, and access to the manager's own views of the help he or she needs.

Table 2.2 ● Managerial roles (after Mintzberg, 1973)

Interpersonal roles	Informational roles	Decisional roles
Figurehead	Monitor	Entrepreneur Disturbance
Leader	Disseminator	Handler Resource
Liaison	Spokesperson	Allocator Negotiator

The six working characteristics relate to the following:

1. The quantity and pace of the manager's work.
2. The patterns of the activities.
3. The relationship in work between action and reflection.
4. The use of different communications media.
5. The relationships with contacts.
6. The interaction between rights and duties.

Mintzberg (1973), Stewart (1977), Dubin and Spray (1964) and Horne and Lupton (1965) all confirm from empirical studies that managers' workloads are substantial. Managers work at an unrelenting pace. This is because the job is inherently open ended and the manager never finishes his or her work.

Managerial work is characterized by brevity, variety and fragmentation. The manager is never able to concentrate on one aspect of the job alone or for any length of time. The trivial and the important are mixed so that mood and tone shift and change continually. Mintzberg found that half of the activities of five CEOs took 9 minutes or less and only 10 per cent lasted more than an hour. The manager is seldom able or willing to spend much time on any one issue. He or she is constantly interrupted. Rosemary Stewart found only nine periods of half an hour without interruption in a 4 week study of 160 managers!

The manager seems to stress the active element of work – activities that are current, specific, well defined and non-routine attract more attention: for example, processing most mail and reading written reports are low-priority jobs. The manager may be seen as the conductor of the orchestra and, conversely, as a puppet pulled by hundreds of strings. To find out the extent to which managers controlled themselves, Mintzberg analyzed whether in each activity managers were active or passive, and found only a small proportion of active work, with managers spending much time reacting. The initial construction of the manager's job may, however, have included decisions to allow these reactions and passive participation as a way of keeping up a flow of work and ensuring the involvement of others in the management process.

Concluding comment: management in action again

This chapter has examined how organizations are structured and managed. It has identified and described various management structures. But structures are not everything. Overlaid on the question of structure are at least six 'dilemmas' of organization. The reality of organizational life is that these 'dilemmas' are constantly presented to managers as the circumstances around them change. In practice, managers have discretion and choice in the work they do. The extent to which they will recognize and exploit this discretion, will be related to the 'corporate culture' of the organization. This is a question to which we will turn in a later chapter of this book. For the moment we conclude by stating that defining an organizational structure is to define a 'moving target'. It only begins to establish the boundaries within which managers act or choose not to act, and within which they can obtain resources and information and be held accountable for what they do!

The above identification and analysis of managerial roles cannot describe the whole, but nor can a manager function who does not fulfil these roles to some degree. This is the real difficulty in team management which requires very careful reintegration and effective communication. Different managers spend different amounts of time on different roles.

To be effective a manager requires the following:

● Self-knowledge and insight.

● Understanding of the managerial job.

● Timely and controlled responses to the pressures and dilemmas which apply.

Managers must also find ways of dealing with the daily dilemmas and pressures of their working lives. Understanding organizations, then, involves understanding both what managers actually do and how it can be/should be structured.

In the next chapter we will develop the concept of a value-added organization taking forward the thinking established in Chapter 1 and building on the ideas set out above. We will seek to set out some of the tools and techniques which have been developed as managers have sought to devise and manage new forms of organization. We shall see that not least of the principles emerging in the value-added organization is the increased application of market mechanisms to induce change. We are in the midst of a shift in the mind-set (see Chapter 4). We need new means of managing changes, moving away from a reliance on planned changes towards an increased use of a mix of planned and market-induced change.

Exercises

1. How does your organization deal with the dilemmas we have identified?

2. To what extent is the commitment model one which encourages innovation and creativity? Can you think of any experience (in a company, at college, in a sports club) which represents a good example?

3. What management structure does your company (or department) have? Why? Is it likely to change? What are the main reasons for change?

CHAPTER 3

Organizations in the twenty-first century

The value-added organization

In this chapter we seek to present a set of practical tools to assist you in rethinking your own organization along the lines set out in Chapter 1. Throughout we combine some explanatory text with a sequence of exercises and instructions. It is intended to help you to think through and apply the ideas set out in the book. You may wish to return to this chapter as you work through the book. The workbook has been designed on the assumption that you are seriously engaged in a process of organizing around the flow of value to customers and intend to adopt 'cluster' structures. However, the techniques can be applied even if you do not propose to apply those specific ideas.

The global business environment is changing faster than ever. We are living in an era where businesses constantly need to reshape their ideas merely to survive. But to achieve sustained success it is not sufficient merely to manage existing operations better: businesses need to do things radically different to secure an advantage over their competitors. Thus, in the future, we shall need to focus not on re-engineering processes but on re-engineering markets, not on restructuring the organization but on transforming it.

If you recognize one of more of the following pressures increasingly impacting on your organization, then the need for radical transformation could be just around the corner:

- The transition from growth to maturity in developed economies, leading to over-capacity, more competition and fewer larger players.
- The need to compete against global leaders, even in once secure local markets.
- The challenge of managing a shift from a wide competence/local market focus to a narrow competence/international market focus.
- The entry of small, aggressive competitors into niche segments, using these as a springboard to challenge the leaders.

● The shift from integration (ownership or control of all elements of the value chain) to specialization (leveraging capability in one key element of the value chain).

● The shift in power or added value from one player to another in the value chain (from manufacturers to distributors or suppliers or vice versa).

● The need to cope with and exploit the increasing speed of business processes, in particular time to market for innovative new products and services.

These are critical issues for competitive organizations. Business transformation is a philosophy which challenges established practices and boundaries in a fundamental way. It involves challenging 'the rules of the game'.

Changing the rules of the game

'We've restructured, we've de-layered, we've got close to our customers, we've achieved zero fault manufacturing and service capability. Now what do we do for an encore?' Questions like this indicate that 'business as usual plus' is no longer an adequate means of achieving sustained competitive success. In future, this will go increasingly to organizations which are able to achieve radical change either internally or externally, or, more probably, both. *This is the central idea of the business transformation philosophy.* This approach to competitive strategy is based on five key propositions:

1. Discontinuity in the market is more likely to result from *radical* rather than *incremental* change, and this is likely to be driven as much by companies themselves as by social and economic factors.

2. Coping with strategic change needs to move from an emphasis on *forecasting* to creating an organization which can *respond to change fast.*

3. Approaches to gaining and sustaining competitive advantage need to shift from *erecting barriers* (vertical integration, proprietary technology, piling up fixed costs to create scale, etc.) to *overcoming or ignoring barriers* (through outsourcing, building strategic alliances, and the aggressive elimination of fixed costs).

4. The basis of strategic thinking therefore needs to shift from an *as is now* perspective of market attractiveness and competitive capability to *changing the rules of the game*, thus destabilizing entrenched players.

5. The role of leadership in this context is to affirm that *'it's achievable'* (provider of a business vision), rather than *'it's impossible'* (controller/naysayer).

By changing the rules of the game, a business may be able to wrong-foot competitors to such an extent that they may never recover; this can be achieved by driving radical changes internally or externally. Thus the competitive breakthroughs of the future are likely to go to businesses which can transform either their market or their organization, or both. This will involve radical rather than incremental change, and needs vision and leadership to bring it about. But before business transformation can realistically be contemplated, a sound strategic basis must be formulated upon which subsequent actions can be built. Strategic thinking must be the foundation of any intention or attempt to change the rules of the game, and the programme will commence with a searching review of this essential management skill.

Techniques for a value-added organization

These are as follows:

- Assessing the value added.
- Process redesign – mapping the value flow to enhance value added.
- The balanced scorecard.
- Activity-based costing and customer satisfaction analysis.
- The 360° appraisal.
- Competence models.

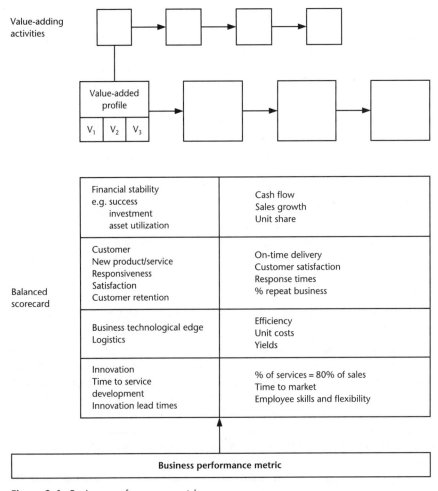

Figure 3.1 Business performance metric

The workbook is designed to focus on the application of the first four steps in the organization design process. The combination of these techniques is shown in Figure 3.1.

The steps are as follows:

A. Assess the strengths, weaknesses and development priorities of the business (business performance metric) and value added from the existing business (value-added metric).
B. Using the business performance metric development priorities as a starting point, develop a balanced scorecard for the unit, business, etc.
C. Assess the process design by identifying the value-adding activities in the business, identifying cost drivers and seeking new business process configurations both to manage cost effectively and to enhance the performance and value-added metrics.

Step 1A: business performance metric

The business capability profile seeks to assess a company's managerial, competitive, financial and business process strengths and weaknesses. The completed profile reveals 'gaps' which need to be corrected and strengths on which to build.

To complete the metric you should first go through each item scoring it 1 to 7 for the current situation (actual). Thus is your company growth rate currently low – high scored 1–7. Having completed that you should then identify no more than 24 high-priority items from the items in the profile.

The exercise should enable you to identify strengths, weaknesses and development priorities. Development priorities are those where the priority is high but the current score is low.

A1: corporate position

	Score (1 to 7)		
	Low	Actual/priority	High
Growth			
Profit (last 5 years)			
Financial stability			
Technological capability			
Asset utilization			
Capital intensity			
Productivity			
New entrants to market			
Other			
	Low		High

A2: organizational factors

Score (1 to 7)

Low **Actual/priority** **High**

Integration across the business
Brand image
Flexibility
Performance focus
Ability to attract and retain
creative people
Ability to change
Investment in new product development
Access to information
Team-based problem-solving
Other

Low **High**

A3: competitive position

Score (1 to 7)

Low **Actual/priority** **High**

Market share
Product quality
Product differentiation
Product life cycle
Selling/distribution costs
Time to market
'Tender' success (bid 'hit rate')
Customer loyalty
Capacity utilization in the industry
Technological capability
Other

Low **High**

A4: financial strength

Score (1 to 7)

Low **Actual/priority** **High**

ROI
Liquidity
Availability of capital
Stability of costs
Order book
Cash flow
Ease of exit
Risk in industry
Other

Low **High**

A5: business processes

Technical skills
Resource utilization
Level of technology used in products
Strength of patents/processes
Operational effectiveness
Delivery performance
Value added to customer
Labour intensity
Economies of scale
Application of information technology
Level of co-ordination
Elapsed to work time ratio
Other

Score (1 to 7)

Low   Actual/priority   High

Low   High

Step 1B: value-added organization metric

If the goal of your company is to create value for all stakeholders, this metric can help you assess how well prepared it is to achieve that goal.

1. *Does the company seek to solve problems so that all stakeholders benefit (customers, employees, shareholders, the local community) or does it consistently favour one or more stakeholder groups?*

Focused on one stakeholder	**Often makes trade-offs between two stakeholder groups**	**Seeks mutual benefits**
1 2 3	**4 5 6 7**	**8 9 10**

2. *Is there an integrated performance measurement framework which links individual level to corporate level performance covering employee, customer and shareholder issues and concerns?*

No framework	**Fragmented framework**	**Integrated framework**
1 2 3	**4 5 6 7**	**8 9 10**

3. *Do we have a good understanding of the value drivers of our business?*

No clear understanding	**We focus on everything**	**We focus on the key value drivers**
1 2 3	**4 5 6 7**	**8 9 10**

4. *Does the company approach market and employee performance measurement as rigorously as financial measurement?*

Financial measures only	**Some of each, but based to one area**	**Balanced**
1 2 3	4 5 6 7	8 9 10

5. *Do we make decisions using a rational approach based on 'the figures' or do we seek to combine factual analysis and intuition in our judgement?*

No analysis at all	**Rational analysis**	**Combine 'facts' with intuition**
1 2 3	4 5 6 7	8 9 10

6. *Is reward based upon tenure or value?*

'Equitable' tenure-based rewards	**Performance pay**	**Rewards linked to creation of value**
1 2 3	4 5 6 7	8 9 10

7. *Is the value created by all parts of the company (from the CEO down) clearly defined and understood?*

Not defined	**Defined only within store operations**	**Defined throughout the business**
1 2 3	4 5 6 7	8 9 10

8. *Does the information, work flow and reward infrastructure support flexible responses or do investigations and studies drive change in the business?*

Nothing changes without a major study	**Lots of data, poor insight**	**Flexibility**
1 2 3	4 5 6 7	8 9 10

9. *Is the organization of work designed around the needs of the customer?*

Defined by the corporate hierarchy	**Designed around teams**	**Designed around the customer**
1 2 3	4 5 6 7	8 9 10

10. *How does the company compare with others inside and outside the industry in value created for shareholders, customers and employees?*

Below average	**Average**	**Excellent value Creator**
1 2 3	4 5 6 7	8 9 10

Thank you.

Step 2: mapping the value flow

It is normal to define value flow (or chain) of activities for customers, distinguishing primary and support activities. Once the value flow is identified you need to decide how to organize these activities, e.g. on functional, product–service geographical bases and either 'command and control' or value-added clusters.

1 Value-added design

1.1 Map value flows.

1.2 Identify important transactions with customers.

1.3 Assess level of input needed from other functions for each activity.

1.4 Estimate/assess customer perceptions of:
cost (high, medium, low; stable, changing)
importance (high, medium, low) and
satisfaction (high, medium, low).

1.5 Estimate elapsed to work time ratio.

1.6 Assess whether to 'cluster': proceed to steps C2 and C3.

2 Estimate value-added problems of 'command and control' mode

2.1 Value flows across functions.

2.2 Narrowly defined tasks.

2.3 Multiple handovers (and queries).

2.4 No 'owner' for the customer.

2.5 High elapsed to work time ratios.

3 Value-added clusters

3.1 A cluster of end-to-end activities which create value for a customer.

3.2 End-to-end activities contain most or all tasks from start to delivery of outputs (note: but shared service clusters may need to be involved).

3.3 *Value* on customer-critical issues such as speed, cost, quality, service, delivery.

3.4 *Customer* – internal or external.

3.5 *Size* – no final answer but in professional businesses 30–40 people the norm.

4 Value-added contributions

Once steps 1, 2 and 3 are complete we can define the value-added contribution each 'cluster' brings to the total business process. For example, a *management team* might deliver the following:

Strategy
● decide and recommend new directions;
● guide and drive strategy;

- develop plans in support of strategies;
- manage the asset portfolio.

Performance management

- monitor and appraise performance;
- manage external image and brand.

Resourcing

- allocate resources;
- agree service levels;
- acquire new technologies, capabilities and people.

A *primary cluster*, however, would seek to achieve a flexible, de-layered and business-oriented approach delivering the following:

- customer satisfaction;
- competititive prices;
- team work;
- high-quality, integrated solutions;
- ability to learn and to change;
- provision of product/service with better functionality and value.

If the business operates internationally and for *that purpose is organised regionally into operating units, then there may be a need for business interface managers* who link the clusters to those operating units via 'service agreements' or contracts. These managers would deliver the following:

- act as account manager for the operating unit;
- ensure that the operating unit's needs are responded to in plans and programmes
- agree contract variations within agreed authority limits
- work with cluster to ensure 'deliverables'
- leverage common technology interests of operating units to ensure maximum benefits to company
- leverage best practice
- spend significant time in the operating units.

A *support cluster* such as an IT group might be tasked to deliver:

- computing infrastructure;
- data management and QA;
- IT integration projects;
- software integration platforms.

The important point is to identify the necessary organizational components *including* clusters *and* to identify how each contributes value added to its customers (internal or external). This facilitates the development of balanced scorecards.

Step 3: the 'balanced scorecard'

This is a technique to measure business unit performance which can also be used at departmental or 'cluster' level. The scorecard uses various perspectives to give a balanced picture of current performance and the drivers of future performance. Typically the four perspectives are financial, customer, business processes and innovation. Many argue that managers cannot operate with multiple measures and therefore argue priority for aggregate financial measures (such as operating income, return on investments, economic value added). These are widely used and provide a basis for unambiguous and objective goals.

The counter-view is that on the whole financial measures focus on past performance, saying little about the drivers of future performance. Moreover, experience with the technique shows that managers can make effective use of the balanced scorecard as a performance management and improvement tool so long as each is limited to around 20 measures. In practice the alternative is to have financial measures plus a bewildering variety of other measures often not understood, not reported consistently and not widely or effectively disseminated.

In addition, in a 'value-added' organization the balanced scorecard is a means of making the organization more transparent. It enables the organization focus on how activities interconnect to provide customer service. It shows the contribution each makes to the total. It provides a better basis for cohesion and integration of activities. The balanced scorecard can be depicted as in Figure 3.2.

The measures selected within each perspective need to be based upon a particular view about the business:

1. What do *customers* value?
   response times
   accuracy
   implementable solutions
   price.

2. *Business process*: at what do we need to excel?
   order processing
   delivery to customer
   flexibility
   integrated service packages.

3. *Innovation*: how can the organization improve?
   transfer of best practice
   training
   development of new services
   delivery of integrated solutions.

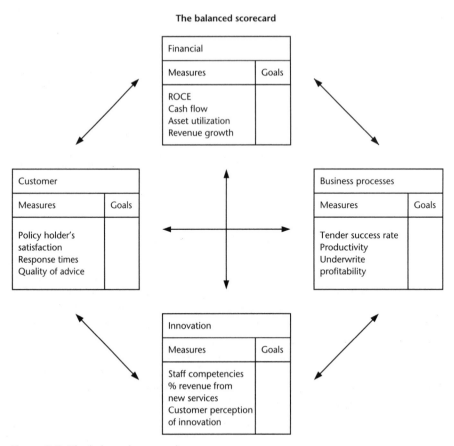

Figure 3.2 The balanced scorecard

4. *Financial perspective*: is the organization creating value?

Typically, creating and implementing a balanced scorecard is part of an overall performance management system in which strategic vision links through unit level balanced scorecards to personal objectives and rewards, plans and budgets and performance review. Building a balanced scorecard is usually undertaken through a programme including senior management with the following objectives:

● to guide the construction and measures for the scorecard;

● to gain commitment;

● to clarify the framework for the implementation and management processes needed to use the scorecard effectively.

A typical workshop to create a balanced scorecard comprises the following stages.

The workshop activity

Agree the vision and strategy and make any decisions necessary to define how resources will be configured into units, groups, clusters, etc., in pursuit of that vision.

Agree the four perspectives to be included and brainstorm possible measures. Discuss each on its merits and not on comparison with the others. Once all measures have been considered select three to four 'candidates', voting if necessary.

Divide into four subgroups, one for each perspective. Each subgroup should identify three to four measures, provide a detailed description for each and propose goals for each (Round 1). The facilitator should circulate a summary of the output.

At the next meeting the subgroups review the measures/goals:

● refine the wording;

● identify the detail for the measure;

● identify sources of information and how to access it;

● identify linkages between measures within the perspective and with other score-card perspectives (Round 2).

Executive workshop to sign off the balanced scorecards (Round 3) as part of the implementation plan.

Selecting the measures

Measures relevant to the activity are essential but the following often appear:

Finance: ROI, profit, revenue growth/mix, cost reduction/productivity.

Customer: Market share, customer acquisition, customer retention, customer satisfaction, customer profitability.

Innovation: Flexibility, percentage of sales from new products/services, time to market.

Business process: Resource utilization.

Creating an implementation plan

Define a detailed implementation plan including training, roll-out of measures and a further executive workshop to sign off the scorecards.

Exercises

1. Can you depict your own organization as horizontal management of value added?

2. To what extent does your company seek to develop its 'social capital'?

3. Assess your own unit, department, division, company, using the business capability profile. What are its strengths and weaknesses?

CHAPTER 4

The learning organization

Ideas and concepts such as 'organizational learning' and 'the learning organization' are widely used by human resources management practitioners. Senior managers express the wish to create 'learning organizations'. At various points throughout this book we argue the view that effective change necessarily involves learning. What does this mean? Can we claim that organizations learn? Does it matter? It is clear that managers may learn as part of the process of change either about themselves or about the company, its environment and so on. This much is illustrated by the previous chapter. But can an organization learn?

Not least of the reasons for interest in the question is the observation that business techniques appear suddenly rather like fashion. Moreover, the use of such techniques ebbs and flows, waxes and wanes. Often one can also readily conceive today's latest technique as comprising old ideas recycled, repackaged and projected as novel to gain attention, or so it seems. In reality it appears that organizations adopt fashionable techniques but are unable to incorporate them as a sustained way of doing business.

At one level, organizational learning clearly is of interest. If only individuals learn, then when people leave an organization the learning they have achieved goes with them. This happens a great deal in practice. On the other hand, learning is often reflected in changing procedures, patterns of behaviour, evolving cultures and so on. Some would argue that these do change and that therefore learning is 'captured'. In that sense organizations learn.

The central point is whether or not we can observe systematic changes in behaviour and culture over time. If we can, there is clearly a basis for arguing that whilst the process of learning may be individual, the consequences may be more wide reaching.

Thus if the individual processes lead to enduring changes in behaviour and culture (in teams and throughout an organization) then the learning is 'captured' at the broader level. So we might refer to 'organization' as opposed to individual learning, and organizations which seek to encourage the 'capture' of learning could be said to be 'learning organizations'. However, there is no accepted model of organizational learning and, moreover, not everyone agrees about whether an organization can learn.

There are two main points here:

1. The debate may be largely irrelevant to those concerned with developing organizational practice.
2. Many ideas about organization and 'organizational learning' are incomplete.

We would accept the following:

> scholars of organisations have developed theories that not only don't work for them but won't work for others.
>
> (Weick, 1991)

In any event, the focus of this chapter is on how an organization can be designed, systems created, and a climate developed to encourage learning and effectiveness.

Changing perceptions of organization

We have already seen (in Chapter 1) that our perception or mind-set related to how organizations are described, designed and experienced is changing. This is due to technological, market and competitive changes and challenges. However, part of the change is associated with the impact of rapid, often discontinuous change and attempts by those involved to find ways of dealing with this increased pace and complexity. In addition, issues such as managing diversity, cross-cultural influences, gender and the environment are creating new challenges to rethink the organization. Finally, the challenge of the long-term switch from a 'career for life' model for at least some employees to a more individually centred concept of career perhaps adds a new impetus to 'learn how to learn'.

In consequence, new ways of describing organizations are now beginning to replace more orthodox approaches. Peter Senge maintains that it is now necessary to think more carefully about what is meant by learning and organization. His work challenges practising managers to recognize that 'mind-set' is a crucial aspect of learning.

> The most accurate word in Western culture to describe what happens in a learning organisation is one that hasn't had much currency for the past several hundred years. The word is 'metanoia' and it means a shift of mind. To grasp the meaning … is to grasp the deeper meaning of learning.
>
> (Senge, 1990)

Some organizations are beginning to rethink the ways in which they relate to the social context within which they operate. Rover now claims its first customers are the people it employs. To keep the workforce, to prepare it for the years ahead, and to give employees a stake in their own future and skills which can be used in other employment, Rover believes it must invest in employee development, based on both company and employees' needs. The second customers Rover serves are the people to whom it sells cars. The sale to BMW will determine whether this policy will continue and work.

There is some evidence that Rover's policy has produced results. Rover took more than 3000 employees off the assembly lines and out of offices and sent them to study management and assembly techniques in companies around the world, including Sony, Sainsbury and Honda. Rover saw this expense showing results in the production of its new Rover 800. This new car was designed and built in just 24 months, compared with the usual 39 month lead time at Rover, and the 35 month average for Japanese car producers. Rover looked seriously at the processes required to produce a car. The result was the scrapping of various functions and a merging of design and manufacturing processes so that faults were ironed out as they happened. By bringing together a project team representing all the major functions there was a 10 per cent saving on development costs.

This is an example of how one firm's ideas about its organizational and operational contexts have been adapted and widened to accommodate activities which, hitherto, have been excluded. But to understand this we need to explore the concept of mind-set a little further.

Looking back at the Ford case study given in Chapter 1, whether or not you conclude that Ford was (or is now) a 'learning organization' it is clear that over a period of time the company believes it has learnt lessons and/or developed systems (e.g. the world-wide engineering release system) which provide an important platform for the global developments now underway.

Van der Erve (1994) argues that evolution is the engine of corporate success. He argues that evolution requires we both understand the changes impacting upon us and know how to ride those changes. Evolution involves a succession of differentiated 'life forms'. Clearly organizational change involves differentiation whether of product features, or target markets or internal capabilities, employee attitudes or customer loyalty or whatever. A chairman of Nestlé offered the following prescription for successful change and growth:

> Be first, be daring, and be different.

But you cannot expect to do so by accident (by random mutation as it were). On this view corporate success demands a high order of cognitive capability or, to follow Argyris and Schon (1974), the capacity for 'double-loop' learning, the capacity to break the mould, to challenge the established norms, policies, objectives, resource configurations and corporate architecture.

All of this argues for the notion of paradigm shift as an important element. Capra (1986) defines a social paradigm as 'a constellation of concepts, values, perceptions and practices shared by a community which forms a particular vision of reality that is the basis of the way the community organises itself'. He goes on to argue that the social paradigm which drives 'the modern world' is evolving from a mechanistic and essentially fragmented view into a new paradigm through shifts on various dimensions, as follows:

● from a focus on the part to the whole;

● from a concern with structure to process;

● from revolutionary to evolutionary change;

● from objective science to an understanding of how we learn;

- from hierarchy to network as the metaphor for knowledge;
- from truth to approximate descriptions;
- from domination and control of nature to co-operative approaches.

The reader should note that I have modified and thereby simplified the Capra text essentially because I seek to summarize these ideas for a particular purpose. It seems to me that we are in the midst of a shift in the mind-set (or paradigm) related to economic activity towards one which emphasizes networks as learning and collaborative resources, which emphasizes proximate to optimal solutions, which emphasizes process and learning through evolution above all and which depends less on a need for certainty to precede action and more on the use of action as a means of achieving certainty.

Van der Erve (1994) describes this paradigm shift thus:

- from quantification and certainty to differentiation and uncertainty;
- from parts to wholes;
- from organization to enable tasks to 'self-organization' to enable creation;
- from single-loop to double-loop learning.

Our view is that this shift in the paradigm has been associated with changes in the language of business which, in turn, has provided the possibilities for new solutions. Where once we talked of organization, tasks, systems, products, technology and customers, we increasingly talk about competencies, capabilities, added value, performance management, process design, information flow. In turn this has happened in consequence of the increased competitiveness of the world post 1970. Increasingly when faced with tough competition, the successful organization is the one which changes the rules of the game. Hamel and Prahalad (1991) conclude:

> Market research and segmentation analyses are unlikely to reveal such opportunities. Deep insight into the needs, lifestyles and aspirations of today's and tomorrow's customers will.

As far as major change is concerned, this paradigm shift has moved our thinking about how to achieve change. Where once the concern was with top-down or 'bottom-up' change with most of our discussion being about why change programmes fail and how to use involvement programmes as a means of buy-in and success, we now seek the following, often via cascade communication programmes, change workshops, performance management programmes and the use of market mechanisms:

- Providing people with a new frame of reference about the company, its performance, its markets, etc.
- Uncovering hidden or 'tacit' knowledge (see below).
- Learning by scoping perceptions.
- Circumventing destructive politics.
- Seeking rapid change via differentiation.

In summary then, achieving mind-set shift is first and foremost a cognitive task undertaken within a social context. Whilst communication, involvement and empowerment will form a part of the process, *unless* we are prepared to engage with the cognitive challenge we are unlikely to succeed. In turn this implies or requires certain skills to be deployed and particular organization characteristics to be in place.

Disciplines for the learning organization

Senge (1990) indicates how such an approach can be generated and identifies what he calls *five disciplines* as the key characteristics which everyone must develop if they wish to create a learning culture which produces an organization capable of facing the challenge of making sense of emerging complexity.

The five skills or characteristics are:

1. *Systems thinking*: everyone must learn how to view things as a whole and that one set of events impacts on others.

2. *Personal mastery*: for Senge this is 'the discipline of continually clarifying and deepening ... personal vision, of focusing ... energies, of developing patience, and of seeing reality objectively. As such, it is an essential cornerstone of the learning organisation – the learning organisation's spiritual foundation.'

3. *Mental models*: these are about 'learning to unearth ... internal pictures of the world, to bring them to the surface, and hold them rigorously to scrutiny'.

4. *Build a shared vision*: this is about everyone holding a shared vision for the future. Leadership is the key to creating and communicating the vision. However, Senge sees leadership being about creating structures and activities which relate to a person's total life activity. The leader creates vision but is prepared to have it reshaped by others.

5. *Team learning*: teams, not single individuals, are the key to successful organizations of the future and individuals have to learn how to learn in the context of the team.

The key observation here is that when an organization faces increased complexity in its environment (caused perhaps by competitive and technological change) there is a need to rethink. This implies a 'mind-set' shift such as that referred to above.

How can this mind-set shift happen? Hurst (1995) argues that faced with complexity a performance organization needs to become a learning organization if change is to be achieved. To this end an emphasis on recognition, networks and teams replaces tightly defined tasks, control systems and rigid structures. One of the necessary conditions, Hurst argues, is crisis, i.e. a clear failure of the status quo which cannot be rationalized away, hidden or denied. He argues that all organizations go through an ecocycle comprising eight stages:

1. Strategic management
2. Consolidation
3. Crisis

4. Confusion

5. Charismatic leadership

6. Creative network

7. Choice

8. Innovation.

Without needing to deny that some organizations will fail, what Hurst's model implies is a renewal process through which an organization recreates itself – more specifically in which people rethink what they seek to achieve, with whom and how, and thereby recreate the organization. Whatever else this may be, it is certainly a learning process.

How does this ecocycle model relate to the coping cycle model discussed in Chapter 10? In effect the coping cycle model deals with the process associated with a single change whereas the ecocycle model presents the same ideas (i.e. initial shock, denial and confusion followed by adaptation and change) in a circular fashion in order to add the dimension of renewal.

Thus we can see that over the medium term change can be part of an overall renewal process. Moreover, we have seen that for this to happen organization processes may need to be rethought. But at the heart of this learning process are people who are either stimulated, helped or hindered by the circumstances which prevail. What do we need to think about as far as the 'fit' between individuals and the organization is concerned if we wish to engender learning and renewal?

One of the oft mentioned but little analyzed issues in strategic change is that of 'timing'. It is often claimed that timing is vital. One sees it in the Ford case (Chapter 1). Hurst's (1995) view of the organizational ecocycle provides one way of viewing the question of timing. By way of introducing this model let us first list Hurst's own summary of its key features:

1. Change is continuous.

2. The pace of change varies, sometimes smooth and linear, sometimes rapid and non-linear.

3. Renewal requires destruction. In a resource-limited world the only way to create new structures, opportunities, possibilities is to dismantle structures which are currently claiming the resources.

4. Emerging structures and processes are a product of a multiplicity of factors including constraints imposed by the environment.

5. However, the organization's people are self-conscious 'actors' capable of rational action.

Whilst the reader may refer to Hurst (1995) for a full treatment, here suffice it to say that the essence of the ecocycle model is to argue that organizations go through crisis and renewal through three phases:

1. Emergent action

2. Rational action

3. Constrained action.

The model starts with the recognition of a market opportunity which turns out to be repeatable. Hurst gives the example of Nike, a company initially established in high-performance track and field shoes, which was able quickly to expand as it moved from basketball to tennis, American football, soccer and many more activities. Also an early mover in the use of endorsements by top athletes, the company exploited a huge, untapped market. By contrast the 1980s saw increased specialization as between sports, new materials and designs combined with flexible manufacturing. Nike were then attacked by competitors such as Reebok (in the aerobics market).

In effect therefore Hurst argues that behaviour (action) is rational at the outset (as we seek to enter a given market), constrained as we proceed up the product life cycle (by competition not least) and then emergent as the need for renewal emerges, often because crisis has occurred or has to be precipitated before significant change can be achieved. By rational we take Hurst to mean the broader rationality we refer to in Chapter 5 rather than narrowly, scientifically rational.

The similarity between the Hurst and the Van der Erve view is obvious enough. Both are evolutionary models. In effect both argue that 'nothing fails like success', i.e. that given a successful formula which then begins to underperform, it is very difficult to get an organization to do more than seek incremental improvements which fail. Clear differentiation is what is needed. For Hurst the cycle is a learning cycle. What he does not analyze is how the learning is captured such that the organization could be said to have learned, but what he does clearly do is show business development and corporate change as a social process within which learning is embedded.

Convergence and the learning organization

Putting these ideas together a number of points appear to emerge. The most important is that if an organization is to achieve long-term benefit from the learning which is undoubtedly achieved through change then appropriate processes are needed. In fact we need *convergent systems* designed to capture and create knowledge. We need to secure a convergence of the IT infrastructure's capacity to capture knowledge, the management structure and systems design focused on the encouragement of learning, and corporate development processes aimed at achieving learning and applying it in new circumstances. All of this needs to be 'energized' by appropriate leadership, vision, rewards and 'mental maps'.

Thus we need a process which facilitates 'productive reasoning'. At root that is hard cognitive work to do with identifying and challenging assumptions, collecting and analyzing data, challenging the status quo, opening up tacit knowledge and converting it to explicit knowledge, bringing in new knowledge and thinking through the unintended consequences of systems, decisions, the status quo, new ideas and so on. New techniques in the field of cognitive modelling can help in training these cognitive capabilities but at root the issue is about overcoming the organizational defences against 'productive reasoning' (see Chapter 5 for more detail).

Of course we need the IT infrastructure to capture learning, e.g. to create a database of customer profile and customer complaints as a resource for product development. But best practice increasingly seeks to provide by electronic means building blocks of management knowledge, examples of best practice, best practice protocols, performance measures, diagnostic tools, etc. But new roles are also implied, see below.

CASE STUDY

Oticon A/S

Oticon is a Danish manufacturer of hearing aids. Having established a dominant position in its sector through the 1950s and 1960s, its performance declined in the 1980s. It was caught out by the advent of In-the-Ear aids which it was slow to develop, but its decline was masked by the steady strengthening of the Danish kroner in the 1980s.

This meant that when finally the need for change was accepted, action needed to be more immediate and wide ranging. Under a new chief executive a turnaround was put in place focused initially on survival but eventually on innovation and change (from 1990 onwards).

In summary the organization has sought to 'think the unthinkable'. In manufacturing it had a flexible manufacturing approach based upon cellular approaches. In head office a 'sphagetti organization' has been created. In essence the organization is an 'internal market'. People are expected to carry out their normal jobs and be involved in projects. *Everyone* is expected to be involved in projects. There is no paper!

But an organization depending heavily on projects may be less effective in professional and technological development, and in particular not good at leveraging technology to maximum effect. Valuable gains in knowledge may be lost or not shared around the business. Thus it was that the role of 'guardian' was created. Guardians, often past functional managers, oversee the development of a specific professional skill (e.g. marketing, finance, technology). They are expected to ensure that Oticon's competencies met the developing strategic rquirements of the business.

But then following Nonaka and Takeuchi (1995) we can conceive of organizational learning as those processes we utilize to capture and convert tacit knowledge into new explicit knowledge and/or to obtain new explicit knowledge. Tacit knowledge is important because when organizations are faced with problems and challenges they rarely emerge overnight. Normally people within the organization have begun to recognize the problems and conceive solutions. Usually these are incomplete solutions and not thought through. They represent tacit knowledge. We need a process to 'collect' that emerging knowledge. The solutions we adopt may need new knowledge as well – say of a new technology. Thus we would seek new explicit knowledge.

Doing so, i.e. capturing and converting tacit and explicit knowledge to integrate it into our business system (into our strategy, structure procedures, product portfolios, etc.), helps the process of shifting mind-sets by adding new possibilities. Here the thought is that mind-set change is unlikely to result from directly challenging people's ideas. Rather it follows by adding new ideas, and therefore new possibilities.

Such a view has something in common with Orgland's (1997) concept of 'vision influencing'. He describes his lack of clarity of the role middle and junior managers had played in a major process redesign change undertaken by a consumer goods manufacturer. He notes that when asked to contribute to a process redesign project driven by consultants, 760 employees submitted nearly 1000 ideas. Whilst we cannot judge the extent to which the 'bottom-up' dimension was substantial, it may well be that, by adding new ideas and concepts, the process redesign methodology created new possibilities for these managers thus helping with mind-set change.

Therefore, the ability to capture and work with knowledge is a pivotal capability creating a:

1. Knowledge base – *capture* and *convert* tacit knowledge to explicit knowledge and create *accessibility* to this knowledge.
2. Knowledge base often *organized* to achieve:
   (a) open *access* to all;
   (b) effective *sharing* of information – conferences, meetings, etc.;
   (c) focus upon *technology*;
   (d) *integration* across corporation;
   (e) systematic capture, analysis and retrieval of *customer* information.

For example, Kao Japlin's leading household and chemical products business handles 250 customer calls a day and now has 350,000 customer questions/complaints stored in the system, which can be analyzed and recalled using 8000 keywords by customer name, product, division, date, geographical area.

Competence development in handling change

We set out a model widely used in the training literature which looks at the stages of competence dvelopment. In any change setting we move from unconscious incompetence to unconscious competence via conscious incompetence and then conscious competence (Figure 4.1).

The typical analogy to draw is that of learning to drive: the process of moving from unconscious incompetence (in which we are not aware of lack of competence or what it means) to a state of conscious incompetence when we first sit behind the driving wheel. In a state of heightened awareness we become immediately aware of lack of competence. This initial process is one of awareness raising. In a change setting, this may come via communication processes, visits and so on, but will often come from facing new demands from customers or sources of competition which cannot readily be met. The latter are generally brought out through diagnostic studies, internal reviews, etc., undertaken by consultants (external or internal), task forces, etc.

The next process is that of skill building as we move from conscious incompetence to conscious competence. Here we have the first stage of implementation. Skills in new

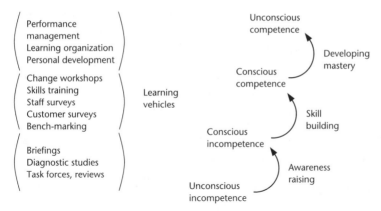

Figure 4.1 Competence development in change

systems, procedures, etc., are developed and practised. The learning vehicles include change workshops, staff training, surveys, etc. Here awareness of the process is high and the level of personal risk taking at its highest. Management support for risk taking is vital as is an understanding that the most important process here may well be experimentation. Early attempts to use a new approach enable us to identify the modifications usually needed to make it work effectively. This is the process within which individual learning is at its highest and is therefore the time during which organizational learning should be maximized. Yet how often do we seek to capture the lessons from early change trials and change workshops in order to transfer systematically the emerging best practice?

The final process is that of developing excellence through long practice. Here the learning vehicle is performance management systems and includes attention to personal development and organizational learning. Now the competence becomes so practised that we no longer think about it. It becomes embedded in the organization, part of the background. Thus it is that further learning demands the specific attention that performance management systems (use of balanced scorecard, value-added approaches, performance appraisal, etc.) can provide. Here, as excellence in performance is achieved, the rate of learning declines.

Overall then there is an obvious dilemma. Compare this model with the coping cycle model. In the middle of the change process, just as learning is at its fastest, self-esteem is at its lowest. Thus it is that people need encouragement, support, role models (the superuser concept) and the security which comes from being able to go through the learning process in clear and incremental steps and at their own pace. *Do things fast by moving slowly* becomes the watchword!

Conclusions

Some argue that we learn too little from history. Alan Taylor, the famous historian, argued that we learn too much – always seeking to adapt structures which earned us past success rather than adapt to changes. The dilemma is that customer service requires consistency, reliability, efficiency and stability whilst change and learning is necessarily a volatile, questioning process. Thus we seek means of combining certainty and stability with adaptability and the ability to 'flex' to changing needs.

Whilst many argue that the key to developing a learning culture is concern for people, this seems not to be obviously true – even though this does not make concern for people undesirable nor vitiate the notion that you may need it for other reasons. As has been argued, learning appears not to be an issue of motivation as such. Rather it may be one of removing constraint in order that a natural tendency to development and learning can be harnessed by the organization. Does this leave us with the thought that learning, both a cognitive experiential and social process, is nevertheless a process largely the preserve of a cognitive elite?

Exercises

1. Is your own organization a learning organization? Explain.

2. Can you identify an example of tacit knowledge – about product, processes or customers – in your own situation?

3. How does your company seek to 'capture' knowledge?

CHAPTER 5

Sustaining organizational effectiveness

Change creates challenges for us all. It brings stress and anxiety as well as opportunities and the possibility for optimism. We have already seen that effective organizational structures are more conducive to change. It is easier to implement change in a more, rather than less, effective setting. Moreover, organizational culture and management style have an important effect, by creating a climate supportive of change. In this chapter we turn to three related issues. Firstly, we examine the blockages to effective change. These operate at individual, group and organizational levels. Secondly, we develop the notion that effective change demands learning. Moreover, effective learning through change requires specific situational conditions (to minimize or avoid the blockages) and a personal and managerial style appropriate to learning and encouraging others to learn. Finally, we examine some ideas on the characteristics of effective organizational structures and designs.

Blocks to problem solving and change

Systematic models of the change process abound. But the issue in planning change is about how to generate creative solutions to what are generally novel problems. We argue that, generally speaking, there is no shortage of ideas about how to reorganize, deal with problems, create new markets and so on. What is usually missing is the framework and support appropriate for encouraging the emergence of creative solutions. We will now deal with a range of 'blocks' to creative problem solving as a means of looking at practical ways of organizing and sustaining the process of planning change.

It is easy enough to say that management support is a key to innovation. We now take this a stage further to consider some of the blocks to problem solving in order that we can better understand how to manage this process. The ideas listed below are from Adams (1987).

Perceptual blocks

1. *Stereotyping*: we see what we expected to see. Over recent years we have become increasingly aware of stereotyping. Women only come to work for 'pin money' – therefore there is no point in reviewing jobs to see if they can be improved. This is an obvious example. There are many, many more.

2. *Difficulty in isolating the problems*: a friend of mine gave a classic example of this. He was a member of a team of consultant designers given the brief to design an apple-picking machine. All sorts of solutions were put forward. None seemed feasible – in general all the machines were too big and too unwieldy. It was a month before a team member said: 'Our problem is that we are focusing upon the wrong problem – we should look at the design of the tree.' Eventually, a new strain of apple trees only a few feet high was created. The problems of designing the machine then disappeared. The height and spread of apple trees had been the essential difficulty, not the design of apple picking as such.

3. *Tendency to delimit the problem area too closely*: all too often we define problems very narrowly. In the 'CAC Consultants case study' (see below) each group of partners defines the problem narrowly; thus neither faces the real problem – their own motivation.

4. *Inability to see the problems from various viewpoints*: increasingly we talk of 'trained incapacity'. As we train and develop professionals (doctors, lawyers, accountants, engineers) we run the risk that people see problems only in terms of their own discipline. Seeing problems from different viewpoints helps to conceptualize the problems. It also helps when we come to attract support for solutions.

5. *Saturation*: data may come in large measures, or in large measures only occasionally, or in the presence of distracting data. It can be difficult to distinguish the relevant information from all the available data.

6. *Failure to use all sensory inputs*: we need all the data we can get, but do we utilize everything that is available to us? Thus when trying to decide on a new organizational structure for a new venture we should try to find other organizations facing similar problems. How have they solved them?

Emotional blocks

1. *Fear of taking a risk*: the fear of making a mistake, to be seen to fail, is a common block. If managers 'punish' failure, then this fear is at least realistic. But often the worst that can happen is pretty minimal. Excessive importance is attached to the risk of failure.

2. *Incapacity to tolerate ambiguity*: the solution of a complex problem is a messy process. The data will be misleading, incomplete, full of opinions, values and so on. While creating solutions, plans, etc., requires that we eventually establish order, too early an attempt to do so may mean that we miss promising ideas.

3. *Preference for judging rather than generating ideas*: judging ideas too early can lead to early rejection. The onus of proof is all too easily placed on the person with the idea. Yet if the idea is novel it may be ill thought out and may not present a good 'fit' with the hazy and incomplete data. Thus rejection is easy. We should recognize that finding reasons to say 'no' is easier than finding reasons to say 'yes' – particularly if we are poor risk takers who are intolerant of ambiguity!

4. *Inability to incubate*: an unwillingness to 'sleep on the problem' often because there seem to be pressures for solutions: 'We must have a new pricing policy because the sales department is pressing for one.' In planning the process of managing change we should plan enough time for ideas to incubate.

Cultural blocks

1. *Taboos*: issues which cannot be discussed and therefore cannot be faced are taboo (see below). For example, at International Engineering (see below), it was impossible to question whether or not the admitted technical excellence of the company was relevant for its new markets.

2. *Focus rather than fantasy*: Adams forcefully makes the point that psychologists have concluded that children are more creative than adults. This might be explained by adults being more aware of practical constraints; however, as he says, 'another explanation, which I believe, is that our culture trains mental playfulness, fantasy and reflectiveness out of people by placing more stress on the value of channelled mental activities'. Worth thinking about!

3. *Problem solving is a serious business*: linked to 2 is the notion that humour has no place in problem solving. And yet humour is often based on the process of associating apparently unrelated ideas. Creativity is the same in that it often involves the association of unrelated ideas or structures. Adams argues, therefore, that humour is *one* essential ingredient for effective problem solving.

4. *Reason and intuition*: we often seem to believe that reason, logic and numbers are good and that feelings, intuition and pleasure are bad. Adams suggests that this is based on our (west European?) puritan heritage and our technology-based culture (which raises the question of how this point applies in cultures without a puritan heritage). This has been complicated by the tendency to assign these characteristics to sex roles, namely, that men are logical, physical, tough and pragmatic while women are sensitive, emotional and intuitive. Creativity demands a balance of these characteristics.

5. *Tradition and change*: traditions are hard to overcome, particularly when people do not reflect on their traditions and their present problems/dilemmas together. We need tradition – it is on our traditions that much of our personal commitment and motivation is based. We need to respect tradition and we also need to recognize the need for change. Adams distinguishes primary and secondary creativity: primary creativity generates the structures and concepts which allow the solution of a family of problems; secondary creativity deploys these structures and concepts to develop and improve particular solutions. He argues that primary creativity

demands more intuition, humour, feeling and emotion; secondary creativity seems more likely to be associated with logic and reason – as the structures already established are deployed systematically to solve specific problems within a now well-understood field. Secondary creativity involves applying rules; primary creativity requires that existing rules be ignored, so that new rules can be generated (precisely what Newton did!).

Environmental blocks

1. *Lack of support*: we have already seen that a non-supportive environment is not conducive to innovation, nor to creative problem solving. Change is often seen as threatening and new ideas are easily stopped, by ignoring them, by laughing at them, or by overanalyzing them too early.

2. *Not accepting and incorporating criticism*: but those with good ideas can create blocks, too, by not being willing to accept criticism. The ability to accept criticism builds an atmosphere of trust and support and leads to improvements in what will necessarily have been an imperfect idea.

3. *Bosses who know the answer*: many managers are successful because they have ideas and can push them through. But only if such a manager will listen to subordinates will he or she be able to utilize their creativity.

Cognitive blocks

1. *Using the incorrect language*: whether mathematical or professional (e.g. accounting, marketing, etc.) or visual. Using an inappropriate language can hinder creativity in problem solving.

2. *Inflexible use of strategies*: there are many strategies available; we often use them unconsciously, but not necessarily to best effect in problem solving, perhaps because of the various blocks we have already discussed.

3. *Lack of the correct information*: clearly a limiting factor. But again balance is needed. Information makes you an expert, which can mean that you think down the lines of that expertise – closing you off from creative solutions?

Working through the blocks

Or, to follow Adams, 'block busting'. Various techniques are available. Here we need to do no more than list one or two very briefly. More details can be found by referring to Adams' own account. Identifying them in the first place helps enormously! A questioning attitude can take us further. Various thinking aids can also be applied, including attribute listing, 'checklists' and list making. Being able to suspend judgement as an individual or in a group can enhance creativity. Another useful technique is 'synectics' (Gordon, 1961).

The following actions seem to encourage creativity in problem solving:

● Stay loose or fluid in your thinking until rigour is needed.

● Protect new ideas from criticism.

- Acknowledge good ideas, listen, show approval.
- Eliminate status or rank.
- Be optimistic.
- Support confusion and uncertainty.
- Value learning from mistakes.
- Focus on the good aspects of an idea.
- Share the risks.
- Suspend disbelief.
- Build on ideas.
- Do not evaluate too early.

The following actions seem to discourage creativity:

- Interrupt, criticize.
- Be competitive.
- Mock people.
- Be dominant.
- Disagree, argue, challenge.
- Be pessimistic.
- Point out flaws.
- Inattention, do not listen, use silence against people.
- React negatively.
- Insist on 'the facts'.
- Give no feedback, act in a non-committal fashion.
- Pull rank.
- Become angry.
- Be distant.

Limits to problem solving

Still more limits or 'blocks' can be listed. At the individual level people may engage in 'satisficing' or 'incrementalism', accepting satisfactory solutions and/or making only incremental or limited changes to previous policies. At the group level we have 'group think' and 'risky shift'. 'Group think' is characterized by complacency and lack of critical evaluation of ideas (Janis, 1972). 'Risky shift' is a condition observed in experimental groups, where groups seem likely to take more risky decisions than the individuals involved might have gone for (diffusion of responsibility perhaps), but still without critical examination. At the organizational level various typical limits can be identified. Some we have already seen. People seem to 'distance' themselves from problems. Where organizations are highly centralized, responsible managers may be 'out of touch'. There can exist an 'illusion of reliability' in existing techniques or people (the

Greeks had a word for this, *hubris*, which means overbearing arrogance). Highly specialized organizations can lead to parochialism, the tendency to conceal dissent or disagreement, and to problems of communication (Wilensky, 1967). Solutions to all these limits involve opening up the problem-solving process, being willing to change and allowing the 'block busters' to operate. Our assumption is that the ideas are there, among the people – the challenge is to encourage them, to help them find expression, then to evaluate realistically, to apply them and learn from our experience and then to change.

Thus a simple model drawn from the work of Argyris is as set out in Figure 5.1. In essence the various counterproductive norms focus decision-makers' attention on the simple issues, often the things we can measure quantitatively rather than the crucial issues – frequently the blockages to change and improvement. This reinforces a risk-averse culture leading to people 'covering up' mistakes etc. Can this be conducive to change? Not if you conclude that the model of planned change provided in Figure 5.2 has any relevance. This illustrates what some would call the 'virtuous circle' of change, i.e. successful experience of change reduces anxiety, lessens resistance and encourages measured risk taking and leads to more change. So far so good, but clearly we will need to examine how to avoid the one and encourage the other.

Janis (1989, pp. 235–64) presents a range of ways in which these counterproductive

Figure 5.1 Organized 'irrationality'

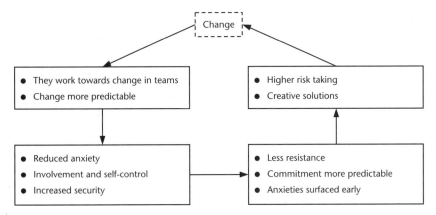

Figure 5.2 Planned change: effects on people

dynamics can be avoided. His advice includes ways of maintaining scepticism about the 'obvious' solution as well as of limiting criticism of 'wild' suggestions. In particular he argues for a willingness to make 'temporary' arrangements with other groups in order to buy time (admittedly his focus and therefore his examples deal with national policy, but one can readily see equivalents in the organizational area – for instance, in the context of mergers and acquisitions, where joint ventures are involved, in difficult technological change situations and so on). Basically the approach he favours is to take any and all measures likely to lead to a more systematic approach to planning, decision making and implementation. Some of his recommendations relate to leadership style and some to the structure of decision making, but all are designed to create or facilitate this more systematic approach.

Organizations and rationality

All the above must lead us to question whether what happens within an organization is rational. Moreover, do we believe that effective organizations are 'rational' organizations? Are organizations designed and managed on rational lines? Can the thorough application of a systematic approach to change planning and implementation lead to a 'rational', perhaps 'optimal', result? Not if we equate rationality with the notion of optima drawn from the scientific method. It all depends on our definition of rationality.

As an example, the idea of 'clinical' rationality is often seen as dominant within health care systems. The decisions of doctors govern the pattern of care provided and the use of resources. This does not mean that all doctors have the same views, beliefs or attitudes, or that they would argue for the same vision of health care. People are not automata, without autonomy or freedom of action. At the outset we must make clear that our definition of rationality owes nothing to the 'scientific method'. There is no simple dichotomy between rationality and irrationality, the former based upon 'science', the latter on emotion, feelings and so on. On this view we suggest that when subject to changed circumstances in their environment (which might be a budget cut or the advent of a new 'bit' of medical technology) people will reflect upon the courses and consequences of the change, developing responses and decisions based upon reason. People use reason based upon knowledge and experience. In turn these emerge through the processes of thought, emotion, action and decision making in the 'practical world'. We argue that there are various 'sources of rationality' which lead to men and women constructing different arguments about, and drawing different conclusions in respect of, the changes which affect them.

Any definition of rationality must allow for the doubts which beset us all, and for the uncertainties, vested interests and ignorance of the world in which we live. Weick (1969: 87) summarizes the position succinctly, as follows:

> rationality is best understood in the eye of the beholder. It is his aims and how consciously he sets out to accomplish them that constitute the clearest, most easily specified component of rationality.

He goes on to argue that people in large organizations are unlikely to employ the same rationality; rather, 'organizations will have several different and contradictory rationalities'. Herein lies the reason why many of us find that discussion about the problems an organization faces (whether about the one in which we participate, or when we listen to others) is often confused and confusing.

The literature abounds with theories of decision making ('garbage-can model', March and Olsen (1976); 'satisficing', Simon (1957); and 'incrementalism', Lindblom (1959)) which reflect this problem (although we note that they are also attempts to deal with different 'problems', including the peculiar difficulties of choice under conditions of uncertainty).

Bryman (1983) suggests that there has been a 'retreat from rationality' as a consequence of attacks on the rational systems model of organization. He identifies two ways of arguing for some form of rational systems model of organization. The first, exemplified by Weber's writing on bureaucracy and by the classical school (see March and Simon, 1958), has been under attack for many years. In recent years a second wave has emerged: namely, the development of the 'contingency' approach. Proponents of both views see organizations as goal-seeking, functional systems: the first adopt a closed-system perspective; the latter adopt an open-system view (Scott, 1981) which has been subjected to critical scrutiny from at least four directions, the 'garbage-can' model, institutional, political and Marxist approaches. Bryman (1983) concludes that scholars in the fields of management theory and economics are now uneasy about their 'rationalist infrastructures'. Here he refers to a rationality placing particular emphasis on notions such as utility and profit maximization, taken from economics.

He notes that this is an extreme form of rationality and goes on to discuss 'soft' rationality, incorporating ideas such as Simon's notion of 'satisficing' and Watkin's (1970) discussion of 'imperfect rationality'. He concludes this discussion by noting the methodological and conceptual weaknesses of the alternative views of rationality, and of alternative models such as the political or Marxist approach. When he discusses one empirical study of the capital investment process which found the economists' version of rationality to be of little empirical use (Bowers, 1970) he concludes that purposiveness had greater usefulness. Here lie reasons for hope, he seems to suggest.

Landes (1967, p. 204) provides us with a clear definition, based upon the idea of purposiveness, as follows:

> Rationality may be defined as the adaption of means to ends. It is the antithesis of superstition and magic. For this history, the relevant ends are the production and acquisition of material wealth. It goes without saying that these are not man's highest ends; and that rationality is not confined to the economic sphere.

Rationality is a way of doing things: the application of the principles of rationalism to action, rationalism being defined as the doctrine that the universe of perception and experience can be understood in terms of thought or reason, as against emotion, intuition or extrasensory modes of apprehension.

We accept the means–end definition of rationality; however, we depart from Landes' equation of rationality and the doctrine of rationalism. We need to recognize the limitations of the individual. We cannot pretend that men and women do not use intuition as well as empiricism. Some may use one or the other to a lesser or greater extent – but not at all? We doubt that. We tend towards Weick's position on this point (see above).

The notion that political models of organization represent an attack on rational models needs careful analysis. Close examination of alternative modes of decision making proposed by Pfeffer (1981) makes this point clear. He compares rational, bureaucratic, decision process/organized anarchy and political power models. For *rational* decision making the ideology is seen as 'efficiency and effectiveness'; for *political power*, the ideology is 'struggle, conflict, winners and losers'. Decisions from the former flow from 'value maximizing choice', from the latter from the result of 'bargaining and interplay among interests', but this is hardly a satisfactory distinction. We must ask what it is that the 'interests' bargain over. Definitions of appropriate action, policies, means–ends sequences and strategies will form the calculus of any answer to this question. By saying that the political power model demands the analysis of interests we immediately adopt a rational model – at the level of the interests themselves. Thus this model differs from the rational model only in that the proponents of the rational model are seen to model choice in essentially unproblematical terms. But Bryman (1983) makes it entirely clear that only proponents of the 'hard' version of rationality could be accused of that. Thus the apparent difference collapses in all but the most extreme of juxtapositions. We conclude that the extreme or 'hard' definition has never had much application for those concerned with the management of organizations. (In parenthesis, it is worth noting the growing number of studies examining the work of F. W. Taylor which cast doubt on whether or not Taylor, for one, ever believed in such a straightforward view – see Rose (1975) and Merkle (1980).) However, by distinguishing 'hard' and 'soft' rationalities Bryman seems tacitly to admit that the latter is not properly 'rational'. Here he appears to be following Landes, equating rationality with rationalism. To do so is to adopt too limited a view of rationality. The concept of multiple rationalities does not imply a 'softer or weaker' view. Ill understood it may be, but we believe it is possible to establish, empirically, rationalities in use.

If we accept that people attempt to make sense of the confusion of the world as they experience it and that they do so by employing a particular rationality, then to understand their attempts so to do we must understand the rationality in use. Moreover, if we are to understand the confusing talk we often hear when problems are under discussion we need to understand the different rationalities and the nature of the contradictions between them.

Finally, when examining a particular institution over a period of time we should be concerned to identify, and then understand, periods during which the dominating rationality, ordering decisions and action in the institution are changed. Such change would represent a watershed in the 'life' of the institution concerned. Here would be a significant period in which to study the institution and its relations to a wider society.

If all this is accepted how do we proceed? In essence we must search for the frames of reference which make intelligible the choices and decisions of people within a given institution. A particular 'rationality' comprises 'rules of action' that are deemed suitable for given circumstances. Thus our approaches require us to observe the choices that people make, and the reasons they give for making them over long periods of time, examining many of them in order to discern the 'rules of action' and 'frames of reference' in use.

Important consequences flow from the existence of alternative sources of rationality which people use to establish and maintain order as circumstances change. Each apparently rational strategy for 'getting things done', for maintaining order, for ensuring that employees work hard, are loyal and committed, obey instructions, and so on, has counter-rational consequences associated with it – that is to say, counter-rational viewed from the perspective of the particular rationality in use.

An example: organization and counter-rational behaviour

Argyris (1982) provides us with a good example of this situation. A group of senior university administrators attending an executive course were examining a case study on a particular college which included a set of recommendations for the future of that college, produced by a working group of senior academics and administrators from the college. The working group had been asked for 'concrete recommendations'. The course members were asked to evaluate these recommendations. Criticizing the recommendations, course members expressed the view that the recommendations were vague and cliché ridden, the typical output of a committee which had not been well briefed. Such an evaluation of working groups, working parties or committees is not uncommon. Argyris suggests that it was based upon several assumptions about organization and management.

The first is that giving people specific goals will lead them to actions which are more relevant and specific (in this case produce more specific recommendations). The second is that goals will motivate people or, if not, will at least make it easier to confront them on the quality of their performance. Finally, it is assumed that effective control of performance requires objective monitoring of performance. Underlying these assumptions is the fear that people will *not* obey, follow the rules, perform their tasks. Many managers see rules, regulations, systematic procedures, objective performance monitoring and control as the basis for order.

So far so good! But implicit in this is the belief that rules, systems, monitoring and control cannot in themselves bring about consequences that are counterproductive to order, that obstruct progress, that make it harder to 'get things done'. Yet we all know this to be false. When we think of bureaucracy, we tend also to think of 'red tape'.

Here we refer to what R. K. Merton (1940) has called the 'dysfunctional' consequences of bureaucracy and what March and Simon (1958) refer to as the 'unintended consequences'. For Merton a bureaucratic structure exerts constant demands upon officials to be methodical and disciplined. To operate successfully there must be reliability, conformity and discipline. However, adherence to the rules, originally conceived as a means, becomes transformed into an end:

> Discipline, readily interpreted as conformance with regulations, whatever the situation, is seen not as a measure designed for specific purposes but becomes an immediate value in the life-organisation of the bureaucrat. This emphasis, resulting from the displacement of the original goals, develops into rigidities and an inability to adjust readily. Formalism, even ritualism, ensues with an unchallenged insistence upon punctilious adherence to formalised procedures.
>
> (Merton, 1940, p. 16)

This may be taken to the extent that conformity to the rules obstructs the purposes of the organization, known to us, familiarly, as 'red tape'.

To return to our example, how did Argyris explain the apparent paradox? Remember that the original diagnosis was that the working-party recommendations were vague and unusable, and that more specific goals and directions combined with methods of monitoring and controlling performance would overcome this difficulty. However, should such a strategy be implemented, the members of the working party may feel mistrusted and constrained. In any event, Argyris points out that faculty members and administrators within a college are likely to pursue different ends and will not work together on critical issues. There is a need for integration between the two groups, the members of which are trained in different ways, work to different rules, with different methods and styles, and are likely to emphasize different views of the college. There might well be advantages in keeping goals vague. Specific goals might be interpreted as limiting and not allowing the freedom to think creatively. They may result in emotional reactions which inhibit performance. Thus actions which appear rational (setting specific goals) may lead people to produce counter-rational consequences (judged in the light of the rationality of those specific goals).

Argyris suggests that these counter-rational consequences can emerge in three ways. Firstly, individuals may distance themselves from the tasks in hand and the responsibilities involved. Not feeling any personal responsibility for producing the problem, they do not see it as their responsibility to solve it. Secondly, tacit acceptance may develop that the 'counter-rational' behaviour is 'undiscussable'. Where motivation is falling, where people feel mistrusted, where behaviour appears to be disloyal, there seems to be a tendency for people to find these issues difficult to talk about openly. So difficult, according to Argyris, that all agree that the issue is 'taboo', in principle undiscussable. Finally, people may prefer counterproductive advice: that is to say, advice which reinforces the counter-rational behaviour. Thus, on the course we have been discussing, members suggested that the college president should play a game of deception in order to save face for himself and the faculty and in order to keep his options open. They proposed that he accept the report, thank the working party and at the same time arrange for a new committee, or implement specific action. Such behaviour would, of course, reinforce the undiscussability of any problem, and the distancing of the working-party members from the issues at stake. It is clearly a form of collusion aimed at avoiding making the issues, or the working party's difficulties, explicit.

It is important for us to recognize that by counter-rational we do not mean irrational or emotional. Counter-rational behaviour may be highly rational from the viewpoint of the individuals concerned, given their situation, the power and resources under their command, and so on. By counter-rational we simply mean based upon different sources of rationality.

Forrester (1969) discusses this problem when he refers to the 'counterintuitive' behaviour of complex systems (such as urban systems or large corporations). He tells us that we have been 'conditioned almost exclusively by experience with first-order, negative-feedback loops [which] are goal-seeking and contain a single important variable'. This form of experience suggests that cause and effect are closely related in space and time. He argues that complex systems appear to be the same, i.e. they appear to present cause and effect close in time and space. However, causes of a problem may be complex, may actually lie in some remote part of the system, or may lie in the distant past. What appears to be cause and effect may actually be 'coincidental' symptoms.

Action to dispel symptoms in a complex system will often leave the underlying causes untouched. Forrester claims that intuitive solutions to the problems of complex systems will be wrong most of the time. He also suggests that change programmes will often have an effect that is less than originally anticipated because they tend to displace existing internal processes. Pressman and Wildavsky (1973) quote one example of an 'underemployed-training programme' training 19,100 people per year which led to only 11,300 people becoming employed, this being a consequence of declining job starts occurring naturally. Based as it was on simulations, this is not an entirely convincing example.

However, Pressman and Wildavsky (1973) describe a programme aimed at developing employment opportunities for ethnic minority groups in Oakland, California. The federal government, through the project, committed $28 million during a 4 year period with little result as far as the aims of the project were concerned. Their evidence suggested that the majority of the benefits derived from the programme went to people other than members of the ethnic minority groups. We do not need to interpret this as failure; we merely offer it as an example of counterintuitive behaviour.

People in organizations, whether representing themselves or their groups, tend to advocate views and positions with a degree of certainty which discourages further enquiry. Moreover, they tend to act in ways which inhibit the expression of negative feelings. We often talk of the need to 'sweeten the pill' or not to overdo criticism in case people are 'upset' by it. Sometimes we offer presentations in such a way as to emphasize that there is nothing new or radical in a set of proposals. People appear to design their behaviour to appear rational. Thus they focus upon what they argue to be necessary and attainable goals, realistic means and clear objectives. All this is to suppress issues that might upset other people. Moreover, people tend to control meetings to maximize winning, minimize losing, minimize the expression of negative feelings and to keep others rational. Following Argyris (1982, 1985), we summarize these ideas in Table 5.1.

All this can have important consequences. People attempt to 'distance' themselves, to treat key issues and events or norms as 'undiscussable' and to offer advice which, while ostensibly aimed at increasing rationality, actually inhibits it. All this tends to hinder the production of valid information for diagnosis and decision making. Yet these behaviours are most prevalent just when valid information is needed – when people are dealing with difficult and threatening problems. Argyris (1985) suggests that we are dealing with a powerful set of individual, group, organizational and cultural forces which are mutually reinforcing. These forces create contradictions. Yet success can, and does, occur. But this will be based upon routine performance, upon stability, which can mean that people do not feel it necessary to pay attention to the

Table 5.1 ● Ineffectiveness–effectiveness patterns

	Behaviour	Response	Outcome
Ineffectiveness	Not defining goals	People become defensive, inconsistent, feel vulnerable, act in manipulative ways, mistrust, lack risk taking or take very high risks, withhold information, adopt power-centred behaviour	Limited testing
	Maximize 'winning' and minimize 'losing'		Issues not discussable
	Minimize the expression of feelings		'Distance' themselves from issues
	Appearing always to be 'rational'		
Effectiveness	Depend on people	Builds confidence, 'self-esteem'	Effective testing
	Allow tasks to be jointly controlled	Creates learning and trust	Informed choice
	Make the protection of feelings a joint responsibility	Leads to less defensive relationships and group dynamics	Internal commitment
	Discuss issues, performance and problems, *not* people	Open confrontation of issues	

deeper issues until the impact of these contradictions becomes so powerful that the stability is itself under threat. Now the organization is seen to be in a crisis. Drastic action is possible; 'turnaround' becomes the objective. These factors will all influence the process diagnosing the need for change, as we shall see in Chapter 9. In essence, therefore, we need to deal with the 'blockages' before we can identify, let alone make progress towards, the organizational changes we need.

Sadly, as Argyris makes clear, people can become highly skilled at maintaining these patterns of ineffectiveness. He calls this 'skilled incompetence' (see Argyris, 1990). He demonstrates the relevance of this to major programmes of change by reference to a study of six large US corporations which had invested heavily in change programmes which had not worked, in which the authors found evidence of the following:

Inflexible rules and procedures.
Managers not understanding customer needs.
Managers not committed to, or skilled in handling change.
Inter-group problems.
Poor communication.
Lack of strategic thinking.
Top managers evidently believing that declining revenue was only temporary.
Low levels of trust.

(Beer *et al.*, 1988)

Here we have the 'blockages' to change all over again.

Argyris goes on to argue that characteristic solutions to these problems seem purposely to avoid the problem. Thus a structural solution will not deal with the real issues, nor will a solution which emphasizes clearer definition of roles and 'better' communication, because neither deals with the causes but rather attempts to deal with symptoms. His main idea to deal with these problems is to get participants to 'map' how decisions are actually made as a means of recognizing their own 'skilled incompetence'. He refers to work by Putnam and Thomas (1988) on a performance-related pay system which was ineffective because too many people received high ratings.

Putnam and Thomas sketch out an organizational action map which shows that various circumstances (e.g. low economic growth), cultural norms such as that of attempting to give all employees equal treatment and the wish not to upset people combine with management behaviour (covering up conflict) to create consequences such as resentment by good performers of poor performers, protection of mediocre performance and so on. Any attempt (e.g. by good performers) to refer the situation to the grievance procedure would simply lead to mistrust, polarized attitudes, less coaching of them by managers whose performance reviews were being criticized and, even worse, the acceptance of mediocre performance. To escape these patterns of behaviour managers map their situation. By making the behaviour and its consequences explicit there emerges a better understanding of the situation, a fuller diagnosis and a greater willingness to engage in what Argyris calls 'productive reasoning'. At the core of this as a successful strategy is the need for all involved to see learning as an essential characteristic of 'productive reasoning', a thought we shall return to as an essential ingredient of effective change (see below).

CAC Consultants

The 'problem'

CAC Consultants is in the business of marketing highly sophisticated knowledge and professional skills, particularly in the field of project management. The key to the firm's success lies in the professionals and the skills they develop and deploy. Attracting and keeping first-rate professionals is a key issue, and senior partners hold strong opinions on it. The company comprises a chairman and six senior partners (each responsible for a major area of business activity); and 14 junior partners, each reporting directly to either the chairman or a senior partner. In addition some 40 professional staff and 60 support staff are employed, all organized into teams within the major areas of activity.

Some senior partners believed that career development was needed to attract high-quality young professionals. Another group had serious doubts about this, believing that the firm could attract people of the right level of skill. In any event, these people believed that it was impossible to appoint more senior partners because of the impact of that on the income of the current partners. Finally, it was felt that career development would retain only the less able professionals; others would 'naturally move on'.

Both groups of senior partners recognized problems, however. For some the problem was how to attract and retain able young professionals. For others it was how to motivate effort and commitment from them in order to increase company income.

The former saw the solution as lying in that of career development, the latter in the field of recruitment procedures. It was decided to hold a 1 day meeting of senior partners to discuss the problem. Prior to the meeting there had been much discussion with individuals often attributing various views or motives to others. People were seen as unfair, emotional, 'empire building', overreacting or overprotective. At least one senior partner had been attributed as using career development as a means of rewarding one junior partner working for him.

The 'meeting'

At the meeting one senior partner proposed that regular reviews of individuals be carried out and that the senior partners should agree a policy regarding career development and promotion, to both junior and senior partner level. It was argued that this was not a panacea but would allow for modest improvement in present practice. It would not undermine existing practices or lead to a fall in the technical competence of staff. Moreover, it was proposed that the process be largely informal and be designed so as not to threaten anyone. One response to these ideas was: 'I'm glad to hear that we intend to move slowly and build on present practices. The most important thing is to ensure that we recruit the right people and ensure that they perform well.' All agreed on the need to build up the firm's position. One pointed out that some of the junior partners were overcommitting

▶▶

themselves in order to ensure promotion. Others felt that this would not matter 'if kept within reasonable limits'.

One partner passionately put the point that the firm's growth and reputation would be harmed unless they could develop new services to allow them to meet rapidly changing needs. It was essential to attract people with ideas. Others responded: 'We don't seem to have any problems attracting people, and in any event we are highly profitable now. What's the problem?'

When the meeting convened several partners proposed that part of it be used to review the performance of the practice. Moreover, other commitments that people mentioned meant that it had to end at noon, rather than go on to late afternoon. The review of performance lasted until 11.20 a.m., allowing only a short discussion of the career development issue. There were constant interruptions as various senior partners were 'called to the telephone'. At the end the chairman summed up. Nothing would be done that was costly in terms of time and money. He proposed that a subcommittee of the partners be formed to develop ideas and a policy. One senior partner asked that the subcommittee's representation should include the range of views. This was agreed. The meeting ended with much comment about the progress made.

Background to the meeting

Interviews afterwards identified the following points:

● The senior partners concerned to see significant progress on the career development front felt they had to avoid anything which made other partners defensive. No mention would be made of the need to develop new ideas, services and business.

● They also wished to avoid overstating their case because this would lead to the issue becoming personalized.

● Overall it was felt important to keep the discussion on 'rational lines'.

● Others clearly felt that the best approach to the meeting was to give those who wished to see career development 'their head'; 'Let them talk so they cannot accuse us of having our heads in the sand.'

● Thus it was that everyone appeared to rule out discussion of the validity of the views being put: 'If people are upset they become emotional and you cannot test their views.' 'After all, we must be rational.'

It is not difficult to see that the key issue is the future of the practice itself. There are two questions to be faced as to what new markets and services can/should be developed? To what extent should the practice grow? Some senior partners are tempted to maintain the status quo. They have built it and it does provide good profits and therefore good incomes, at the moment. Growth and change will be uncomfortable. But will competition mean that the status quo is not a viable option? This point needs careful discussion and analysis.

The question of attracting and retaining new staff is very much a matter of means. A status quo and a growth/development strategy will require different approaches. Therefore, to make progress the senior partners need to discuss the overall strategy and their own motivations. These are the forces relevant to the choice that needs to be made. To make progress there is a need for senior partners to discuss these issues more openly. We will return later to how such progress may be made. For the moment let us merely state that it requires effective leadership and good team working among the senior partners.

The 'block-busting' ideas of Adams (1987) are relevant, as are the practical recommendations to be made in Chapters 8, 9, 10 and 11 of this book. In general, we suggest greater openness, but two points should be made. Firstly, openness and honesty are not the ultimate purposes of learning; rather they facilitate learning in the circumstances that we are considering. Secondly, it is important to enable people to control this process (a point made by Argyris). Only then are we likely to minimize the sources of ineffectiveness that we have discussed. Handy (1983) identifies the following blocks to learning:

- *We don't see the questions*: we do not critically examine our success and failure. We do not habitually question events. Yet to learn we must constantly experiment, trying out new ideas and skills.

- *We see the question but seem unable to come to any answers*: answers do not come automatically. We need to search for them, compare a problem situation from the past, talk to friends and colleagues.

- *We are sometimes unable to see how to put an answer into action in order to see if it works*: here the issue is one of turning ideas into practical action in such a way as to allow for monitoring, feedback and learning. It is important to identify people who can help, provide support, counsel and encourage. This also demands internal motivation and energy. If we can get so far we are learning how to learn.

Contingency, choice and organizational environments

Thus far in this chapter we have seen that various blockages can impede decision making and choice. We have also seen that deeply held assumptions about people and about the need for so-called rational behaviour can limit effectiveness. Assuming for the moment that we can find ways of handling these difficulties, can we define the characteristics of effective organizational structures and design? This seems to depend largely on the 'fit' between the organization's structure and its environment.

The design of organizational structures to suit the needs of the particular business enterprise or organization, which provides for the co-ordination of the diverse activities carried out within the enterprise or organization, but also provides for adaptability to respond to changing circumstances, presents a challenge to management which cannot be overstated in its importance. The structure of an organization allows the pursuit of objectives and the *implementation of plans*. People and resources are allocated to the tasks which must be performed, and co-ordination is provided. Working methods, rules and procedures define the ways in which tasks are to be performed and/or establish criteria for task performance, output or quality. These are typically all related to reward systems, planning and scheduling systems and monitoring systems. The structure of an organization is directly linked to the *information system*.

The structure of the organization provides a *decision-support* system. Arrangements are made for the collection and processing of information relevant to the decisions taken by managers. Specialist posts are often created to provide for such arrangements. Accountants and organization and methods personnel will, for example, collect and process information on various aspects of the performance of the organization. This information will be evaluated and presented to decision makers, either regularly (to a senior management meeting) or in response to particular circumstances (e.g. when a major project is under consideration). The tasks of the organization create decisions to be made. In practice, decision makers decide, from the range of tasks which could be undertaken, those tasks to be pursued and for which a market exists and those to be dropped. For a decision system to be effective, provision for monitoring trends in the market is essential. Changes in technology, in resource markets for capital or labour and in the product market will affect the performance of any organization and will thus require adaptation.

Following Child (1984), the main dimensions of an organization's structure are as follows:

● The allocation of tasks and responsibilities, providing appropriate discretion over methods and use of resources.

● The designation of formal reporting relationships, determining spans of control of managers and supervisors.

● The grouping of individuals into sections and departments, and the grouping of departments into divisions or other major units.

● The delegation of authority with associated procedures for performance monitoring and evaluation, which may either be regular or operate by exception.

● The design of communication and co-ordinating systems, to provide information and participation in decision making.

● The provision of reward systems to motivate individuals.

● The establishment of decision-support systems such as regular management meetings, project teams and specialist posts or departments.

Where the structure of an organization is inappropriate or deficient we would expect to see a number of possible problems emerging, including the following:

1. Low motivation and low morale of employees.

2. Delayed or poor decisions.

3. Conflict between departments.

4. Rising costs.

5. A tendency to stick to the rules and regulations, whether or not appropriate action will follow.

6. Lack of the capacity to adapt to changing circumstances.

If we observe problems such as those listed here (and this is not meant to be an inclusive list), then we have reason to conclude that the structure of the organization is deficient in some way. It is important to recognize that the dimensions of an organizational structure can be designed in different ways and that they vary considerably in practice.

The organizational form with which we are all most familiar is bureaucracy. Bureaucratic structures are characterized by a high degree of job specialization, by reliance on formal procedures and paperwork, by hierarchy, by clear and significant status differentials and by an emphasis on control. Bureaucratic structures are intended to provide for equal treatment for all employees; a reliance upon the expertise, skills and experience relevant to the job; specific standards of work and output; the maintenance of records and files dealing with work and output; the setting up and enforcement of rules and regulations that serve the interests of the organization; and a recognition that rules and regulations are binding upon managers as well as upon other employees.

In environments which are changing rapidly, however, rules, regulations and working procedures can quickly become out of date and irrelevant. Moreover, rules and regulations can become barriers behind which individual managers hide or which they use to justify incorrect decisions. Inflexible systems or procedures can create demotivating conditions for employees and can reduce the ability of managers or employees to innovate. From this we could conclude that a bureaucratic structure might be suitable for an organization dealing with a stable and simple environment. Conversely, an altogether more flexible and innovative structure would be suitable for a changing, complex environment.

Contingency theory is a label applied to a body of research based on the assumption that there is 'no one best way' to design an organizational structure but, rather, that the effectiveness of the design of a particular organization is *contingent* upon various factors. These factors are normally stated to include the technology, the environment, the history of the organization, norms and expectations of employees and/or customers or clients, and the size of the organization. Lawrence and Lorsch (1967) were the first to use the term 'contingency theory' as a convenient way of describing this empirical view of organizational structures and processes; however, the earlier work of Burns and Stalker (1961) and Woodward (1965) are important applications of the approach.

Exponents of contingency theories have advocated a shift in the approach of organization designers from prescription to the creation of the organizational choice. Rather than propose one strategy as being of universal application within organizations, contingency theorists have suggested that design, management and control strategies should be developed to meet the situation within which they are to be applied. The theory suggests that organizational performance depends upon the extent to which the organization secures a good match between situation and structure. Child (1984) summarizes it as follows:

> Contingency theory regards the design of an effective organization as necessarily having to be adapted to cope with the 'contingencies' which derive from the circumstances of environment, technology, scale, resources and other factors in the situation in which the organization is operating.

The components of organizational structure (e.g. the degree of formalization of procedures, centralization of decision making, number of levels in hierarchies and the spans of control of managers) can take different forms. Lorsch (1970) suggests that the 'structure of an organization is not an immutable given, but rather a set of complex variables about which managers can exercise considerable choice'.

The contingency theory approach to organization design attempts to take account of all four factors, uses the organization as the unit of analysis and tends to accept a managerial framework, particularly in respect of organizational purposes. By stating that the components of an organization can be changed, they introduce the idea of choice, called 'strategic choice' by Galbraith (1977). For Galbraith, organization design involves attempts to make the goals of organization, the means applied and the people 'coherent'. The phrase 'strategic choice' is used to emphasize the available choice of goals, means and processes for integrating individuals into the organization and also the choice as to whether some or all of these goals, means and processes should be changed to meet changes in the environment.

Organization design, resources and complexity

From what we have said so far it is plain that organization design is not a precise science. Yet there does seem to be evidence to suggest that issues such as control, resources and the complexity of the environment are important issues in organization design. Lawrence and Dyer (1983) have examined these points in an interesting way. Their argument is that appropriate organization designs are related to the complexity of the environment and the scarcity of resources for the organization. Figure 5.3 summarizes this idea.

In effect Lawrence and Dyer (1983) identify what they feel are the most appropriate

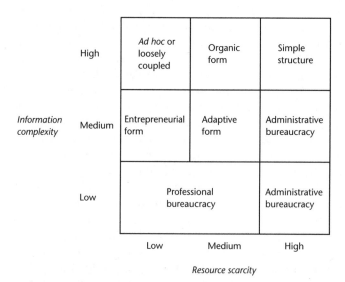

Figure 5.3 Organization design (from Lawrence and Dyer, 1983)

Information complexity	High	Research	Development of new products/services	Sales (short-term revenues)
	Medium	Marketing	General management	Production (unit efficiency)
	Low	Finance (profit management)		Control (cost cutting)
		Low	Medium	High

Resource scarcity

Figure 5.4 Functional tendencies (from Lawrence and Dyer, 1983)

organizational forms for each combination of information complexity and resource scarcity (which might mean high levels of competition for sales in a private sector example or government restrictions on expenditure for a public sector organization). Information complexity refers to the diversity of (uncertainty about) the technologies and opportunities (and threats) in the organization's environment. For example, where the organization is dealing with a complex and changing environment with high levels of competition, then a fluid and responsive organizational structure is essential. A trading company is a typical case. Conversely, professional bureaucracy is an appropriate structure where the organization deals with low levels of competition and well-established technology. However, such organizations experience significant tensions if the environment changes suddenly and dramatically. A typical case would be universities – compare the typical university in the 1960s with the changes that took place in the 1980s.

Figure 5.4 reproduces Figure 5.3 with typical functions substituted for each organizational form. For example, where markets are tight and the environment complex, the emphasis may well be on sales (to generate income) rather than on marketing (which costs money, takes time and may rapidly become outdated). This is a controversial view. Many marketing people will argue the contrary position, yet the situation we describe is that of the trading company – which tends to do little formal marketing. In practice, organizations attempt to control their environments to some degree. Is there a tendency to operate at medium levels? In any event, perhaps most organizations find themselves operating in environments where adaptation and general management are both crucial.

What specific changes are needed to move an organization towards the adaptive structure? These are summarized in Figure 5.5 (again following Lawrence and Dyer, 1983), from which it is clear that these comprise either means of achieving more focus

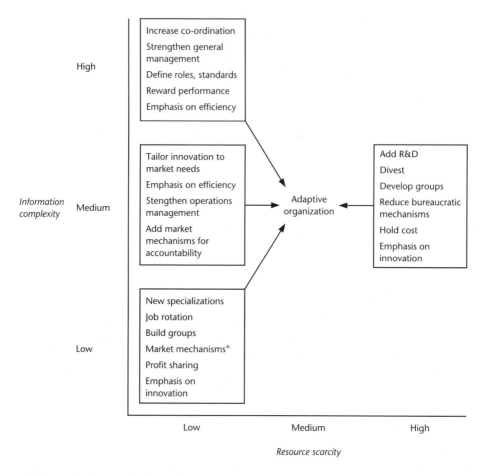

*Market mechanisms, e.g. breaking a larger organization into separate smaller organizations which are treated as separate units or profit centres.

Figure 5.5 Changes needed to achieve an adapting structure (from Lawrence and Dyer, 1983)

and business-orientated effort (or at least efforts that are more attuned to corporate objectives) or ways of developing people and groups to improve the emphasis on innovation.

Criticisms of the contingency approach

Various criticisms have been made of the contingency approach:

● In reality the design of organizations is subject to 'political' and ideological factors as different interest groups come into conflict when defending their own interests (e.g. nurses and managers in health care or, more accurate, different groupings of both 'nurses' and 'managers'). Hence structures are often the result of bargaining and compromise.

CASE STUDY

International Engineering

This company engages in engineering design, consultancy and project management work world-wide. It is wholly owned by a US-based multinational. It employs 2000 people, of which 1500 are based in the UK, 1000 in Central London. This company had enjoyed almost a monopoly position in the 1950s and 1960s and then had benefited from the rapid growth of North Sea oil exploration engineering work in the 1970s. The 1980s had brought growing competition and a declining market in the North Sea. Growing markets required new technology. Overall the company was structured in a relatively *ad hoc* way. Within the engineering departments, and within specific projects, the company was structured as a professional bureaucracy. By the early 1990s the board was concerned that it was losing competitive edge and therefore being unsuccessful in any important bids for new business.

To develop a more adaptive organization various main threads of organizational change were needed. Firstly, the organization needed to be structured to achieve clearer accountability. Various measures were required, as can be seen from Figures 5.6, 5.7 and 5.8. The establishment of business units at regional level was designed to strengthen general management, improve efficiency and focus effort to meet market needs. Organizational changes aimed at elevating the role of projects, engineering and marketing were designed to improve co-ordination, strengthen operations/project management and improve efficiency. Under the old structure, too much depended on the operations director. The changes created a more balanced allocation of responsibility and authority between the various functions. The business unit approach involved the adoption of market mechanisms. For accountability, each general manager was to be responsible for profit, and was

Figure 5.6 Corporate structure, September 1988

Figure 5.7 Regional decentralization: 1989 corporate structure

to be left to be relatively autonomous, as long as profit and market objectives were attained. It was intended that business units buy in services from both group and other business units, or from elsewhere, thus strengthening the market approach.

Developing an organizational structure and an appropriate management style demands attention to a range of issues, including technology. For example, typical 'success' criteria for an organization such as International Engineering are listed as follows:

● Control of factors critical to the successful penetration of existing and new markets, including technology.

● Clear sales accountability.

● Quality control in clearly branded products and services.

● First-class systems support.

● Developing and retaining effective people.

● Management development.

● Effective market development.

These success criteria were developed for the company by the top management team in 1988. We set out the existing structure and two new structures, one for the new regional structure and one for the new corporate structure. The new structures make technology easier to develop, partly because it is now to have board-level representation by having the director of engineering no longer reporting to the overburdened operations director, and partly through regional decentralization, which will allow a more effective marketing approach at regional level. More effective market intelligence from the marketplace, combined with higher-level attention to the development of technology, will provide for a more co-ordinated approach in this field. Moreover, decentralization will provide for and

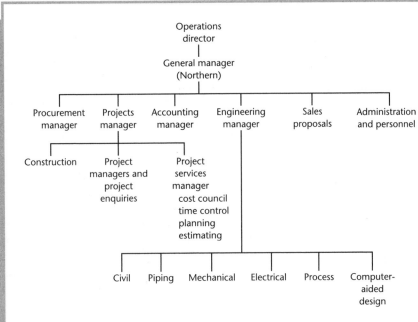

Figure 5.8 Regional decentralization: regional structure

encourage a more open management style, thus encouraging more initiative throughout the organization.

All these changes require the development of new management styles and skills at various levels, and, indeed, many of the managers and engineers will need to develop new skills. Performance appraisal is needed to support these changes. New technological disciplines will be needed. We can readily see from Figure 5.6 how all these changes are intended to move International Engineering to a more adaptive structure. We will be returning to this case study in later chapters to discuss various aspects of these changes and their implementation.

- The environment itself is problematic and cannot be taken as a given determinant of the organization. Instead it requires interpretation and is likely to generate differences within the enterprise. In any event the structure of an R&D department is very likely to be very different to the structure of a production department – note, however, that contingency theory could account for this difference.

- Within given situations it appears that a significant degree of choice exists for managers as to how they structure their organizations, without serious diseconomies being incurred.

- At worst, contingency theory may become a trivial exercise for managers in encouraging a sort of 'checklist' approach which ignores how the variables themselves may interact, often in a complex way.

● Finally, it is worth noting a renewed belief in universal principles of organizational structure. These have been broadly enunciated through a research method which has focused upon 'successful' or high-performing companies and asked whether they have any common organizational characteristics. Peters and Waterman's *In Search of Excellence* (1982) is the best known of this type of work. Some care has to be taken to avoid reading these books uncritically, however; by not concentrating on unsuccessful companies we cannot assert with certainty that a culture of 'success' is due to certain structural forms. It might even be that there is no relationship!

Similarly, some writers, such as Ouchi (1981), have argued that Japanese forms of organization represent a superior model which could be imitated. To some extent Japanese practices such as 'right-first-time' production, flexibility in tasks among operators and participative styles through such mechanisms as quality circles have been tried by many large firms and notably those suffering most from Japanese competition, such as the automobile producers. However, again, care has to be taken in assuming that it is easy to create new attitudes or an improved company culture. Such changes require long-term effort.

The innovative organization

To what extent does effectiveness include innovation? A number of management books dealing with innovation have been published since the early 1980s. Peters and Waterman (1982) attracted particular attention. They identify the following eight characteristics of an innovative organization:

1. Bias to action.
2. Proximity to the customer/client.
3. Autonomy.
4. Productivity through people.
5. 'Hands-on' management.
6. Concentration on strengths.
7. Simple structures.
8. Centralization of core issues, and decentralization of actions/implementation and day-to-day control.

In essence, the emphasis is on getting things done, allowing autonomy as far as is possible to middle-level managers. Linked to this is a concern for individual accountability.

In much the same way it has been argued that 'excellent' or 'high-performing' companies emphasize the following nine characteristics:

1. Concern for the future.
2. A concern to develop human resources.
3. A focus on the product/service being provided.

4. An orientation to the technologies in use.

5. A concern for quality, excellence, service and competence.

6. An orientation to 'outsiders', clients, customers, the community and shareholders.

7. Constant adaptation of reward systems and corporate values.

8. A focus on the basis of 'making and selling'.

9. Open to new ideas.

Here the same concern is shown for the basics of the organization's business, whatever this may be, and the same concern to balance internal and external issues is in evidence. For many organizations the concern expressed for the external environment, combined with quality, involves a new emphasis on service and on marketing as a means of achieving competitive advantage or more effective utilization of resources and public support (notably, but not exclusively, for public sector organizations).

It is interesting to contrast these ideas with the following view of what makes for an effective organization which emerges from the organizational development (OD) literature (see Strauss (1976) for an excellent and critical review):

● Lack of status differentials.

● Innovation.

● Sharing of responsibility.

● Expression of feelings and needs.

● Collaboration.

● Open, constructive conflict.

● Feedback.

● Flexible leadership.

● Involvement.

● Trust.

This makes important additions to the first two sets of ideas. Open and constructive conflict is important, as is the recognition of individual needs. Interestingly enough, the concerns are essentially, if not necessarily, internal concerns. The OD literature appears to give primacy to the staff and rarely mentions clients or customers. Nevertheless, organizations which can create an 'organizational climate' which encourages those latter characteristics and achieves the balance of internal and external concerns referred to above seem likely to establish effectiveness.

If innovation is a central element for improving effectiveness, then we need to understand why some circumstances seem to be more innovative than others. Rickards (1985) has identified the following key issues to be faced when deciding on a strategy for innovation:

● *Innovation is systematic*: all the factors involved (social, economic, political, technological, cultural, commercial) are interrelated.

● *Innovation is non-linear*: it experiences stops and starts and is often characterized by 'accidents' (e.g. penicillin).

- *Innovation is creative problem solving, requiring imagination and flexibility*: managers need to learn how to support people and to facilitate team work and problem solving.

- *Innovation is situational*: there is no one best way. Success will be dependent upon such factors as top management support, sensitivity to market needs, effective communication and technological expertise.

- *Innovation requires appropriate structures*: traditional hierarchies are too rigid. Project teams and task cultures are effective structures.

- *Innovation can be stimulated*: this requires major effort, however, and involves significant learning.

- *Innovation requires various communities of interest*: customers and clients can and should play a part.

- *Innovation is mission orientated*: thus it creates impetus, high viability and 'success'.

- *Innovation involves negotiation and participation*: it will involve conflict which must be resolved through negotiation or participation.

- *Innovation is itself innovation*: it will never go the way of past innovations.

- *Innovation and information are closely linked.*

- *Innovation is personal and global*: it involves and affects individuals and communities.

Concluding comment

In this chapter, we have considered a number of approaches to effectiveness. We have seen how blockages to effectiveness and change can be created and how they can be handled. We have also examined the link between organizational structures, the environment and effectiveness. Most importantly, we have seen how organizational ineffectiveness can hinder progress. We turn now to our treatment of how change can be managed to create and sustain effectiveness. As we shall see, this depends on our ability to generate greater understanding of the issues to be faced, the willingness to face these issues and the ability to learn from the process of more informed choice, from changing and experimenting with new ideas and from the experience which follows.

Exercises

1. Can you explain the problems being experienced at CAC Consultants?

2. How can CAC Consultants resolve their problems?

3. In what ways is International Engineering seeking to encourage adaptability?

CHAPTER 6

Managing complexity

Introduction

Managing change effectively is difficult enough with its attendant uncertainties and the problems along the way. It requires an understanding both of what is and seems likely to happen and of how people react to change, and a skilful management performance. Change management is rather like conducting an orchestra. One must energize and motivate, build cohesion, create a sense of pace and timing, and provide a skilled performance while sustaining the performance of others.

What then is the skilled performance that we say is needed? It comprises the ability to create a personal strategy which integrates 'solutions' to the various issues and problems described in the early chapters of this book. In this chapter we draw together many of the practical conclusions from the book into a profile of the skills and styles appropriate for effective change management. Can any individual expect to develop all these skills and styles? Perhaps not; but if we have a clearer idea of what is needed we can either attempt to develop them ourselves or look for colleagues who might provide the missing skills. Moreover, organizations might develop more appropriate selection and management development policies for senior staff, looking at both the individual and the management team, if preparation for and handling of significant organizational changes were known to be key management tasks in the coming year or so.

Is it possible to manage change perfectly? No is the short answer. But it is possible to provide more of what is needed in a period of change. People in change need empathy, information, ideas, milestones and feedback. They often get authoritarian management, avoidance of key issues, 'rah rah' management (see Woodward and Buchholz (1987) for an excellent, albeit partial, discussion along these lines), no clear milestones and no feedback. Following Woodward and Buchholz, we define 'bolt in, rah rah' change management as based on the idea that managing change requires that we merely bolt in the new system (or technology, or strategy, etc.) and 'fire up the troops'. Ignore the problems, go full steam ahead, 'it'll be all right on the night', and so on. This is true enough, in part, but it is ineffective as a change strategy by itself. We need some 'rah rah' but we need much more besides.

Why is it that people are often managed inappropriately in a period of change? There are two main reasons, examples of which we have already met in this book. Managers managing change are under pressure. This pressure undermines their own performance. Also, organizations often do not possess managers who are sufficiently skilful in handling change. Kotter (1988), for example, suggests one 'syndrome' associated with inadequate leadership, which we might similarly associate with inadequate change management. In summary, the argument is that successful organizations can carry the seeds of their own later decline, unless managers learn to, be both successful and adaptable. The syndrome is set out in Tables 6.1 and 6.2. It is interesting to note that these three stages can readily be traced in ABF Ltd (case study, Chapter 8) and International Engineering (case study, Chapters 5 and 9). In both, the tensions created by declining performance were creating performance problems. Top managers responded by setting up short-term control pressures (ABF Ltd) which made matters worse, or by *ad hoc* changes to the organizational structures, undermining the development of a clear strategy (International Engineering). In both cases top management found it difficult to face the underlying issues of strategy and performance. In ABF Ltd the managing director avoided discussion of performance, wherever possible. In International Engineering the fundamentals of the business seemed to be avoided because people felt the need to protect the feelings of several senior managers. These various pressures can be examined in greater detail, see Table 6.2.

Table 6.1 ● Syndrome of ineffective leadership and change management (after Kotter, 1988)

Stage 1: the firm is in a strong position, with little competition. It develops systems, management practices and a culture which depend on a few capable leaders. The management style is a combination of autocratic, directive and paternalistic

Stage 2: the firm grows and becomes more complex. Competition increases and new technology emerges. The firm now needs strong and capable leadership but does not have enough people with these skills. Many people with good leadership potential left because of the frustrations created in stage 1. However, the firm's performance does not deteriorate dramatically. It remains well placed in its established markets. It 'lives' off its reputation

Stage 3: declining performance leads to a focus on short-term results. Internal tensions lead to conflict which cannot be handled constructively. Senior managers seem incapable of facing these tensions. Functional rather than corporate policies prevail. The firm lacks a co-ordinated strategy. This, in turn, undermines efforts to improve the quality of management

Again, both the ABF Ltd (see p. 149) and International Engineering cases provide examples of this more detailed analysis. Particularly interesting is the point about 'fear of failure'; the pressures are dual in nature. On the one hand the short-term approach combined with a functional or departmental orientation, centralization and autocratic management styles creates a powerful tendency to limit risk taking. On the other, managers moving rapidly through careers and not having to face up to their mistakes do not learn the interpersonal skills needed to do so. They find facing up to performance issues difficult. Therefore, when forced to do so by those same short-term pressures, they often do so inadequately and in a volatile, even primitive, fashion (ABF Ltd). This further reduces risk taking, over time creating an organization within which the 'fear of failure' is very high indeed.

Kotter (1988) identifies a number of the 'characteristics needed, to provide effective

Table 6.2 ● Impact of short-term pressures and functional approaches on the quality of management (after Kotter, 1988)

Short-term pressure and 'functional' management styles

Promote people who need little training, who will obey orders. Little attempt at management development	Departmental managers hang on to good people. People develop very limited experience. Limited training undertaken	Organizational structure is bureaucratic and centralized	Good people get promotion quickly, manage careers for personal gain
Succession problems. Few people with leadership potential, good interpersonal skills or credibility	Most senior staff and managers are very narrow and are credible within their own functional departments	Senior managers are better at operations management and tactical decision making	Some managers move through the hierarchy so quickly that they do not live with their mistakes
Management team, made up largely from internal promotion, is of poor quality	Little understanding or trust between functions. Poor co-operation and co-ordination	Strategy tends to be focused on the short term. A lack of vision	Senior managers do not build the credibility or skills needed to build trust
			Top management find facing up to poor performance difficult. Strong 'fear of failure' builds up at lower levels in organization

leadership', overcoming the problems identified in the syndrome outlined above. To be effective, leaders need a range of knowledge of industry, business functions and the firm. Also needed are a broad range of contacts and good working relationships in the firm and the industry. Linked to this will be a good track record in a relatively broad set of activities. Kotter also refers to 'keen minds' (whatever that means), strong inter-personal skills, high integrity, seeing value in people, and a strong desire to lead. All this is very relevant, but we need to go further than this and try to set out the skills or competencies that managers need to develop.

Managing change: core competencies

We propose a simple model identifying four core competencies that are essential to the effective management of change; these are as follows.

Decision making

This comprises the following characteristics:

● The acquisition and application of information to shape a feasible and focused programme of work.

● Intuition and vision – the ability to make 'imaginative leaps' to see how a given situation can be transformed and the aims and objectives that can be achieved.

● The ability to resist such statements as 'it can't be done, has never been done, was tried and didn't work'. In essence, to discuss people's doubts and concerns while patiently but consistently reinforcing the plans and programmes for change.

● Understanding the practical and political consequences. To understand those activities, changes and systems which can be introduced given the level of internal opposition and the available resources and skills.

● Synthesizing skills – this ability to identify the views, ideas and aims in common between those who wish for change and those who might oppose. The ability to interpret the new system in terms of the existing culture and traditions. These sometimes need modifying or even overturning. However, this is not always nec-essary. If not, then every effort should be made to synthesize the new and the old. Many people's commitment to their employing organization is engaged by these traditions, which should not be unnecessarily discarded.

● Cross-cultural skills – empathy.

Coalition building

Decisions are not made until the support and resources needed to implement them are available. This core competence comprises the following characteristics:

● Clearing ideas – checking out the validity of information and the feasibility of ideas before we become too 'fixed' on them.

- Gaining supporters – selling the ideas ahead of 'going public'.
- Bargaining – identifying and then establishing networks of support and resources from key managers and groups who, while not directly involved, can provide support.
- Presenting – selling the change clearly, linking new concepts to well-tried ideas and projects/systems where relevant.

Achieving action

This comprises the following characteristics:

- Handling opposition – waiting it out, wearing it down, displaying support to those engaged in implementing change.
- Motivating people to try out new ideas, ways of working and systems.
- Providing support for risk taking and experimentation.
- Building self-esteem.

Maintaining momentum and effort

This comprises the following characteristics:

- Team building.
- Obtaining commitment and generating feelings of ownership.
- Sharing information and problems.
- Managing the early 'data' from the new system or project to build credibility.
- Providing feedback on success.
- Flexibility of style, problem-solving approach.
- Trust in the people to solve their own problems.
- Energizing, not directing!

Management styles for change

All the above lead us toward identifying management styles that are appropriate for managing in changing circumstances. This is true whether these circumstances are to do with growing complexity, internally or externally, or where specific changes (e.g. a new product launch) are underway. Broadly speaking, effectiveness and adaptability require strong leadership, the ability to maintain progress and a facilitative and supportive approach. Managers will deploy different management styles with different individuals and groups and different circumstances. Nevertheless, the implications of our discussion thus far are that managers need to deploy management styles which allow greater dependence on their people, but not without accountability.

Giving leadership, supporting action and risk, holding the line on accountability: to develop your style in these directions demands high-order interpersonal skills. It demands that managers can face and resolve the dilemmas posed in Chapter 2. Various management styles are identified in Table 6.3. Against each are shown characteristic values underpinning the style, core assumptions, typical tasks, roles and management skills adopted and developed when that style is used.

The managers involved in the London Underground case study (see p. 185) completed a management-style exercise. When asked what changes in management styles they saw as necessary in the next 2 to 5 years they consistently expressed the view that three styles presently predominate. Top management were seen as autocratic and political. Middle management were seen as co-ordinators. For the future they saw a facilitative style as being increasingly needed.

I have used this same exercise with nine groups of middle managers from an international corporate finance bank, with much the same result. The most interesting point was that in both these cases managers identified one overriding constraint to the development of this new management style: too many middle and senior managers had been appointed on technical and not on managerial merit. Thus progress depends on changes of the type outlined in the health care organization, the case study – 'Developing the professional role in a period of change' presented later in this chapter. Which style or styles best represent you? Not a straightforward question, of course, but one with self-evident importance for the management of organizations.

Agenda for implementing change

To complete this chapter we now identify an agenda for change. This agenda summarizes much of what we have said so far in this book. Following it brings no guarantees of success but should increase its likelihood. The main ingredients of successful change programmes are the following:

● A clear *strategic aim* is needed for implementation. The benefits of change are often slow to achieve and intangible. Unfortunately, the costs are often more tangible and are certainly more immediate. Therefore, people need to understand why. What competitive advantage will the organization achieve if the changes are successfully implemented? I remember working hundreds of hours of overtime trying to get an electronically controlled crane working effectively in 1961. Why? Because the contract under which it was being built had a penalty clause against late delivery. Much more important, however, was the customer, which was one of those companies that launched the 'container revolution' in the 1960s. The factory manager had made clear to us that success now meant major sales in the future. We responded!

● *Support* at top level is crucial to success. Senior managers must be clearly *accountable* for change. New systems, new product launches, new structures are expensive and disruptive. It is important that senior managers are clearly accountable so that people can see how expenditure and progress are being controlled. Increasingly organizations now adopt a *project management* approach to reinforce this accountability.

● Major changes often lead to changes in the *power structure* of the organization. This

Table 6.3 ● Management styles (from Jameson, 1984)

Style description	Characteristic values	Core assumptions	Tasks	Roles	Skills
Autocrat Organization must have clear-cut singular goals	Economic ends demand order, authority, expertise and energy and justify means	People require direction and control to work effectively	Structure work; direct and control people	Decision making. Giving example. Punishing and rewarding	Technical Functional Analytical ('Power')
Laissez-faire (Permissive) organizations are coalitions of differing interests and plural goals	Independence, self-reliance (as distinct from total self-support). Anti-autocratic tendency conventional	People are resourceful but not controllable (i.e. will serve own interest) given opportunity	Set boundaries but prevent bureaucracy. Limited help to others	Peace-keeping. Stabilizing. Giving range to talent within limits	Negotiating Mediating Resourcing Limited systems
Politician Organizations are temporary coalitions of changing goals and interests. Prevailing values determine action	Pragmatism, self-reliance, status or recognition. Freedom from expediency. Facts need interpretation and change	Performance is judged by appearances – things are uncertain – change is inevitable	Problem solving by strategic tactics. Authority by consent	Leader, maintainer, disturbance handler, compromiser, 'fixer'	Interpreting Negotiating Influencing Resourcing Eliminating dissension
Social Organizations are 'social systems' which should put social before economic values	Interdependence, mutual support, caring for others, quality of life. Work is a means to an end not an end itself	Contented people are more productive – co-operation gets things done	Mediating. Motivating. Peace-keeping. Helping and supporting people	Leader–counsellor, maintaining work group cohesion and morale	Social (i.e. interpersonal) Mediating Developing people
Executive co-ordinator Organizations are complex economic systems for getting work done	Efficiency of output and economic results are to the common good. Duty and responsibility must be assigned	Conflict is harmful to common good and is removed by good management and planning	Structuring work and effort. Planning. Co-ordinating. Controlling	Leader and planner allocating tasks and responsibility and rewards	Technical Functional Analytical Planning Administrating 'people'
Facilitator Organizations are highly complex systems with multiple goals, conflicting interests	Accountability Pragmatism Idealism Aesthetic Theoretical Humanist	People are resourceful, creative and have development potential which needs to be well managed	Developing people, their ideas, aspirations and capabilities	Counsellor Innovator Trainer Resource provider Team worker	Counselling Negotiating Interpreting Theorizing Bargaining Conciliating

is another reason why successful implementation requires project management with the involvement of users and line managers.

● Implementation must be carefully planned, and managed. It will take time and will have far-reaching effects. *Achieving ownership* is crucial. Managing the stress induced by change, helping people to cope with change and understanding its impact are all important. Where possible, changes should be designed to depend on existing systems, procedures, cultures and traditions. Ensuring *maximum compatibility* creates a better basis for implementation.

● The main problems to be solved in implementation are *cross-functional* problems.

● The *pace* of change needs careful planning. Longer planning leads to quicker implementation, early success, faster diffusion.

● *Pragmatism*, rather than a technology-driven 'big project' approach, is more likely to deliver success. As we said earlier, 'the excellent is the enemy of the good'. People respond to pragmatism. People respond if the planned changes appear to deal with problems that they recognize.

● Build in systems to *reward* relevant behaviour. Providing early feedback of success helps. Developing reward systems to reinforce change is another powerful means of supporting implementation.

● Recognize the importance of *role modelling*. Changing one's behaviour to provide an example may be necessary.

● Initiate the appropriate *training and support*, but provide flexibility. Allow users control over training. Too little and overrigid training can be a hindrance. Training provided before people have accepted change (Chapter 10) will be of little value.

Corporate culture

Deal and Kennedy (1982) define corporate culture as encompassing how people in a company are likely to act in given situations both inside and outside the organization. It includes a set of beliefs, a code of behaviour and minimum standards of performance and ethics. It will influence service quality and the way in which people are treated, whether customers or clients.

Deal and Kennedy go on to argue that organizations with 'strong' cultures (i.e. clearly identifiable) are likely to be more effective, basing the conclusion on evidence collected on 80 or so corporations in the USA. They believe that a strong corporate culture comprises the following key features:

● Characteristic and clear approach to the corporate environment – markets, clients, stakeholders and so on.

● Values – shared by the people who make up the organization.

● Heroes – people who represent and communicate these values, people who provide others with 'role models'.

● Rites and rituals – systems and procedures which it is expected that people will follow.

● Networks – the informal means of communication often known as the 'grapevine'.

A strong culture is one in which people may have a clearer idea of what is required of them, a clearer sense of the objectives being pursued. Following Itami (1987), it is an important 'invisible asset' (see Chapter 7). Organizations with weak cultures may be less effective, less productive and less satisfying places in which to work.

If all this is true can we then change the corporate culture? This is what is being attempted at International Engineering, for example. The evidence suggests that one can change a corporate culture, but only slowly, and through sustained effort and hard work.

Deal and Kennedy (1982) conclude that an attempt at corporate culture change can only be justified where any or all of the following various conditions apply:

● Where the environment is undergoing fundamental change (say, in health care or banking).

● Where the industry is highly competitive and the environment is characterized by rapid and often turbulent change (e.g. the computer industry).

● Where the organization is growing rapidly, particularly where the organization is becoming very large.

● Where performance has been in sustained decline.

In such conditions sustained changes to attitudes and behaviour will be essential. New 'role models' will be needed; new management styles will be emerging. The 'lists' of change are such that people will need to understand why the changes are needed. Deal and Kennedy identify the following guidelines for those engaging in culture changes; these are worth examining:

● Peer group consensus will have an important influence on acceptance of change. Typically, people do not feel strongly opposed to a given change. However, social ties can be such that resistance to change can build within social groupings and networks. It is important to build support within these networks.

● It is important to convey and build upon trust in communication and in how problems are handled.

● Changes need to be treated as opportunities within which to build skills and develop people.

● Allow enough time for changed behaviour to become the norm. This point is often ignored, with naïve estimates of how much time is needed.

● Encourage people to adopt new approaches, new behaviour patterns, new systems to fit their own local circumstances. Identify the underlying ideas of the change and maintain their integrity but recognize that many elements of a set of proposals are marginal. Recognize the battles you must win! Account for local circumstances. Allow people to modify your changes to help them resolve their own local problems (their own 'rice puddings'!).

The main point here is that the performance we give in a period of change must be consistent with the corporate culture or, at least, we should recognize the 'fit' between our approach to the tasks of managing and the prevailing corporate culture. At

International Engineering, therefore, establishing the new, decentralized organizational structure was only the first step. If the corporate culture was to be changed, the organization needed to develop and encourage new 'role models', greater clarity of how it saw itself and how it related to its markets, and now, in this case, more commercial values. Training and communication were necessary. Recognition and reward for new behaviours were needed for employees who adopt new practices.

We have long known that corporate culture is an important issue for those engaged in major organizational change. Various definitions of culture exist but the essence of corporate culture has to do with values and beliefs about 'the ways we do things around here'. Models of culture tend to relate particular kinds of culture with organizational and market circumstances indicating the forms which appear to emerge and the performance characteristics of each. To the extent that a 'strong' culture emerges they are difficult to change. Indeed it seems clear that to change culture we must work on the mind-set or mental programming within the organization.

It does appear that we can do so. The key seems to be that of getting people to focus on shared problems. Developing new solutions and supporting their successful implementation helps. Most importantly we can aid the creation of new mind-sets by identifying 'tacit' knowledge which already exists in the organization, converting it to new explicit knowledge and encouraging its use in problem solving. Thus are created new possibilities – engendering mind-set change not by seeking to destroy the current mind-set but rather by adding new ideas; by focusing on solutions and not on failure.

Goffee and Jones (1996) offer another approach to the analysis of culture. For them culture is about the presence (or absence) of community. Building upon the ideas of social theorists such as Durkheim they argue that sociability (the extent to which people like each other, mix with each other in and out of work) and solidarity (the extent to which there are shared goals) are important components of corporate culture. These two dimensions lead to the identification of four cultures – see Figure 6.1 below.

Note that I have modified the Jones and Goffee model here. In my version where sociability is high but solidarity is low we have a team culture. Of course the solidarity within the team may be high whilst solidarity for the organization as a whole is low. Where sociability and solidarity are high you see a network culture emerging. These are characterized by easy and effective vertical and horizontal communication and relate to the value-added model described in Chapter 1.

As a case study we may examine Philips NV – Operation Centurion. From 1990 onwards Philips has sought to transform itself as a business. The company has tried hard both to build current performance and to become more innovative. Combining cascade communications with taskforces working on a range of issues deemed important to the future success of the business, the company has attempted to engender a sense of urgency about the need for dramatic change. Also much attention has been paid to the need to create new values based on trust, openness and honesty. Early on it was recognized that culture change cannot be achieved without fundamental change to how the business operates. Projects have been used to change the way people manage. However, it is also recognized that mind-set change lies at the core of the needed changes. In particular the attempt to create a new and shared mind-set requires

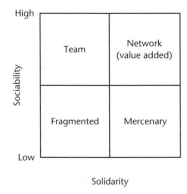

Figure 6.1 Two dimensions, four cultures

attention to creating a sense of urgency, opening minds to what the competition is doing but most of all focusing effort on action projects which can have an impact on the business and which over time may lead to the growth of solidarity.

Here we see an attempt to use changed behaviour as the basic building block of culture change. In summary the new behaviour includes cascade communications, dialogue across all levels of the business, cross-boundary working, a new focus on asset management, bench-marking and so on. Not least of Philips' ambition is to reinvent its culture to emphasize behaviour such as risk-taking, creativity etc.

Managing corporate politics

We have now seen that achieving change requires us to manage effectively in circumstances which include problems of organizational culture, organizational politics and the need to help people to cope with the pressures and anxieties created. All this creates great uncertainty. In this chapter, we extend our discussion by looking at the politics of change and how they can be managed.

Before commencing this task there is one point which deserves emphasis. Changes in organizations are rarely, if ever, neat. One can rarely identify a clear starting point or a clear end. The trends and pressures to which we respond are on-going. Discussion moves forward at varying speeds and in different arenas. There is nothing new under the sun! The ideas incorporated in any particular change will have been considered elsewhere, for other purposes, by other people. Thus it is that organizational change is more process (and muddy process at that!) than event.

To organize our discussion of the use of political skills in the management of change we present a simple model in Table 6.4. Managers and others utilize a variety of resources as they engage in the politics of organization. They may have formal authority (or may be perceived as having such) by virtue of their positions in the organization. Moreover, they may have direct control over resources. The use of resources to negate

Table 6.4 ● Political skills and the management of change

Resources	Process	Form
Formal authority	Negotiation	Politics of:
Control of resources	Influencing	Budgets
Control of information	Mobilizing support	Careers
Control of agenda	Mobilizing bias	Succession
Control of access symbols	Use of emotion	Information
	Ceremony and ritual	Organizational structures
	Professional 'mystery'	Appraisal

change efforts is widely observed. If a change programme needs engineering resources, and if the engineering manager can withhold those resources (perhaps by claiming that other priorities must prevail), then the change programme will be delayed.

Control of information, agenda and access are all important political resources. It is commonplace to state that 'information is power'. This applies in two main senses: power to control the organization internally, and power in regard to the development of policies for the future. Control over the organization is essential for control over policy. This point is made eloquently by Henry Kissinger when he discusses the new role that Nixon and he had agreed for the National Security Council at the beginning of Nixon's first term:

> A President should not leave the presentation of his options to one of the Cabinet departments, or agencies. Since the views of the departments are often in conflict, to place one in charge of presenting the options will be perceived by the others as giving it an unfair advantage. Moreover, the strong inclination of all departments is to narrow the scope for Presidential decision, not to expand it. They are organised to develop a preferred policy, not a range of choices. If forced to present options, the typical department will present two absurd alternatives as straw men bracketing its preferred option – which usually appears in the middle position. A totally ignorant decision-maker could easily satisfy his departments by blindly choosing Option 2 of any three choices which they submit to him. Every department, finally, dreads being overruled by the President, all have, therefore, a high incentive to obscure their differences. Options tend to disappear in an empty consensus that at the end of the day permits each agency or department maximum latitude to pursue its original preference. It takes a strong, dedicated, and fast Presidential staff to ensure that the President has before him genuine and not bogus choices.

> (Kissinger, 1979, p. 62)

Recognizing the narrowness of view which often emerges from specialist, departmental and sometimes from professional concerns, Kissinger demonstrates here the crucial importance of controlling the presentation of options to a president. Without this the president may be at the mercy of departments, which may preclude policy debate by the nature and range of the options presented to the president. They may also structure a policy debate by purposely obscuring differences over policy in the pursuit of consensus. Eisenhower makes his own view on this tendency clear in an acerbic comment in his memoirs about how departmental analysts can elevate consensus over analysis. Political theory contains concepts such as 'non-decision making' and 'organization as the mobilization of bias' (see Bachrach and Baratz, 1963; Schnattsneider, 1960), which help to describe these forms of behaviour. In essence, it is suggested that when considering decision making we should focus not only upon the genesis and process of the decisions actually made. We also need to concern ourselves with options not considered. The power to preclude certain options is power indeed. Moreover, we should be concerned with decisions which were not made, with opportunities forgone, with 'alternative historical possibilities'. Many students of the history of technology point out that technology does not develop in a straight line; rather, it is a series of branches. Over time various branches attract less interest and research effort. This happens less because of a lack of intrinsic merit in the pursuit of a particular line of work and more because one particular line of research has attracted attention.

Corporate political tactics

To manage corporate politics and changes effectively, managers need to recognize and develop skills in deploying various political tactics. We have discussed some of these above. For reference, we list some widely used political tactics before turning to a case study. In the case study we shall be considering a constructive role for a 'political' style of management, in a period of change.

Political tactics involve the following actions:

- Selective use of performance criteria to manage credibility.

- Use of outside experts and consultants.

- Control of the agenda including the order of business.

- Building internal alliances and coalitions.

- Working with external groups, stakeholders and opinion leaders.

- Use of promotions.

- Co-operation.

- Information access and control.

- Control of access to key decision makers.

- Group pressure for conformity.

For the moment we merely note that tactics like these are used in the real world of organizations. Let us now turn to the case study.

CASE STUDY

Developing the professional role in a period of change

This case study is based upon a large health district in the UK. Subject to a complex set of changes, management faced major problems as a consequence of the complex tasks facing the various professional groups involved in health care. During the period under review an array of financial, systems and management changes were underway. Budget restrictions constrained, or were seen as constraining, service provision. A major budget reallocation process moving resources from this district to other districts required spending cuts over a period of years. Yet, at the same time, new money was becoming available, sometimes to meet specific problem areas, from either regional[1] or central government.

The finance department occupies a central and powerful organizational role. The treasurer/director of finance carries statutory responsibility for the stewardship of public money. Finance is required to ensure that money is used properly and effectively. This places finance in the role of both guardian and investigator: guardian of funds and investigator of 'spending departments', use of those funds. Changes to the management structure in recent years have brought decentralization of finance to unit level. Nevertheless, the central finance department occupies a key and powerful position within the district. Given this position it seems likely that the finance department might give the lead to achieve more general changes to the managerial climate for the organization as a whole.

We now list the specific proposals to be effected from within the finance department before turning to a more general discussion of their impact in the longer term.

Stop promulgating 'false' information

During the early part of each financial year it is common practice to present exaggerated spending trends. The 'overspending' predicted is aimed at placing pressure on spending departments. Some managers will curtail activity in order to avoid overspending. Thus 'slack' is created. While some departments will still overspend, others will not. Moreover, each year 'savings' tend to be more than overspending, thus providing resources. These resources provide the treasurer with the patronage by which he or she can manage the organization's politics. Through the ages patronage has been a key form of influence. This approach has very real dangers. In a complex and changing world it encourages departments to take parochial and defensive views. It frequently means that important issues will not be discussed openly. Finance staff are less able to play a positive role in the development of services. The credibility of financial information becomes untenable. Thus line managers and finance managers increasingly lose control.

In effect, the finance department becomes the only budget holder. The advantages of patronage are 'bought' at the cost of lack of co-operation, absence of control, limited access of finance staff to line managers (who will be defensive), and thus inadequate support for planning and service management. Moreover, the reliance on patronage, while

---

[1] The service is organized nationally into regions, each of which comprise a number of districts.

▶▶

resulting in some influence, often leads to a diminution of respect and credibility for and of those who do so. As we have already agreed, the deployment of political strategies in management is more credible if the intentions behind them are seen as constructive and if the strategy and its related tactics are not too crude.

This cannot be changed overnight, while in the long run one of the objectives of achieving change would be to improve the credibility of financial information. To change too quickly may lead people throughout the organization to experience great uncertainty about financial data in the short run. Most managers will believe some of the financial data, others because they have struck up a good working relationship with a middle-level financial manager. Too rapid change risks the credibility of all financial data (of 'throwing away the baby with the bath water'). Finally, too rapid change may undermine confidence in the district elsewhere in the service, e.g. at regional or at national level. This is not to say that managers and others at these levels do not recognize the existence of these problems. There is a strong tacit recognition, unstated because people are leaving the district to resolve its own problems, at least for the moment. Also widely understood is the notion that these problems need resolving in a not too public way. Too rapid a change risks too much attention, perhaps leading to the problems taking on too high a 'profile'. On the face of it this sounds appropriate but in reality it could lead to a loss of control over the problems, polarized positions and, in consequence, their resolution may take longer and involve more stress and difficulty.

What is needed is a systematic approach. Senior financial managers need to explain how the financial data are developed, explain the assumptions and their limitations and how the information can be interpreted. Many line managers and/or professionals may choose or pretend not to understand. This can be a convenient defence. Persistence and greater openness will, over time, lead to improved understanding. From there, decisions can be taken on a joint basis.

Demonstrate understanding that finance may be no more or less efficient than other departments/functions

Identifying inefficiency and ineffectiveness is a key task of a finance function. To do so credibly means that finance staff must be seen to review and improve their own departmental performance. The department should co-operate with reviews by other organizations and methods professionals and by external consultants.

Play a positive role in performance improvement

A key danger to overcome is that of allowing too many reviews (of other departments) to highlight weaknesses without recommending remedies. This problem is made worse if reports are published before departmental management have had the chance to improve performance. To take a key example, audit staff need to be trained to work with departmental staff. Their task is not merely to identify weaknesses; also, they should be encouraged to use their expertise and experience to work with line management. Discussing solutions at this stage can lead to more rapid implementation and improvement. Then when the findings are published the picture is of weaknesses remedied.

▶▶

Increasingly, finance staff need to work with line managers, helping them to resolve their own problems. Too narrow an approach does not encourage co-operation. Instead, defensiveness and departmentalism are fostered, making changes and improvements harder to achieve.

Work with people in the hospital

Traditionally, meetings involving senior financial staff were held in the finance department. This served to symbolize the department's power. Moreover, it reinforced the somewhat 'punitive' image of the department *vis-à-vis* other functions. Meeting people on their own territory demonstrates interest in them as people, and in their work. It helps to eliminate the distance between finance staff and others.

'Distancing' is a major impediment to effectiveness, as we saw in Chapter 9. It allows people to reject the input, ideas and contributions of those who are 'distanced'. Furthermore, hospital finance staff appear remote if they are not seen regularly in the hospital. Senior finance managers have much to learn both in and from other departments, but only by seeing them in action. Finally, encouraging more junior finance staff to visit the hospital would give their work more meaning and create stronger commitment to the organization as a whole.

Resist traditional financial control arguments

Traditionally, finance officers were believed by others to resist changes, which appeared to undermine the historical pattern of financial control. For example, revised arrangements for joint finance with local social services organizations allowed local authorities and/or housing associations to run some community services in some circumstances. There are sound arguments for such developments. These organizations have relevant experience, can ensure effective co-ordination with other local-authority-managed services and can avoid duplication. All too often the response is 'We cannot give them our money, they will waste it!' What is needed is joint exploration of problems to ensure effective control of spending.

To this we should add two points. Financial control is essential. But should financial control play a constructive role in the deployment and development of services or should it merely be a 'gate-keeper', allowing projects which meet traditional control requirements and thus risking turning down innovative ideas? The second point is that it is important to apply financial controls to the finance department, and to be seen to do so.

Avoid jargon

It is essential that the information provided should be intelligible. Great care must be taken to assure that unnecessary technical jargon is avoided. Jargon is another means of 'distancing' finance from other functions. We hope to recognize that contentious reports are sometimes filled with jargon just because they are contentious. This should be minimized although the start may well be best made on the more mundane documentation.

Changing the culture

Changes of the type described would go some way towards changing the culture of the organization. It would become less defensive and departmental in its style and in its managerial politics. Greater openness might be possible. This would take time. People are 'entrenched' in ideas, attitudes and positions. Years of distrust and departmental in-fighting cannot be overturned quickly. But many positive relationships do exist and these can be built upon. Stronger relationships and a more open decision-making style will be a better basis for dealing with the on-going conflicts of views and ideas which will inevitably exist.

Conflict and organizational politics are inevitable. Moreover, both are likely to be heightened during a period of change. The case study summarizes one example of how it is possible to develop a more open approach to management. The purpose is not to avoid conflict but, rather, to create a more open and collaborative approach in order that conflict and politics can be handled constructively. That is not to say that this always happens. Often, individuals (or even coalitions of individuals) and departments pursue narrow interests. This seems to be inevitable and even desirable. Without it people might lack the energy to argue, question, put forward ideas and so on. What is needed is a credible way of moving forward amidst conflict. As we have already suggested, it seems likely that longer-term credibility and organizational effectiveness flow from the ability to establish a more balanced, constructive approach to conflict.

Leadership and corporate politics

The ideas examined in the case study needed the full commitment of senior financial management. The style and approach of the finance function is to be changed and this demands leadership, partly to 'sell' the ideas throughout the function; partly to provide 'role models' for other staff, i.e. leading through example; partly to manage the relationships between finance and other functions. No matter how gradually the changes are made, people from other functions will recognize the different approach and may exploit the new situation. Years of low trust and interdepartmental conflict leave a legacy.

The task of the leader in this situation is multi-faceted. In Chapter 7 we shall be dealing with leadership, but because of the obvious relationships between leadership, the constructive management of conflict, corporate politics and power we will deal with these aspects briefly.

Few, if any, prescriptions for effective leadership can be offered. Leadership has been linked to individual traits (e.g. intelligence and charisma) and to specific types of behaviour (e.g. focus on the tasks, focus on the people). Currently, much attention is devoted to contingency approaches to leadership, which link effective leadership to features of the situation in which leaders and others operate, such as technology, organizational structure, the environment, characteristics and needs of subordinates, etc.

This approach leads us to suggest that leadership style should be varied to meet the varying circumstances in which leaders lead.

Effective leadership is an elusive concept. In practice, it is also difficult to determine the criteria underpinning effective leadership. It is clearly linked to power. The following concepts seek to identify the following five social bases of power:

1. *Legitimate power*: deriving from the manager's position and therefore formal authority.

2. *Expert power*: deriving from the knowledge and experience of the individual (thus a doctor can influence the patient's behaviour because he or she exerts expert power when giving advice).

3. *Referent power*: deriving from the ways in which people identify with others (often involves a charismatic individual).

4. *Reward power*: deriving from the individual's control over rewards such as pay, promotion and task assignments.

5. *Coercive power*: deriving from the capacity to sanction individual behaviour.

Thus power is not simply a matter of position; people appear to vary in their motives for power and can thus exert personal power. Power is inherent in bargaining, negotiation and political processes. The effective use of power is central to effective management and leadership. Kotter (1978) suggests that individuals who make effective use of power are likely to possess the following characteristics:

● Be sensitive to what others consider to be legitimate behaviour acquiring and using power.

● Have good intuitive understanding of the various types of power and the methods of influence.

● Tend to develop all the types of power to some degree, and use all methods of influence.

● Establish career goals and seek out managerial positions that allow them successfully to develop and use power.

● Use all resources, formal authority and power to develop more power.

● Engage in power-orientated behaviour in ways that are tempered by maturity and self-control.

● Recognize and accept as a legitimate fact that, in using these methods, they clearly influence other people's behaviour and lives.

Coping with conflict

What can managers do to cope with conflict? We can look at this question by considering first what a middle manager can and cannot do, what top managers can do directly and how top managers can support implementation indirectly.

CASE STUDY

Oticon (see p 92 above)

Oticon is a Danish manufacturer of hearing aids famous for having created 'the Spaghetti organization' through which it seeks to create new ways of working in pursuit of innovation and reduced time to market. It has a record of substantially improved financial performance since restructuring in the early 1990s.

In the midst of a turnaround strategy begun in 1989–90, a proposal came forward to relocate head office to western Denmark so that it would be located with Oticon's principal factory. The new design provided for appealing working conditions, paperless offices and so on. There was considerable opposition. Eventually this change was not forced through over the opposition of staff. At the same time top management pressed forward with the reorganization plan – once staff were settled into the new head office the change was widely publicized in the press, on television and eventually on CNN. Was this about creating a sense that there could be 'no turning back?' To what extent was all of this about managing perceptions? To what extent was the concession on location as much about recognizing that some battles are not worth fighting and that ensuring that people felt engaged in the process and *listened to* was important in focusing attention on the future? If change requires that new routines be accepted and problems be solved, then a platform of high self-esteem is needed. To what extent is the management of the politics of change about managing perceptions and expectations to that end?

Some things that managers cannot do much about

Decision making is neither a rational nor an orderly process

This is particularly so in periods of change, characterized as they are by uncertainty and involvement of emotions. We now know a considerable amount about the process of decision making, enough to know that a wide range of individual, group and organizational factors can affect the process (see Janis and Mann, 1976; Hickson *et al.*, 1986). Selective perception, uncertainty, organizational politics and time pressures are but some of these factors. Moreover, decisions are not discrete events; they are fluid. A group of people 'decide', but in implementation the decision is often modified, scaled down or delayed. Decisions have both intentional and unintentional consequences. These may occur rapidly and the latter may lead to changes to the original decision. Decisions are part of a 'stream of decisions', connected either directly or indirectly, because they are part of the same programme or project or because implementation demands that those involved compete for scarce resources. Add to this the tendency of many to dissociate themselves from failure and we begin to get a picture of the real-life complexity involved.

Example: Union Carbide and the Bhopal disaster

On 3 December 1984 a cloud of deadly gas was released into the atmosphere around the Union Carbide Corporation's pesticide plant in Bhopal, India. With a death toll of over 1200 people, and many more injured, this was the world's worst industrial accident.

On the other side of the world, in Connecticut, USA, Union Carbide managers faced the prospect of coping with the disaster. A complex set of issues had to be dealt with quickly: how to establish the cause; how to ensure it could not be repeated; how to help the victims; relief agencies; how to reassure investors; how to control the issue of legal liability; what to announce.

With only two telephone lines into Bhopal and the plant supervisors under arrest, hard information was difficult to come by. Much of the information coming through seemed barely credible.

Hellreigel *et al.* (1986) quote this as a case of complex decision making. They describe it as a convoluted action process because of the following four points:

1. The nature of the problem was unstructured – the managers had never faced a disaster of this magnitude before.

2. The problem will go on for years – litigation alone is likely to continue over a period of years.

3. Many vested interests were involved – the company, the Indian government, the USA, the heirs of the dead, the injured, the shareholders of the company.

4. Many people were involved in different ways – to fix responsibility, report the story, compensate victims, avoid repetition of this type of accident, look at the future of the Bhopal plant.

In this process all manner of trade-offs, bargains, compromises, misunderstandings and conflicts were likely.

Conflicting demands

In a world in which resources are finite, there will always be conflicting demands for resources, attention or priority. Moreover, it seems likely that managers and others will conflict over the goals to be pursued and the means of use. Finally, disagreement will have both cognitive and emotional dimensions. While conflict can be a positive force to change, the first point to note about it is that it cannot be (and indeed should not be) eliminated.

Example

In the Bhopal disaster described above it was always clear that the demands of victims, the governments concerned and the company would be in conflict – the interests were so different.

Uncertainty

This point hardly needs emphasizing! We live in an uncertain world. Managers must necessarily deal with uncertainty.

Bias

Again, the point hardly needs emphasis. We all have incomplete perceptions and stereotyped attitudes, and this can lead us to adopt biased views. Moreover, departmental as well as personal bias needs to be considered. The different departments reflect the concerns and views of that department, which are not necessarily a corporate view.

External forces

The changes in markets, technologies and legal frameworks external to the organization need to be dealt with by managers. While companies can set out to influence these external factors by lobbying, advertising and so on, they tend to be insurmountable at any given time.

Some things that managers can do

If these are the things managers can do little about, what are the things *that managers can do*?

1. They can *choose the problems to work on*, the battles to fight, when to act and when to wait. Timing can be an important skill (see below).
2. They can develop a broad and detailed *knowledge of the organization, its clients or customers and its people*. Knowledge is power!
3. They can try to *develop their own self-awareness*. What are my strengths and weaknesses? What do I wish to achieve? What does all this tell me about 1 and 2, but about 1 in particular?
4. They can set out to *develop their own skills* in order better to influence others.

Some things that top managers can do

Set and sustain values

By setting appropriate values top management can influence people throughout the organization. The chief executive of International Engineering (see Chapter 5) constantly discussed, communicated and supported people working towards a more commercial set of values for the company. The traditional values of engineering excellence were insufficient as a basis for meeting increased and global competition.

Support problem solving and risk

Once again, taking the example of International Engineering, here we had a low-risk-taking culture, an engineering culture which had been managed in a fairly authoritarian way and in which the operations department dominated, and had reinforced the 'fear of failure' very powerfully indeed. People were afraid to take risks because the price of failure was known to be high. Directly or indirectly, people who 'failed' felt that they were being punished. Typically, this was carried out by assigning them poor jobs on 'low-profile' work or projects. Such assignments have a powerful impact on career, promotion, job interest and even pay. This was a 'reality' that many managers were not prepared to face. After 10 to 15 years of that style of management, present-day senior managers bemoan the fact that managerial succession is a problem. Why so? It is clear how that came to be. Under the circumstances described, the better people try, fail and leave!

Design systems to support action

The most important thing is to get on and do things; to get action. Only then can people try out new ideas, learn and develop. Pilot schemes can allow for this approach. Reporting systems should be designed to encourage it. The attention of managers should focus on action. Plans, targets and milestones should be clearly defined and consistent with a well-understood longer-term strategy.

    Q: How do you eat an elephant?
    A: In slices.

Focus on the manageable

The excellent is the enemy of the good! Managers rarely start from an ideal position and rarely have enough time, resources or knowledge about what they either can or should do. Thus it is crucial to focus on manageable issues. Managers can communicate these to their own people; they will be credible and will support action and progress. It is important to have and to articulate a clear longer-term vision. But people need to work out how *they* are going to get there.

In an uncertain world managers cannot be everywhere

They must rely on others. This means that they must create opportunities to help people develop. *They need to support learning and development.*

Top management actions to support the implementation of major change

Spend time on the problem/project

There is no better way of focusing attention, effort and energy in support of change than by top management devoting time. This needs to be done carefully. Top managers should provide support, interest and resources. They should not interfere because this will demonstrate lack of trust in the manager on the spot. This is a difficult balance to draw because to ignore change may well be taken as a signal of low priority.

Interpret the traditions of the organization around the new systems, procedures and solutions

Give powerful emphasis to how the traditions of the organization support and are sustained by changes. I work for a business school which pioneered distance learning in management education in Europe. One of the school's key traditions has always been its concern to deliver and establish learning situations which meet the needs of course members, in a practical way. Throughout the early development of distance learning the need to design the new material on this principle was always paramount. Also emphasized was the idea that distance learning was a practicable and flexible means of providing management education to the large numbers of managers who never attend business schools. The rapid growth of distance learning clearly demonstrates that this was not because the managers had no need or desire for management training. For us the point is to note how the traditions of the school were linked to the development of new systems for delivering management education.

Manage the timing effectively

Managing the timing of change is very important. A number of considerations apply. How much expertise does the organization possess? The more established the necessary knowledge and expertise, the quicker will be the changes. To what extent is there opposition? How powerful is it and what control does it have over resources and decision making? Are other significant changes likely? If change creates disruption, then it is worth looking at how to time various changes so that they occur together. Managing the timing to manage the stresses induced also deserves attention (Chapter 10) to balance this latter point. Finally, attention must be given to logistics, resources and other commitments. We tend to underestimate the time, resources and energy needed to achieve change. More attention to these issues is invaluable, particularly if realism prevails!

Managing corporate politics

Managing the politics of change requires us to consider the interests of the various groups involved in the changes, but it also requires much more than that. Ultimately, it involves us in finding ways of making sense of the 'booming, blooming confusion' around us. Creating effective organizations is not about eliminating corporate politics. There is too much uncertainty for that to be feasible. It is about finding principles of action which allow politics and conflicts to be handled constructively and thus harnessed for corporate change.

Exercises

1. What core competencies will be important for Philips NV in the next 5 years?
2. Does corporate politics play a positive role in change?
3. How would you characterize the culture of your organization? What implications does this carry for successful organizational change?

CHAPTER 7

Leadership in practice

Introduction

Can we identify the key elements of effective leadership? Can we assess individuals on those elements, looking at their skills and performances? Can we help individuals to become more effective leaders? Are leaders born or made? Or both? In this chapter we answer these questions. Leadership is a key to managing organizations in periods of change and crisis and is thus important to all of us working within organizations.

Hersey and Blanchard (1988) say that leadership occurs when one attempts to influence the behaviour of an individual or group. They go on to state that there are three general skills (or competencies), as follows:

1. *Diagnosing*: being able to understand the situation as it is now and knowing what can reasonably be expected in the future. The gap between these two – sometimes known as the 'performance gap' – is the problem to be solved. This is what the effective leader will attempt to change. Diagnosing is a *cognitive* skill.

2. *Adapting*: involves adapting one's behaviour and other resources in ways that help to close the 'performance gap', a *behavioural* skill.

3. *Communicating*: even if one knows what needs to be done and is able to adapt oneself to meet the new needs, this will fail unless one can communicate all this to others in ways that they can understand and accept, a *process* skill.

Warren Bennis (1984) has completed an interesting study of 90 outstanding leaders. Based on this, he identifies the following four areas of competence shared by all 90 leaders:

1. *Management of attention*: the ability to communicate clear objectives and direction to others.

2. *Management of meaning*: the ability to create and communicate meaning clearly, achieving understanding and awareness.

3. *Management of trust*: the ability to be consistent in often complex circumstances fraught with dilemmas (so often the potential trap for the unwary!) so that people can depend on them.

4. *Management of self*: the ability to know oneself and to work with strengths and weaknesses.

Leaders empower their organizations to create an environment where people feel significant, where learning and competence matter, where there is team spirit, flexibility and excitement. Also where quality and excellence matter and are something to strive for.

All things to all men!

In a period of great uncertainty, and change, and amidst the outward evidence of the rewards available to both the individuals and organizations who seize 'opportunities', it is not surprising that there has been a resurgence of interest in leadership. The study of 'great leaders' seems to provide little evidence on how to select, develop or encourage potential leaders. Self-evidently, perhaps, 'leaders' need not be 'selected' or 'trained'. Nevertheless, if we are to understand the role of leadership then we must understand why only some succeed and how they emerge as successful.

The notion of 'transformational leadership' is both appealing and uninspiring. If 'managers are people who do things right and leaders are people who do the right thing' (Bennis and Nanus, 1985, p. 21), it hardly helps us to understand what corporate leaders do to achieve these transformations. That said, it is clear that individual corporate leaders can and do play roles in periods of change which enable dramatic transformations to take place.

It is commonplace to mention outstanding corporate leaders such as John Egan of Jaguar, Richard Branson at Virgin or Sir John Harvey-Jones of ICI (see Pettigrew, 1985) as examples. But any careful study sees the corporate leader firmly in context. This is described plainly in Stewart and Chadwick (1987), an excellent study of change in the Scottish Railway network. For these authors, large organizations experience 'systems crisis' through overspecialization, bureaucracy and low risk taking. Organizations capable of overcoming this crisis seem to share the following characteristics:

● Decentralization.
● Combined with Decentralization, evolution of roles for head office as consultant, power-broker and financier rather than direct controller.
● Positive attempts to encourage the entrepreneurial spirit and risk taking.
● Breaking down of interfunctional barriers.
● More emphasis on leadership, and on people.
● An evolving client or customer focus.
● Established informal links at all levels.

● A move from controlling to enabling approaches. Systems control the minimum necessary, rather than controlling each and every activity.

Trust turns out to be central. If leaders seek new ways of dealing with clients, deploying services and products, and of negotiating change, then people must trust them.

Thus it is that Burns (1978), in his seminal work, was concerned with 'followership' as the other side of the coin to 'leadership'. How do leaders establish the conditions under which people will follow? Writers often mention vision. Successful corporate leaders are capable of articulating a clear vision of the future. Capable of engaging support to that vision, they work with the values and ideology of the business or organizations. But what does this mean? Itami (1987) adds the key concept of 'invisible assets': technology, consumer loyalty, brand image, control of distribution, corporate culture and management skill are all invisible assets. Physical, financial and human assets are essential for business to be transacted but the invisible assets of knowledge, values and skill are needed for competitive success.

Itami tells us that invisible assets are the key to adaptability and competitive advantage for three reasons: they are hard to accumulate, are capable of multiple uses and grow through further use. Developing brand image or technical skills is time consuming and costly. Money cannot buy a change of corporate culture. Thus a firm can differentiate itself from the competition by developing its invisible asset. A firm's reputation with customers will impact on its business across a range of products and sectors.

People are important assets of the firm, largely because they develop knowledge and experience; they are the accumulators of invisible assets.

Leadership, vision and strategy

Following both Stewart and Chadwick, and Itami, the corporate leader enables people to contribute, solve problems, learn from and by experience, and accumulate invisible assets. The leader must do so both by making strategy explicit (vision) and by using the process of strategy formulation to mobilize the organization.

The need for explicit strategy is clear enough: it allows for co-ordination of activity; it provides direction to people; it can boost morale and sustain self-esteem; it can provide a shield against anxiety in a period of change. Explicit strategy also fosters better planning. Rather than merely reacting, people can plan change. Thus explicit strategy allows people to plan, create change and then learn from the experience. Explicit strategy allows for the development of invisible assets.

Corporate leaders must make strategy explicit and ensure its diffusion throughout the organization. Words and actions are important. Repeated attempts to inform and persuade must be supported by appropriate actions. Selecting people with strong reputations to lead new projects can help. Visits to departments with key roles display the importance of the new strategy with powerful symbolism. Reward systems designed to recognize excellent performance are important (see Stewart and Chadwick, 1987), just as are slogans. IBM's 'right-first-time' campaign articulated the company's concern for service with a powerfully simple slogan. Finally, charisma or personality features in both Stewart and Chadwick's, and Itami's, views. It may be dangerous for organizations to become overexposed to, or too dependent upon, charismatic leaders. Nevertheless, we live in what seem to be times in which individual values have gained growing recognition. People will respond to personality. Can system, order and consensus not feel dehumanized?

If the strategy is made explicit how may its content mobilize the organization? From Itami we see that this operates at the three following levels:

1. By providing a unifying focus.
2. By creating momentum.
3. By sustaining creative tension.

The strategy should be simple and clear, based on an identifiable core concept, priorities should be clear, resources should be clearly allocated, continuous adaptation and improvement should be stressed and it should match the corporate culture. To create momentum, leaders must sell the core concept, ensure and reward early success, involve people in clear tasks and pay attention to timing. Accumulating resources and people can create the invisible assets so crucial to the launch of a major new activity. To avoid complacency the leader will put continuing pressure on the organization. Constantly seeking new methods and procedures, improvements, new products and services is an excellent means of sustaining creative tension. Strategy formulation should seek the limits of the organization's consensus and explore beyond it. Generally, consensus is agreement that the policies successful in the past will continue to be so in the future. This consensus needs careful but continual pressure and questioning. Finally, placing people in conditions where the resources are inadequate can encourage a creative effort to resolve the problems so created, usually a very uncomfortable working situation. This can encourage the development of the invisible assets needed as people seek their own ways out of the impasse thus created.

Leaders and situations

From this sketchy analysis it seems that the effective corporate leader uses skills, knowledge, charisma and much else besides. These are deployed to encourage the development of the invisible assets so central to competitive advantage. In turn, this development flows from involving people in change, enabling them to act, allowing them to learn and develop, sustaining them with confidence and with vision.

Can we identify corporate leaders as individuals? Cooper and Hingley (1985) studied 17 'change-makers' in the UK. From this study the following pattern emerged:

● Early childhood experience: early feelings of insecurity and loss led to a subsequent drive and need to control their own future.

● Lower childhood experiences also developed self-reliance.

● Motivation and drive: a recurring element was strong motivation and drive.

● Value system: each had a well-developed value system and clear vision and purpose.

- Early responsibility: development of executive careers had been facilitated by early high-level responsibility.
- Charismatic leadership: leadership style and charisma were unimportant for the individuals studied.
- Communicator: the ability to communicate was a powerful element that all change-makers possessed, particularly the ability to be open and honest about feelings and attitudes.

Another survey (Norburn, 1988) focused on 108 chief executives and 30 executive directors from the *Financial Times'* 500 companies. From this study key features which distinguished chief executives from other members of the top management team were as follows:

- The length of tenure within their organization.
- The early stage at which their grooming for senior management responsibility began.
- The variety of managerial functions they experienced.
- The rapidity of promotion to a general management position.
- Their exposure to overseas cultures and business.

Both studies point to early responsibility as a key feature. Perhaps the ability to communicate and clear vision flow from breadth of experience. There seems little doubt that the successful leader brings wide experience and varied knowledge to the tasks of leadership. Perhaps, then, the individualism to which we respond is the credibility flowing from wide experience?

But if we know little enough about the individuals who are successful, what do we know of the circumstances within which success is more likely? Are some circumstances better than others? Also, how? During the last 50 years the focus of leadership studies shifted first from studying the traits of successful leaders, to looking at leadership style, and finally to focusing upon the idea of contingency.

Figure 7.1 outlines the contingency approach. In essence the approach argues that the effectiveness of any given leadership style or behaviour will be contingent on the situation. Various models exist. Fiedler (1967) offers one which looks at leader–member relations (quality of personal and effective relations between leader and group

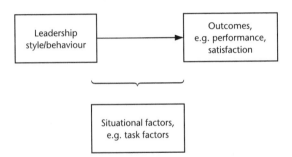

Figure 7.1 The contingency approach to leadership in outline

members), task structure (structured vs. unstructured) and position power, as situational variables. Vroom and Yetton (1973) offer a contingency model of leader decision making. The focus is a positive one. The model offers a framework by which leaders might improve both the quality and the acceptability of decisions. Hersey and Blanchard (1988) offer an outwardly practical approach to situational leadership. Little researched, it has become very popular among practitioners (see Bryman, 1987). These authors identify the 'maturity' of followers as a key factor in deciding on an appropriate leadership style. They believe that the leader's task behaviour (providing guidance and direction) and relationship behaviour (team building, providing socio-emotional support) should accord with the maturity of followers. They define maturity as the willingness and ability of people to take responsibility for defining and directing their own task behaviour. The theory is set out in Figure 7.2. Four leadership styles are defined: delegating, participating, selling and telling. Each style represents a different combination of task and relationship behaviour by the leader. The diagram proposes a particular combination of style and maturity of followers. A 'telling' style is proposed for those of 'low maturity', namely for people who are unable or unwilling to take responsibility. A 'selling' style is recommended for those who, though willing to take responsibility, are unable to do so. By 'selling', Hersey and Blanchard seem to mean

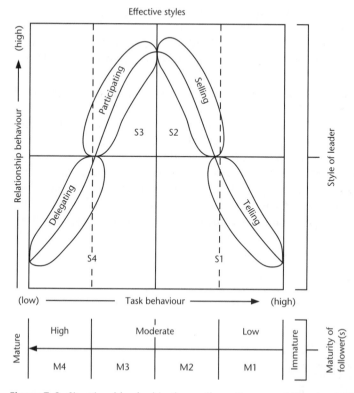

Figure 7.2 Situational leadership theory (from Hersey and Blanchard, 1977, p. 170. Reprinted by permission of Prentice Hall, Inc.)

providing direction combined with explanation, support and feedback to maintain motivation. A 'participating' style, described as appropriate for those with 'high maturity', they suggest is appropriate for able people whose motivation and commitment might be increased by involvement in decision making. Finally, a 'delegating' style leaves 'high-maturity' followers to take responsibility for what needs to be done.

The approach has powerful intuitive appeal. It is a development of various situational models but still lacks credible research support. Yet I know a number of major international companies which use this approach within internal management development programmes to good effect, at least as far as the reactions of the managers of the programmes are concerned. However, the model considers only the situation 'below' the manager, relating it to leader behaviour and effectiveness. What of the context *within* which the manager operates? At whatever level of management, managers are often concerned about crises, problems and opportunities in other units, divisions and organizations. Thus the divisional manager is concerned about what happens at group level; the managing director is concerned about what happens in client companies or in government. For example, I spoke recently to a senior manager of a major manufacturer of precision machinery. This company had never sold equipment to a major potential user in its own country. It had always bid but had always been beaten by competitors. In the preceding year it had decided to change this position. It 'targeted' key managers within the company concerned and other key 'players' in government and consulting firms used by that company. It identified major upcoming projects and analyzed its own strengths and weakness *vis-à-vis* those projects and its own competitors. Thus it attempted to deal with the problem of not having worked for a major potential purchaser by creating and working with networks of people and organizations. This it followed by managing the uncertainty through competitive analysis to identify the most appropriate targets to bid for – and while bidding for all projects across the board the bid effect was more effectively targeted and co-ordinated to be successful in target projects. Managers operate within real constraints, which they work with to create new business, organization change, and so on.

The context of leadership

The real context of leaders thus involves much more than their 'followers'. Leaders find themselves in complex and often changing networks of people, institutions, opportunities and problems. Thus, if we are to understand or even assess top managers as leaders we need to view their actions in context. What can they do? What can they not do, at least immediately, or even in a longer-term perspective?

In Chapter 6 we examined this question in some detail. If the context within which leaders work is pretty unsuitable in the short term, what actions can they take? The following five sets of actions appear to be open to them:

1. Set values.
2. Support problem solving and risk.
3. Design systems to support action.

4. Focus on the manageable.

5. Develop skills in people.

By setting the overall 'values' of the organization they provide ideas to people about the issues that are important and the priorities to pursue. I spent some considerable time working with the top management team of a large, international process engineering group (International Engineering). The work focused on the development and implementations of new corporate strategies. One of the key values that the chief executive emphasized throughout is that of 'delivered service'. The company delivers a high-quality engineering service in a range of industries and in a variety of forms. All too many senior staff saw the company as producing engineering structures. The chief executive was doing two things here: firstly, he was opening up the definition of 'the business we are in'; secondly, he was setting new values. Value of technically optimal design was replaced by the value of high-quality engineering service. The one leads us to develop sophisticated engineering solutions, the other to combine technical with commercial factors in delivering a service, on time, to cost and appropriate to the client's needs.

Top managers support problem solving and risk because it is from these that innovation is born. Innovation requires risk taking, but most fundamentally it is driven by commercially defined needs. The innovator is the manager who can translate the creative idea into commercial or organizational reality. Possessing perhaps some of the attributes of the 'dreamer', first and foremost the individual is the 'mandarin' (Kingston, 1977). Such people solve problems, obtain resources and support, achieve action. They get things done!

Top managers can design systems to support action. Reward and appraisal systems can focus on and support action. Corporate strategy formulation can be designed to encourage and achieve action. I once spent a day with the project manager of a large off-shore development (installed value £800 million), only to observe that this manager spent 2 hours 'signing off' expense claims. On asking about this I discovered that he 'approved' all expense claims, roughly 700 each day. Was this system designed to support action?

We can focus on the manageable. We cannot change everything overnight. So let us focus on the issues we can deal with, which give us some scope for improvement. A company facing losses this year and next will probably be best advised to focus on rationalization, the use of resources, cost, cash flow and the like. The development of costly technology centres might attract rather less attention *in the short term*. Of course, this is not to say that the latter are not needed but, rather, that in the circumstances the survival of the company seems to demand a different approach.

Finally, we come to development of skills in people. Ultimately, in all companies people are a limiting resource. Development, improvement, performance, managerial succession all depend on people: development of people to engage in problem solving, to be willing to take measured risks (i.e. to assess the risks and take them consciously), and to achieve action, focused on improvement. All this combined with appraisal and feedback can contribute to the effectiveness of the business.

Other things that managers can do include focusing attention and support on key people and projects. Partly, this involves simply paying attention to them, and being seen to do so. Key values can be articulated through simple phrases; 'right first time' is a simple and memorable phrase which various companies (e.g. IBM, Rolls-Royce) have used as the title for quality improvement programmes.

But perhaps most fundamental of all, top management can pay attention to timing. New programmes, new product launches, organizational changes, new strategies should, where possible, be planned with timing in mind. Where is the likely opposition? Can it be isolated? What other 'events' are likely? Will they be relevant? Do they provide opportunities as far as the current project is concerned? Behind all the argument, presentation of the case, and 'selling' of the programme, how much analysis has been undertaken? What pattern and profile of resources are required? What is available or capable of being obtained? Which are the limiting resources? Shorter implementation periods can create confidence and lead people to feel that top management really support the change. But longer periods may be needed if more experience is needed, or if the resources are not available.

Thus pilot programmes may form part of the process, along with fuller involvement and clear communications. Have accountabilities been made clear? By identifying the leadership of the project or programme we clarify its implementations. Attention to these issues can aid top managers in finding the means to achieve action, even in complex circumstances. The timing of announcements is a crucial issue. Whether we want more or less immediate attention to be paid to our announcement will influence both how we market it and how we time it.

Managers and leadership

In looking at the leadership aspect of managerial jobs we have focused upon the context within which managers work. We turn now to the whole job. How do management and leadership 'fit' together? Managerial performance is a combination of knowledge and skill applied in practice. Management is about getting things done, about action.

Managerial work is surrounded by circumstances which create problems, including uncertainty, incomplete information, change in the environment or elsewhere in the organization and conflict. Mintzberg (1973) has developed a comprehensive, empirical picture of the nature of managerial work through observing and recording what managers actually do (see Chapter 2).

Managers seem to stress the active element of their work – activities that are current, specific, well defined and non-routine attract more of their attention: for example, processing most mail and reading written reports are low-priority items. The manager may be seen as the conductor of the orchestra and, conversely, as a puppet pulled by hundreds of strings. To find the extent to which managers controlled themselves, Mintzberg analyzed whether in each activity managers were active or passive; he found only a small proportion of active work and that managers spent much time reacting. However, the initial construction of the manager's job may have included decisions to allow these reactions and passive participation as a way of keeping up a flow of work and ensuring the involvement of others in the management process.

The effective leader may well be the 'mandarin', i.e. politically shrewd (in the ways of his or her own organization). Ready to respond to the needs of others, such leaders control enough of their time to give the lead, to sustain effort, to maintain momentum, to motivate others, to articulate vision and so on. The effective leader may well be the person capable of meeting the varying demands made on him or her while undertaking a workable balance of the various roles, workable for the given organization at a particular point in time. It has to be said that we do not know. Many of the biographies produced by well-regarded corporate leaders might be read along these lines, but we are woefully short of clear evidence. What we have attempted to do in this chapter is piece together the various ideas and some relevant evidence to illustrate what we do know about corporate leaders as people and about the situations within which they work. If the picture turns out to be rather complex, at least we have the outline of the emphases that effective corporate leaders might provide for their organizations and their own people. In later chapters we will develop this into guidelines on how to analyze situations, recognize the management and leadership options available and assess the likely advantages and disadvantages of each.

However, what seems clear is that Deal and Kennedy (1982, p. 8) may well be right when they suggest that: 'Business certainly needs managers to make the trains run on time; it more desperately needs *heroes* to get the engine going.' They go on to say that heroes do the following:

- Symbolize the company to the outside world.
- Preserve what makes a company special.
- Set a standard of performance.
- Motivate employees.
- Provide role models.
- Make success attainable and human.

Perhaps this last point is the key. The effective corporate leaders bring human scale to risk, change, success, challenge and crisis. They translate the pressures that can confuse or paralyze so many into acceptable levels. They are not afraid to fail. Nor are they afraid to question, to ask why. Their approach to leadership is both skilled and thoughtful (following Mant, 1983). Thus it is that they become credible and successful.

Ben & Jerry's is a company which created a new vogue in ice cream. It was created by two friends, Ben Cohen and Jerry Greenfield, and grew quickly to rival Haagen-Daz in the premium market. In 1995 they appointed a new CEO. The appointee famously produced a poem called 'Time, values and ice cream' as part of his submission for the appointment. It seems clear that in seeking a new CEO they looked for operational experience and a commitment to the values which had driven Ben & Jerry's which sees prosperity emerging out of commitment to the product, to a social mission in the community and to an economic mission. How can a new leader expect to provide the necessary unifying focus without similar beliefs? But that is not enough. Also needed is the operational credibility to create momentum for change and to bring to bear new ideas to achieve improved performance. But a belief in the product was also essential – thus the poem. Was the most convincing aspect of the new CEO's contribution that he brought human scale to the process of leadership?

Leadership and 'human scale'

What do we mean when we say that effective leaders are those who bring human scale to risk, challenge, success and crisis? Tennyson captures part of our thought in the line:

> Pray God our greatness may not fail, thro' craven fears of being great.
>
> (Tennyson, 1885)

We argue that the effective leader is not afraid to fail. The fear of failure can be as paralyzing as the fear of freedom (Fromm, 1944).

Summarizing Fromm's powerful argument very briefly, modern industrial capitalism (he makes no distinction between state and corporate capitalism) has freed us from traditional bonds of nature, caste and religion. It contributed tremendously to the increase of positive freedom, to the growth of an active, critical, responsible self; however, it also made the individual more alone and isolated, creating in the individual a sense of insignificance and powerlessness. Isolated and powerless, many individuals are afraid to depend on themselves; rather, they attempt to submerge the self. Taking risks, trying out new ideas, experimenting, bring attention to oneself. This is difficult for many and, as we have already seen, much of the way in which we structure and manage organizations serves to reinforce this already powerful tendency. What then can the leader do? Fromm (1944) suggests that 'progress ... lies in enhancing the actual freedom, initiative and spontaneity of the individual ... above all in the activity fundamental to every man's existence, his work'.

In our view the leader who can bring human scale to organizational problems can do two things: firstly, cope with the pressure on the self, the leader's fear of failure, the stress and pressure of the circumstances to be handled; secondly, find ways of helping others to cope with the pressures on them. In practical terms this means facing the issues addressed in Chapters 4, 5 and 6. Fromm identifies three escape mechanisms which are directly relevant to our argument.

People experiencing the fear of freedom will also experience the fear of failure because they must take risks in order to build their own selves. Those incapable of doing so rely on three principal escape mechanisms: authoritarianism, dull conformity and destructiveness. How many times have you come across managers, at all levels, who become more autocratic as the pressure upon them builds? ABF Ltd is an example of both the situation and its consequences, a vicious circle leading to decline. How many times have you noticed that employees subjected to changes respond with apathetic conformity? One has the changes 'bolted in' but does one have commitment? How many times have you seen opposition to new ideas before they have been given a chance? These are the three mechanisms to which Fromm refers – emerging out of the pressures and uncertainties of a changing world.

Bringing human scale to the problems of organization and change is about pragmatism. It is about resolving today's problems today. One needs to give people a vision of the future, but one also needs to help them to see the stepping-stones along the way. The leader needs to cope with change, so do followers. It seems to me that this is the ultimate defining characteristic of effective corporate leaders. They can energize and sustain people to act, to try things out, to get on with the job in hand. They can energize people to try. Thus to conclude this chapter we argue that the practical side of leadership depends not on grand theories but, rather, on the ability to encourage others into action. This depends on the management of attention, measuring trust and self, as Bennis (1984) makes clear. But it also depends on credibility. The leader's vision needs to be credible. People need to perceive the credible actions that they can take and that they feel they can control. Thus we bring 'human scale' to leadership and change.

Few would argue that risk aversion has not been a common characteristic of organizations, particularly larger organizations. Many may think that this is changing. One fairly recent survey suggests that the problem lives on. A survey of the role of IT (Birchall, 1993) examined 'barriers to change'. A sample of respondents from large and medium-sized companies was asked to list barriers to IT implementation. Items such as 'staff prefer structured organization' (60 per cent of respondents), management control of homeworkers (50 per cent), organization risk averse (38 per cent), rigid organization hierarchy (15 per cent) all may well be linked to risk aversion. The leadership challenge is all too clear given also that other barriers linked to perceived lack of IT capability. Clear vision and leadership will evidently be needed where risk aversion is combined with perceived lack of capability. As we shall see, success here includes the leader's cognitive style (see Chapter 11) which here we suggest may relate to the ability to create 'human scale'.

Exercises

1. From your reading of the business press available to you can you identify a key corporate leader? How does this leader display the competencies we have listed?

2. How important is the situational model of leadership as a training and development tool?

3. What do you think are the behaviours required of successful leaders in a period of change?

Managing organizational change

CHAPTER 8

Strategies for change

Introduction

*Our problem, in essence, is a simple one. We never have enough time to do anything,
but we always find time to do it twice.*

(President, French Pharmaceutical Company)

In a changing world the only constant is change. So why write a book about managing
change in an organizational world which is already changing at a dramatic rate? I run
workshops on managing change for management audiences around the world. Over
the last 10 years or so managers have gained more experience with, and more confidence in, the management of change. The reality is that the stability which seemed to
characterize the corporate world in the 1950s and 1960s has given way to increased
and global competition, technological innovation and change, limited resources,
deregulation, privatization of public sector organizations and change in much more
besides. But with that growing confidence I see a growing interest in learning how to
manage change more effectively.

What does all this mean to us, as employees and as managers? How can we seize
advantage from the process of change? How can we help ourselves and others cope
with the often stressful experience of change? How can we ensure that we manage
changes well? How can we create more effective organizations? Is it possible to do so
and still encourage people to learn, develop and fulfil themselves? Can we do all this
and make money as well? By gaining a better understanding of why certain approaches
to management seem to work we can pursue each of these objectives more fully.

In today's world, managers face complex and challenging pressures and opportunities. They must ensure the efficient use of resources and, at the same time, find ways of
guaranteeing the long-term effectiveness of the organizations for which they work.

Effectiveness includes the ability to identify the right things to do in the future (the right products and services to offer, the appropriate technologies to exploit, the best procedures and structures to introduce, to find, recruit and retain people with appropriate skills). Effectiveness also requires the ability to adapt in order that we can achieve these new tasks. Effectiveness, therefore, comprises the ability to adapt to changing circumstances.

Planning, implementing and coping with change has been, and seems likely to remain, one of the main challenges facing managers, in both the private and public sectors, today. In manufacturing, banking, education and health care change is the norm. The merger and acquisition boom of recent times brings change on its trail throughout industry and commerce. Frequently, for many, these changes must be undertaken in testing circumstances. Sales and profitability may be falling rapidly. A merger bid may lead managers to review performance and strategic plans. All this might form part of a defence against the merger. In any event whether or not the merger or takeover succeeds, change seems likely. Many organizations face deregulation. Banking is a good example of this but not the only one. Transport deregulation has had a dramatic impact in some European countries (e.g. the Republic of Ireland). Central government spending decisions can create powerful pressures on expenditure within public service organizations, often with dramatic effects on the attitudes of staff and clients.

BMW bought Rover from British Aerospace because (amongst other reasons) it believed that Rover has manufacturing facilities which operate more flexibly and at lower cost than much of its own plant in Germany. Japanese companies source units in Taiwan and Malaysia for much the same reasons. An international consultancy firm identifies its Singapore operation as a centre of excellence in software design. It project-manages design projects but utilizes the services of designers in the USA and Europe, all linked by electronic means. Thus the Singapore centre manages a design process which is going on 24 hours a day. No one can dispute that the world of work and working is seeing dramatic changes. Still less would anyone argue that the challenge of managing in a changing environment is getting any easier!

Growing competition, privatization and deregulation across many parts of industry, commerce and the public sector have led many organizations to try to develop in their staff more commercial awareness and more concern for quality. Managers are concerned with value for money, the development, launch and marketing of new products and services, greater flexibility of design, manufacture or service, and in less definable issues such as corporate image and identity. Customers and clients are ever more vocal and critical. The main focus of management is switching from largely internal concerns to a more balanced focus on internal and external concerns. This part is concerned with understanding how managers can create more effective organization in a world of change. It examines why and how approaches to management have been changing and sets out practical guidelines for management action in today's world.

For instance, when five long established corps of the British Army were merged to form a single Royal Logistics Corps, this presented substantial change issues. As members of each corps struggled to position themselves in the new corps, a number of important issues were faced. Not least important was what badges and uniforms were to be used? How best to make such decisions? It was decided to establish a working group of senior non-commissioned officers to resolve these issues – partly because they were seen as less likely to fight 'turf' wars over the issue but also because the army culture places senior non-commissioned officers as a source of continuity within the regimental system. Thus the approach was seen as even handed as between the five corps about to be merged but diffused what might have been quite disruptive conflict over these highly symbolic and, in a uniformed service, very contentious issues.

However, the objectives of this part of the book are pragmatic. The intention is not to develop a grand theory of how organizations should be structured and arranged in any 'ideal' sense. Here the reader will find no elaborate propositions, hypotheses or theories. Rather, I have attempted to synthesize what I take to be the most useful approaches to the problems of managing changing organizations. Through that synthesis we intend to achieve a rather better understanding of what can and cannot be achieved and to point the way towards improved managerial practice and performance.

In Figure 8.1 we propose an 'outline map' of the organizational change area. It sets out the key influences on the nature of any organizational change. This relates to the scope, scale and complexity of change, these being important determinants of many of the issues which arise for those managing major changes. For example, the greater the

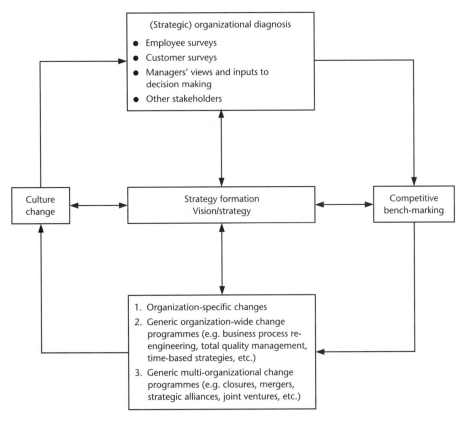

Figure 8.1 Strategic change

complexity of change the more likely we are to adopt a radical approach to change. The more concerned we will be to develop a clear programme of change with account-abilities, project plans, milestones, task force inputs, etc., the more likely we will be concerned to achieve change quickly. All of this we will explore later in Part 2; at this stage our concern is to identify some of the issues the book will address.

At the core of any major change programme is the process of strategy formation. Some say strategic choice or strategy formulation, but that implies a conscious as well as rational process of choice, whereas in many organizations that would be an incom-plete view of how strategy 'emerges'. Here we follow the widely accepted view expressed in Mintzberg (1994). This sees strategy as emerging without necessarily being wholly or even partly the outcome of explicit strategic planning activities. This does not mean that it is necessarily irrational, nor that processes of choice may not be involved. Strategy may emerge from a succession of 'choices', some explicit some implicit (i.e. in people's behaviour) and therefore directly a consequence of the corpo-rate culture (see below).

In a period of major change there is more likely to be an explicit process of strategy formation. Our argument here is that such a process will be more effective if careful diagnosis is involved. Here we argue that the 'acid test' of strategy is implementation. Preparation for implementation will obviously be more effective if we have identified the 'stakeholders' involved in the changes, assessed the impact of change on them and involved them in diagnosis and planning where possible and appropriate (not always possible, see below). Moreover, careful diagnosis provides a partial assessment of the capability of the organization for change and improvement.

Furthermore, diagnosis of the capability for change is enhanced if we also carry out competitive 'bench-marking'. Measuring your own organization on dimensions such as marketing capability, logistics, operations people and organizational issues can and will lead to the generation of ideas about strengths and weaknesses and how perfor-mance can be improved. But will it mean that we can readily identify the maximum potential? One way of doing so is through the technique of competitive bench-marking. Two definitions offered are:

the continuous process of measuring products, services and practices against the toughest competitors or those companies recognised as industry leaders.

an ongoing process of measuring and improving products, services and practices against the best that can be identified world-wide.

(Milborrow, 1993)

Bench-marking therefore involves a comparative audit of your own and one or more organizations. For example, a US white-goods manufacturer was concerned about high distribution cost. It compared the design of its North American distribution facilities and the fact that all return journeys were empty with the performance of freight for-warding companies. This has led the manufacturer to introduce changes which have achieved dramatic reductions in distribution costs, not least by utilizing route planning to ensure that many of the 'empty' return journeys are 'filled' through contracting to carry goods inward to its own plants.

A Coopers and Lybrand survey of 105 board members drawn from the London

Times' Top 1000 companies draws the following conclusions:

● 67 per cent of the companies used bench-marking;

● 82 per cent of such programmes were seen as successful;

● 88 per cent of companies using bench-marking do so regularly;

● 66 per cent of bench-mark users started within the last 5 years.

The main areas regularly bench-marked were the following:

Human resources	60%
Customer service	72%
Manufacturing	68%
Information services	35%

Similarly the senior vice-president of a major teaching hospital in Chicago responsible for total quality management regularly bench-marks on management costs, treatment costs and quality/service.

At best, bench-marking allows us to assess the organization's performance. This becomes an integral part of the diagnostic phase of performance improvement and change. Comparison with direct competitors (if feasible) and/or with the 'best in the world' in a particular field (e.g. distribution) is a worthwhile part of this process. It promotes organizational learning. It can motivate people to tougher yet realistic goals and it can provide early warning of competitive disadvantage. There are many good reasons to include bench-marking in the change process, therefore (see Watson, 1993).

Whilst this may lead to the introduction of a number of *organization-specific* changes (e.g. a new information system, a new product, a new factory, etc.) it may also lead to the development of a more *generic organization-wide change programme*. Examples of such programmes include business process re-engineering programmes, total quality programmes, just-in-time manufacturing programmes, time-based strategies for product development, empowerment (including 'de-layering') strategies and culture change programmes. These are particularly important because success in implementation typically involves, and has impact throughout, the organization. Changes to the corporate culture are necessary for each of them, which is why we have separated culture change from the others in the 'map'.

Finally it is worth noting that closure programmes and merger/integration programmes are major changes in their own right, as are the adoption of strategic alliances and joint ventures. These present problems of strategic change which we will touch on in this book but of which time and space do not allow full treatment. We will suggest some additional reading, however. These we refer to as *generic multi-organizational change programmes* because more than one organization will be directly involved. This may be true for a generic organization-wide change programme – for example, a consulting firm may be utilized, a trade union may be involved – but in the multi-organizational case such involvement is unlikely to have as important an influence on the outcomes as in the single-organization case. Note, however, that a closure programme (clearly a single organizational case) is on the borderline in that whilst a union may be involved it may have little practical impact. However, closure programmes often attract significant and often 'political' attention, regionally and even nationally, with the consequence that other 'organizations' become involved (e.g. government nation-ally or locally, other organizations seeking to purchase the activity due to be closed, management buy-outs, etc.). For example, the closure of a naval base in the USA attracts immediate attention and is never straightforward (indeed some would cer-tainly argue that this is quite right on public policy trends). Achieving strategic change can thus be described as a 'learning loop' (see Figure 8.2) comprising organizational vision and strategy and understanding of 'stakeholders' and of the organization's capa-bility.

To be successful we suggest that strategic changes need to be managed in such a way that three necessary conditions for effective change are in place:

1. *Awareness*: stakeholders understand and believe in the vision, the strategy and the implementation plans, etc.

2. *Capability*: stakeholders involved believe they can develop the necessary skills and can therefore both cope with and take advantage of these changes.

3. *Inclusion*: stakeholders involved feel that they value the new jobs, opportunities, etc., and *choose* to behave in the new ways (new attitudes, skills and ways of working).

Much of the remainder of this book will deal with how to create the conditions for effective change. To conclude this section, however, we will consider one vital element: namely, the importance of achieving an effective 'fib' between corporate and 'functional' strategies if effective change is to be achieved. At root most major changes fail in implementation and often because the impact of the new strategy on the differ-ent functions and activities (strategic business units, divisions, etc.) has not been con-sidered, nor indeed have we thought about the interaction between functional (or divisional) strategy and overall strategy.

We turn now to an illustration, that of ABF Ltd. This case presents a company wherein changes in organization, manufacturing methods and management and reward systems could only be made if tensions with the management team could be

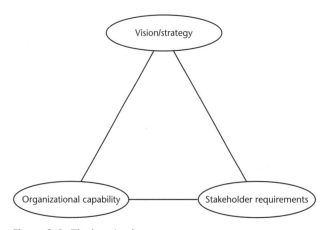

Figure 8.2 The learning loop

resolved. It demonstrates that the idea that change *will only* be possible with support from top management is a serious oversimplification. This is true enough as far as it goes but it begs the question of whether or not top management need to change themselves as part of the process of change.

CASE STUDY

ABF Ltd

ABF Ltd designs, manufactures and markets hydraulic filters. It comprises two product groups (industrial and process control). It is a relatively autonomous subsidiary of a larger group. The company employs 350 people. Its turnover in 1994 was £22 million, with a profit of 8 per cent of turnover. The managing director of ABF Ltd reports to the group board and is held accountable against a set of targets of profit sales volume, capital spend, market share and growth. In the late 1980s, profit had been slowly declining, both absolutely and as a proportion of turnover (since 1984), and this despite reasonable growth in turnover.

At the time of the study the current managing director had worked with the company for 21 years, 10 as managing director. All his senior colleagues were long-service employees. During late 1985 the group chief executive had begun to devote increasing attention to ABF, visiting on several occasions, and asking for more detailed performance figures. Following discussions between the group chief executive and the managing director, it was decided to bring in a team of management consultants to review procedures throughout the company. There was growing concern about both direct and indirect costs. The consultants were asked to look at the following five areas:

1. Planned maintenance policies.

2. Quality levels and quality assurance.

3. Utilization of machine setters and technicians.

4. Information and control systems.

5. Manufacturing organization.

As this review proceeded, a number of significant changes were introduced, particularly to tighten up quality control procedures and to provide improved information. The finance director (who was also responsible for personnel and administration) was the prime mover behind many of these changes.

The management team uses also experiencing a range of what we often refer to as 'human relations problems'. Confrontation between managers was a regular occurrence. Often, managers would adopt an aggressive approach in discussions, taking entrenched and always 'departmental' positions. Conflict between the production director and staff in the sales department was particularly prevalent. On the face of it there was little under-

▶▶

standing (or attempt to understand!) by each department of the objectives and problems of the other.

Communication was also very poor. Rarely were the production departments notified of priority orders in good time. Little attempt was made to co-ordinate sales plans with production plans. There had been several instances of large orders agreed, with short delivery schedules, without any consultation between the two departments. This often led to disrupted schedules within production departments. Machine utilization was poor, ranging from as low as 11 per cent to rarely more than 45 per cent.

Managers tended to treat subordinates autocratically, issuing orders but allowing no discussion. Ideas were either suppressed or ignored, particularly if they came from younger employees. People were expected to conform to 'the way we have always done things around here'. Managers appeared to feel that change was both a threat and an implied criticism of their own personal performance.

Managers seemed obsessed with objectives set years ago. For example, in production, the main concern was with the sales value of output and with efficiencies. The disrupted schedules made both harder to achieve. Little concern was directed at quality of output. In fact deliveries were often late and there was a high level of returned goods. Attempts to start discussion of these latter problems led to intensely defensive reactions by production management. However, much patient work by the finance director, with the production director, created some movement here. A review of quality control procedures led them to agree to appoint more quality inspectors who were to be located at the problem areas in the production sequence. One of the concerns was that quality problems were being discovered late, subsequent to further work having been carried out on the already defective items.

The company had originally experienced strong growth between 1978 and 1986, but since 1986 profits had stagnated, and even begun to decline. The morale of the company appeared to be low. Delegation to middle and junior management was very limited. No management training ever took place. Promotion was entirely from within. The managing director expressed the view that someone who had been promoted would 'know what to do or else we should not have promoted them'. Discouraged in taking the initiative or in promoting ideas, and thus lacking in self-confidence, many junior or middle managers tended to leave decisions to the directors. In consequence, the directors were often vocal in their criticisms of the managers, and felt that the managers were unable to make effective decisions.

As can be readily seen, there is something of a 'vicious circle' at work here. Given the management style in use it seems quite likely that the growth between 1978 and 1986 placed senior managers, directors and the company's various systems under pressure, leading to declining performance. This appears to have led to a redoubling of the directive management style in an effort to regain control. However, instead of gaining control, this merely made matters worse. More staffing in key areas would help and the recently agreed increases in the number of inspectors was the first such increase. In fact, the declining performance meant that the managing director had always opposed increased indirect staffing. Ultimately, of course, more staffing was not the answer. An approach to improving style and managerial effectiveness and performance needed to be developed.

▶▶

The finance director often suggested that management performance needed improvement. He thought that management training was worth investigating. The managing director tended not to listen to other people's views; thus there was very little exchange of ideas. People tended not to approach the managing director to discuss problems, the only exception being the finance director, who had worked with him as a senior colleague for 16 years. The managing director and others found discussing attitudes and feelings difficult and they thus avoided doing so. This was often explained as a means of protecting other people's sensitivities: 'We don't want to press the point for fear of upsetting X, who is under a lot of work pressure.' There was very little open statement and testing of views. The finance director's early attempts to discuss quality were hindered by the managing director claiming that quality was a production responsibility and refusing to talk about the problems with anyone other than the production director so as not to undermine him. However, if an important customer complained about the level of returns, the managing director would often criticize production bitterly, aggressively and openly. Eventually, the finance director's attempts to discuss quality problems were welcomed by the production director with a great sense of relief. Someone was interested! Someone was listening!

Appraisals of senior staff were not carried out. Indeed, recording performance reviews on paper was seen to be counterproductive. However, the managing director had, and was known to have, strong views about individuals and often discussed them at length with other senior colleagues: it seemed that he liked to get general confirmation of the views that he felt unable to confirm with the individual. Consequently, he formed views of people which he did not share with them. In conversation with these people he gave the impression that he did not trust them; they then felt unable to approach him to discuss this because he always avoided such discussion.

All this became very clear to the finance director. It must also be said that the managing director had a wealth of contacts and experience in the industry and had generated, mostly by his own efforts, much of the business growth from the late 1970s. He was widely respected in the industry. The consultants were making it clear to him that changes were needed within the production department. They were reporting very low productivity, rising costs and poor motivation of employees. They were now proposing a package of changes to deal with these problems. However, the consultants had indicated that their greatest concern was the views of shop-floor and clerical employees. There was a general rejection that the problems were anything to do with them. If problems existed, this was entirely a consequence of poor management! They felt that any change of programme would have to be managed participatively. While management performance needed improving, many of the changes that the consultants wished to introduce would have a direct bearing on shop-floor employees. Their acceptance was going to be important if change was to be implemented quickly.

The 'vicious circle' was now complete! Unless management style could be changed no-one could possibly expect other changes to be handled participatively. The company needed to work on management style, managerial effectiveness, management team working, management systems and structures and changes to manufacturing organization.

The finance director and the managing director were beginning to realize that some fundamental changes were needed.

As a first stage it was agreed that the finance director would develop a system of performance appraisal for senior managers, working with his other board-level colleagues. He and the production director were beginning at last to make inroads into the quality problems. Return rates and *rework* costs were falling and improvements in information were providing production managers with better control over production schedules and progress. By working together, improvements were being delivered, as a result of which the self-confidence of production managers began to improve. A more open and systematic approach to performance appraisal seemed to be leading to some more honest discussion of performance and problems. Slowly but surely a less defensive approach was being adopted.

Once improvements began, the finance director was able to convince the managing director that he and the production director, supported by the consultants, should now carry out changes within manufacturing. A key and highly contentious problem was the bonus system; it was outdated. Direct employees were paid a productivity bonus representing, on average, 60 per cent of gross pay. The link between productivity improvement and bonus payment was unclear. Moreover, the bonus in the industrial product group had risen more slowly than that in the process section.

A strategy for change

As a first stage the finance and production directors met with union representatives to discuss these problems. The representatives firmly rejected the idea that the bonus system itself needed changing, although they did hope that the disparities in bonus could be resolved. The directors provided very detailed information showing productivity, cost, pay, quality and other relevant data. They gave guarantees that no cut in pay or redundancy would result from a review of the bonus system and that employees would be involved in any effort to resolve the problems. However, they made it clear that they were determined to improve both productivity and quality, and that, in the long term, *factory numbers* would depend upon performance. The position of the company was becoming increasingly uncompetitive. Something needed to change.

It was agreed to bring in the consultants to work to the following brief agreed between these two directors and the union representatives:

1. To undertake a survey of attitudes in the production departments.

2. To provide an independent check on the problems of productivity and rising costs.

3. To design a wage system acceptable to management and employees *and* equitable as between the process and industrial product groups.

4. To indicate any further areas where significant improvements to industrial relations might be achieved.

For the first time for some years a more open management style was in use. This appeared to be creating some 'movement' by both managers and employees.

The attitude survey revealed some surprises. Employees seemed to prefer higher basic pay and lower, but still significant, bonuses. They felt that much of the low productivity stemmed from inadequate control by supervisors and managers. There clearly was some truth in this (see above). It was agreed to establish joint working parties to devise a means of achieving the following amendments over a 6 month period:

1. New working practices and improved quality.

2. A bonus system using the 'added value' concept to link company performance to bonuses.

3. Revised standards based upon methods study.

4. The introduction of new technology.

Now followed a period in which many of the initiatives were moving forward together. In practice, there were many problems along the way. In general, however, a more open approach by senior management and more effective team work involving various functions and departments were leading to dramatic improvements. Increasingly, the various initiatives were becoming mutually sustaining. The early success of the first quality changes and more effective information and control meant that production schedules were less disrupted and manufacturing therefore somewhat more orderly. This meant that production managers were under less constant pressure. That being so, they were less autocratic, partly also because of the changing examples coming from the finance director and the production director. The managing director, by recognizing that change was needed and by trusting the finance director, was also changing his style.

Over a period of four years (to 1993) productivity increased by 60 per cent. Costs were first curtailed and then reduced. New machinery and new staffing could now more readily be justified. Self-confidence began to build, sustained by positive feedback, both informally and through the performance appraisal system. The case raises a number of issues which typically must be addressed when significant organizational change is needed.

Management performance and learning

One thing is clear from this case. Senior managers needed to *learn* that preceding systems and styles were no longer working. A narrow focus on outdated objectives was one problem, the autocratic management style another. Until they learned that change was needed their approach was simply more of the same, only making things worse. Where fundamental changes are needed we must first look at how managers see the problems. What feedback systems are used? How do they monitor performance? What do they monitor? What strategies and approaches are they using to effect improvements? How do they monitor and review these strategies? Do they modify their approach in the light of feedback? Are new ideas encouraged? Are they examined carefully? Are the needed resources available? Do the existing systems of performance appraisal, promotion, product development, pay and benefits training, corporate culture and management style encourage or inhibit either the achievement of corporate objectives or improved performance? First and foremost, therefore, we need to review managerial performance.

Effective team work

I well remember hearing a senior manager from an international oil company state that 'the problem of managing change is, in essence, a multi-functional problem'. We have worked hard in our organizations to develop highly competent and professional functions, but as the functions have changed, developed and improved, so we have more and more problems in obtaining collaboration between them. Integration becomes a key task. Thus we must add to managerial performance and learning the need to gain more effective collaboration across functional boundaries.

Partly, this is a matter of attitudes and understanding. Partly, it is a matter of effective information and control. In ABF Ltd it was vital to integrate the work of sales and production. Partly, it is a matter of jargon. The oil company manager referred to above gave the management of data processing (DP) projects as an example. He argued that it is now increasingly recognized that the key to success in such projects is to gain effective user and specialist collaboration. This is often made the more difficult given the specialist jargon that both DP and user departments may use. Going a stage further, he noted that his company, in common with many others, now always allocated responsibility for managing DP projects to user department managers.

Effective organizational structures and systems

Next there need to be an effective structure and systems either to sustain existing strategies or in order to implement new ones. There need to be appropriate accountabilities, reporting systems, information and authority, and resource allocation. Revised systems, performance appraisal, promotion and so on need to be defined in order to sustain or improve performance against the organization's objectives. Without effectiveness here, other changes (say new products or new technology) cannot be properly deployed or exploited.

Organizational change

All the above may of course give rise to the need for change. However, without effectiveness in the above three areas, other changes will be more difficult to implement, such as new strategies, new products/services, new markets or client groups and new technologies. It will be more difficult to measure where we are, to decide what we wish to achieve, or monitor progress and problems unless these three core areas of management and organization are on the right lines. It will be difficult to generate effective new strategies, let alone achieve acceptance of the need for change, unless the above is right. We introduce changes either to improve effectiveness or to adapt to external changes. The present level of effectiveness of our organization provides the context within which we wish to introduce change. The more effective the present organization the readier employees will be to accept change. Thus we are concerned with both effectiveness and change.

Learning from changing

The effective organization is the one which encourages and supports learning from change. This means that an open management style, encouraging initiative and risk, is needed. However, the ability to measure and monitor progress and problems is also required. What did the managers of ABF Ltd learn from the changes they introduced? Below, we set out the main conclusions of the finance director:

- There must be a clear set of objectives, linked to pressing problems which people do actually recognize.
- Planning and participation must focus on specific issues and problems.
- Employees will respond to a sustained initiative from senior management.
- It is essential to make improvements in managerial performance at an early stage.
- Creating success early on, supported by positive feedback, enables the building up of self-confidence.
- Managing change is often a slow and difficult process.
- Managers must be seen to act on solutions/ideas derived from employees.
- Monitoring and evaluation are important means of following through with change seeking further improvement.
- Managing change is a learning process for all concerned.

Looking at the ABF case study in retrospect it is clear that the company represents a good example of our 'map' of change. There was a systematic diagnosis which did lead to an organization-wide change programme. Culture change was very much to the forefront of this case. It is perhaps not surprising that bench-marking does not feature in the case – it was not a feature of change programmes in the early 1980s. What the case study does provide (both here and in Chapter 12) is an excellent example of the dynamics of change and managers' role in major change. The lessons are as relevant today as they were in 1993. But looking back, it is probably true that a company dealing with these problems today would have included bench-marking in the diagnosis, would have been more explicit about the need for culture change and would have 'sold' the changes as a single and integrated programme of change with clear accountabilities, more extensive communications planning and so on. Some argue that by doing so you can attract more attention, more resources and more commitment to change and therefore proceed more quickly. Again we will return to the question of how to design successful change programmes later on in the book. For the moment let us merely observe the comparison and move on!

> ### CASE STUDY
>
> ## SmithKline Beecham
>
> The early 1990s have seen dramatic shifts in buying behaviour regarding health care costs in general and pharmaceuticals in particular, whether through government action (in countries such as the UK, Germany and New Zealand) or through the actions of insurance companies (e.g. the USA). Spiralling expenditure has lead to significant attempts to control costs. Since the creation of SmithKline Beecham from the merger of SmithKline and Beecham, a major change programme focused upon enhancing SmithKline Beecham's ability to change and to achieve change faster than the competion has taken place. Known as 'the simply better way', it comprises a clear change architecture within which *core concepts* such as process thinking, quality improvement, evidence-based management, continuous improvement, waste elimination, are articulated via local level *improvement processes* developed within a 3 year strategy. In turn the 3 year strategy spells out *strategic initiatives*, *breakthrough programmes* and *improvement themes*. Longer term there is a 10 year statement of strategic intent focused upon achieving sustainable competitive advantage in terms of customer satisfaction, innovation, integrity, people satisfaction and performance.
>
> Thus there is a long-term vision linked to carefully integrated moves – 3 year strategic changes, 1 year process improvement projects and daily improvement actions. Clearly the intention is to make sure that everyone understands how it fits together. Within this architecture much of the improvement momentum arises from the 'daily improvement system' through which continuous improvement is sought. Here methods and techniques, team activities, measurement and recognition/reward are combined to activate improvement efforts.
>
> All of the above has been 'rolled out' according to a 'road map' over the period 1990 to date. The road map specifies key elements as the focus of successive years and indicates the processes of conferences, communications, education, training, support, change roll-out over time. The clear purpose of the road map is to show how the architecture is being put in place over time.

Managing the changing organization effectively

Following Woodward and Buchholz (1987), we conclude the opening chapter of this part with a final pragmatic thought. Let us pretend that there is a scale of the extent to which we manage a changing organization (in a changing world) effectively. At one end of the scale is ideal, well-planned, sensitively handled, carefully timed, sufficiently resourced change; at the other end of the scale is 'bolt on, rah rah management'. Here the idea is that the new system, procedure, structure, or whatever, can be 'bolted on' to the existing system from a technical and logistic point of view. Once that is arranged we need to sell the new system, and this is what 'rah rah' management is all about: 'You'll like this system'; 'It'll solve all your problems'; 'Don't worry, you won't lose out' are some of the things managers may say. The idea is to 'fire up' the enthusiasm of staff and to press on, regardless of problems: 'It's a great success' and 'It'll be all right on the night.' Selling *is* a part of change management, yet to be effective it must be sensitive to problems and to people's needs. Only then can the real problems, uncertainties and anxieties of change not merely be handled but, rather, be harnessed in support of the change itself. This book attempts to demonstrate how this can be done *but* we start from a pragmatic position. The 'ideal' state will not be achieved. Our view is that through better understanding we can do a *little better*, no more! To return to our opening quote, by being a little more careful about how we handle change, doing it a little more effectively, we can ensure earlier and more effective implementation, creating the capacity to manage change more effectively in future.

Exercises

1. What do you think are the key features of ABF's change strategy?
2. How important is bench-marking as a component of change strategy?
3. What management styles might promote more effective change in the case of ABF Ltd?

CHAPTER 9

Diagnosing change

Creating acceptance for change

To achieve change we must first recognize that change is desirable and feasible. We must get people to recognize that changes are needed: 'We've always done it this way', they say, when you ask why a particular procedure is used. But is the fact that we have always done it this way good enough reason either to continue to do 'it' (whatever 'it' may be) or to continue to do 'it *that way*'? There is a famous story in a company I know. It is known as 'The chairman's rice puddings'. This story will help us to identify the key issue here.

A senior manager had been given the task of leading a review of head office systems and procedures. As he and his team proceeded with the review, all manner of good ideas were identified and implemented. Then, one day, the team examined the chairman's kitchen. They found that every day two rice puddings were made at 12.15 p.m. The same two rice puddings were thrown away at 2.45 p.m. When asked about this the chef said that they had always made two rice puddings. No one had ever eaten one, to his knowledge. This had been happening since he joined the company 8 years before. They never included the rice puddings on the menu! Further investigation revealed that 17 years before, the then chairman had chosen, on a whim, to visit the kitchen. In conversation with the chef of the day he had said that his favourite sweet was rice pudding. When he left, the chef gave instructions that two were to be made each day but not included on the menu. The head waiter could then offer the chairman a rice pudding. Being a shrewd character, the chef asked for two, thinking that if the chairman did ask for one, then so would someone else! Four years later that chairman had retired, 5 years further on the past chairman died. But 8 years later on the chef still made two rice puddings every day.

The point is that people become 'locked' into patterns of behaviour, systems and procedures. Once entirely sound and effective, in a changing world they may become much less so. Yet recognizing that something is no longer effective involves the willingness to consider evidence of ineffectiveness and then to question *why*, how and what might be done instead. All organizations have 'rice puddings'. What we need are systematic and workable means of monitoring performance, measuring effectiveness, measuring potential for improvement, monitoring the environment for new products, markets, distribution channels, technologies, etc. We shall see that making change is not simply a rational process. Yet diagnosing change involves and requires systematic effort, even if the diagnosis itself may need 'selling' if we are to gain acceptance for it. Having the right diagnosis is of no use if we can do nothing about it. The diagnosis must not only be right, it also needs to gain acceptance enough to make implementation feasible.

Monitoring performance, measuring effectiveness

What do we mean by effective? How do we assess whether or not our organization is doing well? What do we mean by 'doing well'? Are we concerned with profit? Or sales value? Or market share? Or service levels? If so, what level is satisfactory? The same as last year? Last year plus 5 per cent? Profit expressed as a percentage of turnover? Rate of growth of sales volume or of profit? Satisfactory for whom? Shareholders, managers, employees, clients, customers? What about comparing our performance with that of competing, or at least similar, organizations? A manufacturing company would compare itself with other companies in its own industry and sectors. A hospital would be compared with other hospitals of a similar size and case load and mix. We can readily see that the question of how well we are doing becomes quite complex.

We need to assess effectiveness for two reasons: firstly, identifying sources of ineffectiveness might lead us to restructure or reorganize in order to improve; secondly, because ineffective organizations present a tougher context in which to implement technological, product or service changes. We are often involved in both. We need to introduce new technology and discover that progress will be impeded by lack of in-house expertise and by poor attitudes to change. Part of our preparation for the new technology involves bringing in the expertise (whether by forming a new department, through secondments or transfers or by hiring consultants). Also involved may be a training programme designed to introduce people to the new technology carefully, partly to allay any fears they may have about the impact of change.

Dealing with sources of ineffectiveness as part of the implementation of change provides us with two advantages: firstly, it will allow us to implement change more effectively, and more speedily; secondly, it will make future changes easier to implement because the organization will have become more adaptable. In essence, this will be because the people involved will have learned through the process of change, learned about themselves, about the new technology and about how to prepare people to cope with change. A positive experience of change, properly exploited by all those involved, leaves people more capable of handling future change. Following Itami (1987), this means that the organization has developed its 'invisible assets'. Invisible assets are the knowledge base from which all employees operate. To quote

Itami (1987, p. 4):

> Invisible assets are the real source of competitive power and the key factor in corporate adaptability for three reasons: they are hard to accumulate, they are capable of simultaneous multiple uses, and they are both inputs and outputs of business activities.

Developing the knowledge base from which people operate takes time and energy. Once accumulated a knowledge base has multiple uses. If a retail company develops an excellent reputation for merchandising high-quality goods, then it can use this reputation to promote products in new sectors, e.g. financial services. The reputation will attach to new stores, and this may help the company attract high-quality staff. Invisible assets are both inputs and outputs.

Having attracted high-quality staff to aid its development of a new market, these staff bring in new ideas to the company. This enables the company further to improve its operations and therefore enhance its reputation; thus being more effective as an organization is both an input to and an output of organizational change. More effective firms are more capable of handling change. Handling change effectively helps to sustain and create effectiveness in the future.

Efficiency and effectiveness

Most people distinguish between efficiency and effectiveness. Efficiency comprises achieving existing objectives with acceptable use of resources. Effectiveness means efficiency plus adaptability. The effective organization is both efficient and able to modify its goals as circumstances change. It can solve one of the dilemmas of organization: 'When we are doing well, why change?' 'Why break a winning streak?' 'Why upset a winning team?' These are everyday expressions which capture the dilemma. If we are doing well people will find it hard to justify change with all its potential costs and disruption. Yet in a changing world we must continue to adapt and when better than while we are doing well? Doing well provides us with the resources, the time and the confidence to accept change.

Consider a company manufacturing electromechanical weighing equipment in Europe in 1970. To be efficient it needed to manufacture its products at economical costs. It needed to market its products with competitive pricing and service support. Above all, it needed to achieve 'acceptable' profits (although we must define what we mean by 'acceptable'). To be effective that company would also need to be developing electronic technology. In the 1970s electromechanical weighing machines were replaced by electronic designs which were more accurate, more reliable and smaller in size. To be effective in its market sector the company needed to be looking to electronic designs in 1970, indeed before then. It needed to be training people in the design, manufacture, sales and servicing of such equipment. The technology was available and would be applied to secure specific product improvements. Thus competitive advantage would be secured through this technology. Effectiveness implies the ability to recognize and respond to changing market or other environmental circumstances.

In looking at effectiveness, Argyris (1962) focuses on the following three core activities relevant to any organization:

1. Achieving objectives.
2. Maintaining the internal system.
3. Adapting to the external environment.

Achieving objectives is the accomplishment of the objectives specified by managers in budgets, targets or corporate plans. These include profit, turnover, market share, quality, delivery and many more. However, we need to add resource utilization here. Merely achieving objectives, at any cost, is a recipe for ineffectiveness, in the long run certainly, and usually very much in the short run in competitive markets or where costs are under close scrutiny (say a police force in a city in which budgetary pressures are severe and creating impetus for 'cuts').

Maintaining the internal system includes activities and systems such as performance appraisal, management development, training and reward systems. The ability to attract and retain high-quality staff at all levels is crucial and forms a useful indicator of effectiveness.

Adapting to the external environment includes marketing, product/service development and public and community relations. How adaptable is the organization? What external reputation or image does it create? The ability to adapt springs from generating income and confidence (through achieving objectives), and developing invisible assets or learning, and through the attention devoted to the internal system. Therefore, these factors interact. In monitoring effectiveness we need to take account of all four factors: *achieving objectives, resource utilization, maintaining the internal system* and *adaptability*. But what should we monitor? There are a number of quantitative and qualitative measures available. In general, quantitative measures help us assess *the past*, although we can establish trends over time which may help us look at the future. Most importantly, quantitative measures may have a tempting but rather illusory certainty about them. The quality of a set of figures on, say, costs is only as good as the data input, and the assumptions (regarding, for example, overhead allocation) involved in the cost calculations. Yet they can appear to be 'hard' data.

However, that is not the key point. All data have their limitations. The most important thing is to avoid narrow, or even single, measures of effectiveness. A famous retail store was reputed to assess the effectiveness of its store managers on 'shrinkage' (the loss of stock from stock rooms and shelves). Taken to the ultimate, the best way of minimizing shrinkage is to lock the stock room, even to lock the store. There are no sales but also no shrinkage! There is a famous story of a Soviet nail-making factory which for many years exceeded its annual target in successive 5 year plans. The factory director was assessed on the weight of nails produced. He had discovered that with the machinery available to the factory, output would be maximized by producing nails 1 foot long. He did so – millions and millions of them!

Recently I was working in a famous furniture manufacturing company, a household name world-wide. The company had quality problems with a high rate of rejection. Most rejection took place predespatch, but after the whole manufacturing process was complete; 35 per cent of faults occurred at the first stage of an 11 stage production cycle. Considerable value added was being built into this furniture, wastefully. Yet departmental managers were achieving their targets. They were assessed on volume, not volume and quality!

Narrow approaches can be misleading. What is needed is a broad approach to assessment. If we are making profit are we making as much profit as we can? How are our competitors doing? Where can we improve? Is there any evidence of ineffectiveness? Also, we need to avoid the tendency to concentrate only on that which we can readily monitor, such as the weight of nails produced! In a rapidly changing world we must work harder than that. Quantitative measures are important and measuring quantitatively creates an analytical discipline. But experience and intuition are also important. Thus we need to make qualitative judgements of employee satisfaction and attitudes, of management style, of adaptability and of management development. We need to monitor a balanced set of indicators over all four quadrants of the effectiveness matrix (see Figure 9.1).

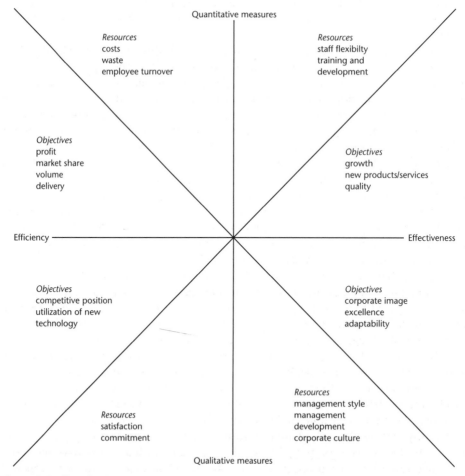

Figure 9.1 The effectiveness matrix

Looking at the matrix allows us to consider an appropriate set of factors with which to assess organizational effectiveness. We need to monitor a balanced set of factors for the reasons stated above. Yet we must recognize that assessment itself costs money. We cannot assess everything. What we choose to assess will vary from organization to organization. The most important point is to recognize that to monitor effectiveness we must look at factors in all four quadrants, in a systematic way, and that we must look at both objectives and resources. The use and development of resources (maintaining the internal system, or building invisible assets) is the main impulse to effectiveness. Identifying the right strategy is not enough if we lack the people and the commitment for its implementation. As Will Rogers once said: 'You can be on the right track but you'll get run over if you just sit there.'

Many organizations are pretty good at the top left-hand quadrant. Information systems have been developed to provide managers with quantitative information on various aspects of performance, both objectives and resources. That said, I often make this point to audiences of managers and then ask: 'How well is your organization doing?' 'Not well enough' is one way of summarizing their response! Few organizations systematically monitor factors in the other quadrants. However, organizations are increasingly moving in this direction. Some monitor the extent and scope of training and development. For example, at least one European bank monitors staff development regularly because it recognizes the challenges that the bank, and therefore its staff, must meet on the IT front. Training and development form a central feature of this bank's strategy in this area.

An international computer company assesses attitudes and satisfaction of staff to various aspects of the company, the policies, the work-setting, and so on, every 2 years (bottom left-hand quadrant) and instructs all employees to appraise the performance of their own manager every year. This latter, combined with performance appraisal carried out by managers with superiors, provides a regular input to the bottom right-hand quadrant.

Techniques for assessment

The problems we face are changing and complex. If you cannot measure them you cannot manage them. This is why we need to develop a balanced set of measures.

We turn now to techniques for monitoring effectiveness. These comprise a checklist for completing a functional analysis of the organization and a diagnostic questionnaire. The data to be collected are often expressed quantitatively. However, these techniques are really focusing on factors within the qualitative end of the matrix; not all the data obtained are quantitative – at least some qualitative comment is generally either asked for or received when techniques like these are used; moreover, the limitations of these kinds of data mean that interpretation is always and ultimately a matter of judgement and experience.

In the next section we present an exercise for assessing organizational effectiveness with typical data drawn from International Engineering, a large engineering design and project management company discussed previously. These data were collected by me as part of a consultancy assignment undertaken in 1988.

Assessing organizational effectiveness: exercise

This exercise presents an internal analysis of the organization in order to identify its strengths and weaknesses. In presenting the techniques, we have included data from International Engineering which we will analyze later in this chapter. We include the average score on each question derived from 92 managers who completed the exercise. This will allow us to identify the organization's capabilities and resources, and how well it is exploiting them. It will also help us to understand how effectively the organization is adapting to changing environmental circumstances. The exercise is divided into two parts: functional analysis and organizational diagnosis.

Part 1: functional analysis

The functional analysis questionnaire in Table 9.1 has five sections that deal with five key elements within the organization, namely people, marketing, finance, operations/service and business/corporate development. Each section comprises a checklist of questions to consider and assess how well each supports the company's corporate objectives. Responses can be recorded as ticks or in note form. Score responses as follows:

5. Fully supports corporate objectives.

4. Adequately supports corporate objectives.

3. Does not support corporate objectives.

2. Makes achieving corporate objectives difficult.

1. Makes achieving corporate objectives very difficult.

Following the blank questionnaire is one showing average scores and comments relevant to International Engineering. Before examining these results you may wish to complete the functional analysis for your own organization.

Closer examination of the functional analysis reveals a number of key organizational weaknesses. The pay, training, promotion and performance of staff are relatively low. This particularly applies to pay, where the company pays at or below current market rates. Its technical training is excellent, but management training is widely felt to be inadequate. These points are problematic on two counts. Firstly, the company essentially exists to sell the services of its engineers. They specify, design and detail process plants and/or provide project management, maintenance management and, increasingly, operational management services. Secondly, the company increasingly provides the latter three management services. More and more, the company sells technical and managerial expertise. One estimate has it that halving the rate of staff turnover could return as much as £150,000 each year into the profit and loss account, taking into account the costs of recruitment, lost time, induction and training against the costs of pay and other changes to reward systems.

A second area of weakness lies in that of management control information. The company has elaborate information systems but does not yet have systems on which managers can and do rely. Therefore, managers tend not to utilize information very effectively. This also impacts on performance. Little attempt is made to use feedback from the management information system to motivate higher levels of effort, or even as a basis for solving problems.

Marketing and marketing information is a further weakness. The company has only limited competitor information. More fundamentally, it does not seem to make good use of the information it does have available. Principally, the weakness lies within the bidding process. Bid teams appear to be put together in an *ad hoc* manner. There is no guarantee that a bid team will have a high-level input from engineering, project management, estimating, commercial or marketing functions. The organization keeps estimating and commercial functions separate and currently has neither a commercial nor marketing director. The chief executive, the technical director and the engineering director lead the bid process, although they may not lead the bid team. There seems to be scope to improve this process as a means of beginning to grapple with the company's core commercial weakness. It is unable to obtain high-value projects. It has obtained a record level of work but at relatively low staff-hour rates for its engineering personnel. The implication of this is that the company could combine record levels of activity with record losses.

All this links back to performance yet again. Engineers often feel that the contracts obtained have ridiculously low staff-hour rates, tight delivery dates and project milestones. Many of the contracts specify staff-hours and staff-hour rates. Yet engineers and managers feel no incentive to seek improvements in engineering work structures and systems: 'It's impossible to make profit from this project' is the response. Yet if we could find ways of achieving the same milestones with fewer staff-hours the company would, firstly, reduce its losses and, secondly, improve its market standing. The latter could help it gain more profitable contracts, and these exist. Other companies in the group are attracting profitable, high-value work. International Engineering's competitors are not all in the same situation. Many are very profitable.

The analysis of operations/service supports this conclusion. The main point is that there is a clear lack of integration between project management, engineering and marketing. This seems partly to be a problem of systems. The appropriate information is not available to various departments as people make decisions which have an effect across departments. More fundamentally, the *ad hoc* nature of the bidding process vitiates such integration as is often achieved on an informal basis.

Finally, the company has lagged behind in key technologies and is therefore less credible in certain areas of work such as nuclear engineering and pharmaceuticals. The company is seen as capable of responding to competitive pressures but this applies mainly to the markets in which it has been well established. These include the oil industry, a market which is relatively mature. Contract prices have been under downward pressure, partly as a result of the oil price situation with all its consequences.

Part 2: organizational diagnosis

This exercise is provided to assist readers in making a structured analysis of their own company's internal system, processes and their effectiveness. Readers are asked to complete the questionnaire. The average scores are for the 92 managers from International Engineering referred to in the discussion above.

Table 9.1 ● Proforma for organizational analysis
(a) Functional analysis

	Fully supports corporate objectives (Score 5)

1. *People*
1.1 The relationship between individuals and the enterprise regarding
  Pay
  Promotion
  Training and development
  Performance improvement
1.2 The skills, training and experience of personnel
1.3 The organization's policy in respect of selection and placement of employees
1.4 The organization's relationship with trade unions represented within the enterprise
1.5 The extent to which human resources are considered strategically when formulating and implementing strategic decisions

2. *Finance*
2.1 The process of budget preparation
2.2 The level of involvement of key staff in budget preparation
2.3 The extent of consistency between divisional (unit) budgets and overall organizational budgets
2.4 The extent to which financial budgets and strategic plans are compatible
2.5 The effectiveness of management control information in terms of accuracy, relevance and timeliness
2.6 The attitude of managers to management control information
2.7 The extent to which managers take corrective action to remedy problems of ineffective control
2.8 The extent to which feedback from the management information system is used to motivate improved performance

3. *Marketing*
3.1 The contribution of each product/service group (division, unit) to sales and profit. (Note: You may wish to tackle the question for each group, division or unit)
3.2 The market position of each product or service group (market share, growth, maturity)
3.3 The extent to which this organization competes in
  Price
  Quality/service
  Delivery

Adequately supports corporate objectives	Does not support corporate objectives	Makes achieving corporate objectives difficult	Makes achieving corporate objectives very difficult
(Score 4)	(Score 3)	(Score 2)	(Score 1)

(Continued)

Table 9.1 ● Continued
(a) Functional analysis

	Fully supports corporate objectives (Score 5)

3.4 The quality and extent of our knowledge of competitors

3.5 The use made of market research and its impact on product development

4. *Operations/service*

4.1 The level of co-operation between marketing and operations/service

4.2 The extent to which the information received from marketing and finance is useful for managing this function

4.3 Management understanding of long-run trends in costs and performances

4.4 The extent to which management are able to control costs

4.5 The level of inventory in relation to output and sales (and the relationship between raw material, work in progress and finished goods, stocks)

4.6 The adequacy, age and state of repair of plant and equipment

4.7 The flexibility of use of plant, equipment and facilities

4.8 The level of investment compared with the average for the industry

5. *Corporate/business development*

5.1 The organization's investment in development

5.2 The ability of the organization to respond quickly to market or competitive pressures

5.3 The organization's ability to exploit new products

5.4 The extent to which the organization pursues opportunities for product/service improvement

5.5 The integration of development with market, operations finance, design, etc.

5.6 The extent to which the organization is able to exploit outside sources for development purposes (e.g. joint ventures, consultants)

Adequately supports corporate objectives	Does not support corporate objectives	Makes achieving corporate objectives difficult	Makes achieving corporate objectives very difficult
(Score 4)	(Score 3)	(Score 2)	(Score 1)

Table 9.1 ● (b) Results: International Engineering

	Average score
1. *People*	
1.1 The relationship between individuals and the enterprise regarding	
Pay	2.24
Promotion	2.68
Training and development	2.56
Performance improvement	2.10
1.2 The skills, training and experience of personnel	3.28
1.3 The organization's policy in respect of selection and placement of employees	3.10
1.4 The organization's relationship with trade unions represented within the enterprise	
1.5 The extent to which human resources are considered strategically when formulating and implementing strategic decisions	1.42
2. *Finance*	
2.1 The process of budget preparation	3.48
2.2 The level of involvement of key staff in budget preparation	2.91
2.3 The extent of consistency between divisional (unit) budgets and overall organizational budgets	3.88
2.4 The extent to which financial budgets and strategic plans are compatible	3.04
2.5 The effectiveness of management control information in terms of accuracy, relevance and timeliness	2.87
2.6 The attitude of managers to management control information	1.96
2.7 The extent to which managers take corrective action to remedy problems of ineffective control	2.72
2.8 The extent to which feedback from the management information system is used to promote improved performance	1.84
3. *Marketing*	
3.1 The contribution of each product/service group (division, unit) to sales and profit. (Note: You may wish to tackle the question for each group, division or unit)	2.71
3.2 The market position of each product or service group (market share, growth, maturity)	
3.3 The extent to which this organization competes in	
Price	3.98
Quality/Service	4.08
Delivery	3.68

Comment

The company pays at or below the normal rate for engineers and is experiencing 15–20 per cent staff turnover per year. It promotes almost entirely from within. It has excellent technical training but limited management training. Performance appraisal is in use but is not very effective

The company has loyal, committed and experienced staff, is technically excellent and is perceived as such in the marketplace

Problems of recruitment and rotation of staff have meant that the use of 'agency' staff has increased to approximately 40 per cent of the requirement for engineers

Not relevant

Not at all

The company has a well-developed budget system

Often key staff have only limited involvement partly because of time pressures

The budgets are consistent (on paper!)

On paper, yes!

While a large amount of data is available, their usefulness is limited

There is a widespread lack of a commercial approach. The company has been making losses in recent years

It is engaged in a considerable amount of work at prices which are not profitable

(Continued)

Table 9.1 ● (b) Continued

	Average score
3.4 The quality and extent of our knowledge of competitors	1.62
3.5 The use made of market research and its impact on product development	1.44
4. *Operations/service*	
4.1 The level of co-operation between marketing and operations/service	1.82
4.2 The extent to which the information received from marketing and finance is useful for managing this function	2.17
4.3 Management understanding of long-run trends in costs and performances	2.04
4.4 The extent to which management are able to control costs	2.92
4.5 The level of inventory in relation to output and sales (and the relationship between raw material, work in progress and finished goods, stocks)	
4.6 The adequacy, age and state of repair of plant and equipment	3.42
4.7 The flexibility of use of plant, equipment and facilities	3.47
4.8 The level of investment compared with the average for the industry	2.91
5. *Corporate/business development*	
5.1 The organization's investment in development	2.11
5.2 The ability of the organization to respond quickly to market or competitive pressures	2.76
5.3 The organization's ability to exploit new products	1.91
5.4 The extent to which the organization pursues opportunities for product/service improvement	2.07
5.5 The integration of development with market, operations finance, design, etc.	2.01
5.6 The extent to which the organization is able to exploit outside sources for development purposes (e.g. joint ventures, consultants)	2.71

Comment

There is a strong feeling that contracts are agreed at prices and staff-hour rates which are not economic, and which do not provide sufficient profit margin
Schedules, which bear little relationship to what is achieved. This means that project managers take on agency staff at high costs and also accept some disruption in consequence. There is limited incentive to improve cost performance

Not relevant

The company has 'state-of-the-art' computer-aided design facilities

The company has lagged behind in technology and is therefore less able to enter or be credible in key new markets (nuclear energy, pharmaceutical applications, etc.). Little effort is devoted to innovation and improvement. Product/service development is inadequate. Little attention is paid to feedback from the marketplace through marketing department, operations department, etc.

Organizational diagnosis questionnaire

This questionnaire is designed to help you determine how well your own organization works, in a number of related areas.

Assess how far you agree or disagree with the following statements as they apply to you within your own department or section, using this seven-point scale, and circling the appropriate number:

1	2	3	4	5	6	7
Agree strongly	Agree	Agree slightly	Neutral	Disagree slightly	Disagree	Disagree strongly

In answering the statements, try to be as honest as you can. This is not a test, and there are no right or wrong answers. The only correct answer is what you decide yourself. *The average score shown in the right-hand column is from International Engineering.*

Statement		Average score
1.	I understand the objectives of this organization. 1 2 3 4 5 6 7	4.62
2.	The organization of work here is effective. 1 2 3 4 5 6 7	4.21
3.	Managers will always listen to ideas. 1 2 3 4 5 6 7	2.11
4.	I am encouraged to develop my full potential. 1 2 3 4 5 6 7	2.84
5.	My immediate boss has ideas that are helpful to me and my work group. 1 2 3 4 5 6 7	2.91
6.	My immediate boss is supportive and helps me in my work. 1 2 3 4 5 6 7	3.78
7.	This organization keeps its policies and procedures relevant and up to date. 1 2 3 4 5 6 7	2.82
8.	We regularly achieve our objectives. 1 2 3 4 5 6 7	2.94
9.	The goals and objectives of this organization are clearly stated. 1 2 3 4 5 6 7	3.61
10.	Jobs and lines of authority are flexible. 1 2 3 4 5 6 7	4.12
11.	I can always talk to someone at work if I have a work-related problem. 1 2 3 4 5 6 7	3.72
12.	The salary that I receive is commensurate with the job that I perform. 1 2 3 4 5 6 7	2.04
13.	I have all the information and resources I need to do a good job. 1 2 3 4 5 6 7	2.98
14.	The management style adopted by senior management is helpful and effective. 1 2 3 4 5 6 7	3.17
15.	We constantly review our methods and introduce improvements. 1 2 3 4 5 6 7	2.61

(Continued)

Statement		Average score
16.	Results are attained because people are committed to them.	1 2 3 4 5 6 7 3.82
17.	I feel motivated by the work I do.	1 2 3 4 5 6 7 4.24
18.	The way in which work tasks are divided is sensible and clear.	1 2 3 4 5 6 7 3.61
19.	My relationships with other members of my work group are good.	1 2 3 4 5 6 7 4.17
20.	There are opportunities for promotion and increased responsibility in this organization.	1 2 3 4 5 6 7 2.71
21.	This organization sets realistic plans.	1 2 3 4 5 6 7 2.56
22.	Performance is regularly reviewed by my boss.	1 2 3 4 5 6 7 4.21
23.	There are occasions when I would like to be free to make changes in my job.	1 2 3 4 5 6 7 2.08
24.	People are cost-conscious and seek to make the best use of resources.	1 2 3 4 5 6 7 2.92
25.	The priorities of this organization are understood by its employees.	1 2 3 4 5 6 7 3.71
26.	There is a constant search for ways of improving the way we work.	1 2 3 4 5 6 7 4.62
27.	We co-operate effectively in order to get the work done.	1 2 3 4 5 6 7 3.50
28.	Encouragement and recognition is given for all jobs and tasks in this organization.	1 2 3 4 5 6 7 2.51
29.	Departments work well together to achieve good performance.	1 2 3 4 5 6 7 2.46
30.	This organization's management team provides effective and inspiring leadership.	1 2 3 4 5 6 7 4.28
31.	This organization has the capacity to change.	1 2 3 4 5 6 7 3.78
32.	The work we do is always necessary and effective.	1 2 3 4 5 6 7 3.42
33.	In my own work area objectives are clearly stated and each person's work role is clearly identified.	1 2 3 4 5 6 7 4.01
34.	The way the work structure in this organization is arranged produces general satisfaction.	1 2 3 4 5 6 7 3.95
35.	Conflicts of views are resolved by solutions which are understood and accepted.	1 2 3 4 5 6 7 3.07
36.	All individual work performance is reviewed against agreed standards.	1 2 3 4 5 6 7 3.61
37.	Other departments are helpful to my own department whenever necessary.	1 2 3 4 5 6 7 2.82
38.	My boss's management style helps me in the performance of my own work.	1 2 3 4 5 6 7 4.58
39.	Creativity and initiative are encouraged.	1 2 3 4 5 6 7 2.71
40.	People are always concerned to do a good job.	1 2 3 4 5 6 7 2.93

In the following questionnaire, eight areas are assessed, each with five statements as shown on the check-sheet below.

Check-sheet

1. For each numbered statement, enter the score recorded on the questionnaire.

2. Work out the total for the five statements in each area.

3. Divide by 5 to find the average score in each area.

I Key tasks	II Structure	III People relationships	IV Motivation
1	2	3	4
9	10	11	12
17	18	19	20
25	26	27	28
33	34	35	36
Total			
Average			

V Support	VI Management leadership	VII Attitude towards change	VIII Performance
5	6	7	8
13	14	15	16
21	22	23	24
29	30	31	32
37	38	39	40
Total			
Average			

For a sample of n people, first add together all the scores for a particular statement, divide the total by n, and proceed as above.

The results of the diagnostic survey were analyzed by groups of managers from International Engineering. From this analysis it appears that the definition of key tasks, organizational structure and management leadership are all seen as areas of weakness. People do not understand overall objectives or how their jobs fit into the whole company picture. They do not feel motivated by the work they do, partly, it appears, because of this latter problem.

The organization is not seen as being very effective, for reasons covered under the functional analysis. Most important, jobs and lines of authority are seen as inflexible and little attempt is made to achieve improvements. The organizational structure is seen as inappropriate.

Management style is not seen as helpful to individual performance and, overall, people perceived relatively weak leadership. Conversely, there was a relatively positive attitude to change. Indeed, it might be argued that the perceived lack of leadership was felt to be particularly frustrating to employees who felt strong commitment to the company and a positive attitude towards change.

Increased competition led to declining economic performance. Greater attention to cost control and internal conflict within the organization meant that corporate policy reflected increasingly short-term pressures. Declining performance, short-term perspectives, limited investment in management development all contribute to the growing difficulty of improving the quality of management in the organization.

The functional analysis checklist and questionnaire results can then be subjected to more detailed analysis. For example, in the engineering consultancy firm 92 managers and engineers completed the assessment exercise. The data were reviewed by the executive committee in a senior management workshop. They concluded that a number of priority issues needed to be addressed, as follows:

1. *Commercial focus and accountability*
   (a) focus commercially both in defining accountabilities and in the management of the business;
   (b) decentralize responsibilities, clarify individual accountability.

2. *Performance appraisals*
   (a) to ensure more rigorous enforcement of appraisals;
   (b) to develop more commercially orientated targets;
   (c) to ensure that remuneration is linked to performance.

3. *Effective systems and information*
   (a) to ensure relevance to individuals;
   (b) to be user-friendly;
   (c) to provide a commercial focus.

4. *Effective communication*
   (a) of strategies;
   (b) of responsibilities;
   (c) of commercial requirements.

Understanding the 'human' dimension of change

Diagnosis for change is partly a matter of analysis and partly a matter of understanding the human dimension of the organization. While it is important that any diagnosis gives full weighting to the commercial and organizational issues, this is not enough. Attention must also be given to the people involved. Can they work more effectively? Could they be managed more appropriately? Can we engage their commitment to change? These questions turn on whether or not we believe that there is potential for improvement within our people. If the expectations that managers have about their people are relatively low, then the response elicited will be low. Achieving higher levels of performance involves believing in the potential of the people involved, equipping them appropriately, training them where necessary and much more besides. Therefore the assumptions that managers make about people are very important. The wrong assumptions may tend to lower managers' expectations and thus lower performance. The wrong assumptions may also lead to the use of management styles not conducive to commitment and change.

The jobs that people actually perform are the fundamental 'building blocks' of any organization. Moreover, they form a key aspect of the experience of working. The extent to which valued skills are used, the discretion available to the individual, the degree of specialization, the extent to which the individual produces a 'worthwhile' product are all important. At the same time, however, individuals appear to differ in the extent to which they would wish these various attributes to be present in their job. There appears to be no simple link between the type of job that an individual does and his or her satisfaction with that job. Similarly, there is no simple link between job satisfaction and productivity. Other factors are also important. Nevertheless, many people find the jobs they do repetitive and boring, or at least will tell an interviewer that this is the case! In the 1960s and 1970s there was much concern over the design of jobs. Today the introduction of new technology provides organizations with the opportunity to review jobs, and perhaps improve them.

Both managers and employees have expectations about each other and in particular about what motivates them to work. Schein (1965) has identified four sets of managerial assumptions about employees, and the implications of them for management and job design strategies. These assumptions and the implications are set out as follows.

'Rational–economic man'

The rational–economic model is clearly associated with the principles of 'scientific management' and, historically, its approach is founded in the early decades of the twentieth century. The model assumes that people evaluate the outcomes of different courses of action and select the one which maximizes the benefit they receive, i.e. they exercise rational judgement based on economic criteria. This general assumption can be broken down into the following eight specific assumptions about employees:

1. Employees are primarily motivated by economic incentives, and will pursue those activities which result in the greatest economic benefit.
2. Employees are passive and can be manipulated, motivated and controlled by management, since management control economic incentives.
3. Feelings are essentially irrational, and must be prevented from interfering with the rational calculation of self-interest.
4. Organizations should be designed so that people's feelings, and hence their unpredictability, are controlled and neutralized.
5. People are inherently lazy and must be motivated by external incentives.
6. People's own goals run counter to those of the organization, and external forces are needed to channel efforts towards organizational goals.
7. People are incapable of self-control and self-discipline because of irrational feelings.

8. People can be divided into two groups: those who fit these assumptions, and those who are self-motivated, self-controlled and less dominated by their feelings. This second group must assume responsibility for managing the others.

The main thrust of these assumptions is that emotions have no place in management –employee relationships, and must be prevented from interfering in the work situation. This implies a management strategy of financial and economic rewards for the employee's contribution and a system of authority, controls and punishment to protect the organization and the employee from irrational feelings (the 'control' model described in Chapter 2).

In the field of work design the main emphasis is on efficient task performance, since this leads to the greatest economic benefit. Rules and procedures must be established, and methods of improvement sought, so as to achieve maximum efficiency, and it must be possible to identify shortcomings so that incentives or punishments can be used to correct the situation. Provided that the method of working is specified, and employees conform to it, adequate motivation and output will be ensured by manipulating rewards and punishments, and using adequate supervision.

'Social man'

These assumptions may be listed as follows:

1. People are basically motivated by social needs and achieve a sense of identity through relationships with others.

2. The rationalization of work processes has removed the meaning from work, and meaning must thus be sought from social relationships while doing the job.

3. The peer group with its social pressures elicits more response from the employee than the incentives and controls of management.

4. For people to respond to management the supervisor must meet the individual's social needs and needs for acceptance.

In the work design area this set of assumptions leads to a major change in approach. The manager should not direct attention solely to task efficiency but should consider employees' social needs. The manager should accept social interaction as a means of improving motivation, rather than as something which interferes with efficient performance, and should regard work groups as being an essential and contributory factor to employee motivation rather than as being a disruptive influence.

The assumptions about 'social man' lead to two related, though rather different, emphases. The first of these is an emphasis on human relations. The manager, instead of being a controller and creator of work, becomes a sympathetic supporter of the employee and enables him or her to do the job rather than ensuring that it is done by direct means. This leads to the need to adopt less autocratic/directive and more supportive management styles. The second is the socio-technical systems approach. Here a deliberate effort is made to integrate the social needs of the employees and the technical needs of the job, usually by designing work for groups of employees, rather than individuals, and often by using group rather than individual incentives.

'Self-actualizing man'

These assumptions about people can be summarized as follows:

1. People are not inherently lazy or resistant to organizational goals.
2. People seek to be, and are capable of being, mature on the job, exercising a certain amount of autonomy, independence and responsibility, and developing skills and adaptability.
3. People are primarily self-motivated and self-controlled and do not need external incentives and controls to make them work.
4. There is no inherent conflict between self-actualization and effective organizational performance. Given the opportunity, people will voluntarily integrate their own goals with those of the organization, achieving the former through working towards the latter.

The implications of these assumptions for management are fundamentally different from the earlier two. Both rational–economic and social assumptions lead to a strategy which requires the provision of extrinsic motivation to elicit performance, while self-actualizing assumptions lead to a strategy which requires the provision of opportunities for the employee's existing motivation to be used. The former needs extrinsic rewards (economic or social) to be exchanged for performance; the latter needs the exchange of opportunities to gain intrinsic rewards (the satisfaction of higher-order needs within the work situation) for performance. In addition, the performance criteria used would differ. In the former, the emphasis is on compliance with desired behaviour patterns but in the latter emphasis is placed on quality and creativity.

The implications for work design are also radically different. Instead of telling people how to do the job, managers using this approach explain what is to be achieved and allow the employee to exercise his or her own discretion. Emphasis is placed on making the work itself more challenging and meaningful and management relinquish much of the direct control of work to the employee.

'Complex man'

There is a certain amount of evidence to support all the assumptions outlined so far. In many cases the models can be used to explain and predict some behaviour, but there is also considerable contradictory evidence. People not only are more complex than the models suggest, but also differ.

Schein (1965) outlines the following five assumptions on which this model of 'complex man' is based:

1. People are complex and variable. They have many needs, arranged in a hierarchy of personal importance, but the hierarchy varies over time and according to the situation. In addition, their motives interact and form complex motivational patterns.
2. People can adopt new motives as a result of their experiences and hence the individual's pattern of motivation and relationship with the organization result from a complex interaction between individual needs and organizational experiences.

3. People's motives may vary in different organizational situations. If they cannot satisfy their needs within the formal organization they may do so in the informal organization or in other activities. If the job itself is complex, different parts of it may engage different motives.

4. People's work involvement may stem from a variety of motives and the outcome in terms of their performance and satisfaction is only partly dependent on their motivation. The nature of the task to be performed, relations with others, abilities and experience all interact to produce particular outcomes. For example, a highly skilled, poorly motivated worker may be as effective and satisfied as an unskilled, highly motivated worker.

5. People will respond to different management strategies in ways dependent on their own motives and abilities and the nature of the task. Therefore, no single correct managerial strategy exists.

The overall lesson of these assumptions is not that the earlier models are wrong, but that each is right with particular people in particular circumstances. Hence the implication for management is not that there is a single strategy to adopt, but that management must be flexible in adapting to a variety of abilities and motives. This in turn means that management must be sensitive in diagnosing the differences, and must have the ability to vary managerial style and behaviour. This sensitivity is an important part of the interpretation of data collected from the organizational assessment techniques described.

Let us return to International Engineering for a moment. The management style had been autocratic and directive. Yet it is clear enough from the data presented here that the company was not organized to be fully effective. Part of the answer lies in restructuring. Partly, it lies in developing a 'sharper', performance and commercially orientated culture. Thus, in part, it is about placing increased demands on people. Any attempt to interpret these data through assumptions of either 'rational–economic man' or 'self-actualizing man', or a combination of these, may not help.

It seems likely that management have adopted some combination of these assumptions in the past. They may have believed that the engineers wish to pursue technical excellence alone. In any event the technical training was admittedly excellent: 'Let the engineers get on with the technical work and all will be well' seems to have been the view of many managers. In an increasingly competitive world, this has proved to be inadequate. It is risky to believe that these engineers cannot be trusted beyond the technical contribution they offer. There needs to be a recognition that the situation is more complex, that many engineers can and will respond to performance and commercial orientation. Creating change at International Engineering involves the adoption of new organization structures and management styles compatible with the implications of the assessment data.

The change equation

But we can only go one step at a time. We must first create recognition that something is wrong. Moreover, change creates risks, uncertainties and costs, both economic and psychological. To engage commitment to change we need to generate a shared vision of how the situation can be improved, and shared aims for the future. We also need to generate a clear understanding of the first practical steps forward. If I recognize that what I am doing is ineffective I need to be able to visualize a better way *and* see some steps that I can take to make progress towards that vision. Many people believe that generating the commitment to, and energy for, change depends on all these factors.

The change equation provides a useful way of dealing with questions such as 'Should I attempt to make change?' and 'What more can I do to improve the chances of introducing change effectively?' It can be expressed as follows:

$$EC = A \times B \times D$$

where *EC* is the energy for change, *A* is the felt dissatisfaction with the present situation, *B* the level of knowledge of the practical steps forward and *D* the shared vision.

Dissatisfaction with the present will only lead to high energy for change if there are high levels of shared aims and knowledge of what to do next. Without these shared aims and knowledge, dissatisfaction will lead to demotivation, despondency and apathy. There is another equation, however. For change to occur:

$$EC > Z$$

where *Z* is the perceived cost of making change.

The energy for change must be greater than the perceived costs of making the change, both economic and psychological. In fact, if we have no shared aims and no knowledge of what to do next there will be so much uncertainty that people will expect the 'costs' of change to be high. We shall see in later chapters that it is all important when designing and managing change to ensure that both the means of introducing change and the impact of change are designed to build the energy for change. This chapter aims to demonstrate a way of approaching organizational diagnosis and assessment and the importance of ensuring that any attempt to diagnose the need for change is carried out with the recognition that the appropriate end-point is acceptance of change and energy for changing.

To return to International Engineering, one of its main problems was that many of the engineers who developed management and leadership potential were believed to have resigned from the company, frustrated by ineffectiveness. This left the company less able to create the energy for much needed changes. It had lost many of the people who might have been involved in developing new business, new technology and the like. The ability to attract, motivate and retain people is an important aspect of the effective organization.

Now we turn to the use of a survey to assess the ability to attract, develop, retain and motivate leadership talent. Kotter (1988) has developed a very useful questionnaire for use with senior managers.

The first part of the questionnaire deals with the managers' assessment of how well the systems and practices within the organization supported the objective of attracting, retaining and motivating a sufficient number of people with the leadership potential to fill senior management positions. Table 9.2 shows the results obtained from

Table 9.2 ● Attracting, retaining and motivating leadership potential

Factors assessed	Less than adequate (%)
1. The quality of career-planning discussions with superiors	87
2. Availability of jobs with development opportunities	78
3. The information available to managers on job vacancies in the company	77
4. Management development offered to individuals with identified high potential	70
5. Outside training opportunities	66
6. The strategic/business and human resource planning processes which help clarify what kind of company will exist in 5–10 years, and thus how many and what kind of important management positions will need to be staffed	66
7. In-house training opportunities	61
8. The ability of managers to identify and select people with high potential	60
9. The promotion opportunities offered to people with high potential	56
10. The firm's performance-related pay scheme	52

International Engineering. Listed on the left are the factors that the managers were asked to assess. The right-hand column shows the percentage of managers who felt that the factor was *less than adequate* to support the objective.

The questionnaire also reveals the managers' assessment of how well the organization's systems and practices contributed to its ability to develop leadership talent. Table 9.3 shows the percentage of managers who felt that, on the factors listed, the company was *less than adequate* in spotting high-potential people and identifying and meeting their developmental needs. When interviewed about the ineffective systems and processes reported in the questionnaire responses, senior managers often referred to short-term pressures by way of explanation. Management development was seen by some to have no immediate payoff and was therefore not used. Rotation was not practised because managers did not wish to lose good performers or people with potential. Ineffective and inadequate feedback was common. Senior managers would *not* face poor performance and development needs directly. Recruitment was carried out on the basis of technical competence, *not* management potential. Hard-pressed managers needed to meet their targets! Middle management were sometimes seen as ineffective. Promotion and reward practices did not encourage high levels of performance.

Table 9.3 ● Identifying and meeting developmental needs

Factors assessed	Less than adequate (%)
1. The way managers are rewarded for developing subordinates	94
2. The advice given to people on how to manage their own career for long-term development	90
3. The use of lateral transfers made for development purposes across divisions	88
4. Assessment schemes aimed at identifying the development needs of managers	82
5. The mentoring and coaching provided to managers	79
6. The amount of carefully planned time and effort the company expends in trying to manage the whole process of developing people	79
7. The way special jobs are used to develop people with high potential	77
8. The way feedback is given to subordinates regarding their progress	76
9. The capacity of the firm's managers to identify the development needs of people with high potential	71
10. The way responsibilities are added to a manager's job for development purposes	69
11. Formal succession planning reviews	67
12. The firm's participation in outside management training programmes	66
13. The opportunities offered to people to give them exposure to higher levels of management	64
14. The capacity of the firm's senior managers to identify people with potential	59
15. The firm's use of in-company management training programmes	52

Managers wanted obedience, not the threat of excellent performance (see Kotter, 1988, pp. 72–3).

Yet these same managers were concerned about the ineffectiveness they had reported. They recognized the changes in technology, competition, expectations and so on: 'To continue to succeed we must become more effective in these areas' was a powerful message coming through these interviews.

Now let us turn to a short example of another organization with which I have conducted an organizational diagnosis and assessment.

CASE STUDY

London Underground

This organization operates an underground or 'metro' service in a major European city. It was a public sector organization, but in the 1990s it changed. Senior management reorganized to achieve a more commercial approach to its management. The organization had been dominated by engineers. Top management had followed a primarily technical approach. Much of its support work (e.g. track maintenance, capital projects) was being put out to tender with no guarantee that internal departments would get the work if they were to bid. Now, for the first time in their careers, technical managers needed to understand costing and pricing. These were dramatic changes.

Part-way through this process, the board and senior management (approximately 100 people) completed an organizational diagnosis and assessment as a means of taking stock and looking to the future. All those involved completed the diagnostic questionnaire, described earlier in this chapter, in preparation for discussion of how to achieve further change in the future. In Table 9.4 we summarize the strengths and weaknesses of the organization as defined by these managers from the questionnaire results. They identified key tasks, people and attitude to change as strengths. People understood their own and the organization's objectives, felt motivated by their own work and understood priorities and their own work role. Relationships between individuals and within teams were good.

There was a strong commitment to the organization and the need for change among employees. Technological change had been a regular feature of the organization's history. It had an international reputation in its own field.

Structure and performance were identified as neither strengths nor weaknesses. The managers generally felt that the management structure had changed dramatically and that

Table 9.4 ● Strengths and weaknesses of the organization

Strengths		Weaknesses
Key tasks		
People		
Attitude to change		
	Structure	
	Performance	
		Communication
		Support
		Motivation
		Leadership

▷▷

these changes had yet to stabilize. Performance had declined somewhat because of the energy absorbed in making the changes that were already underway.

Communication, support, motivation and leadership were all rated as weaknesses. Managers felt under considerable pressure in consequence of the changes being made. Moreover, the changes had included staffing reviews which had led to staff reductions in many areas.

This combination of staff losses and pressure of work led to many managers reporting support as a weakness. One consequence of these problems was that many departments took an increasingly departmental focus, doing only those things that they needed, giving work for other departments (e.g. providing information) a lower priority.

In using the change equation idea we must thus be careful to consider the impact on it of changes already underway. We must avoid trying to view change in isolation. We are not dealing with discrete events; rather, we are dealing with organizations experiencing many changes, each at different stages. As we said at the outset, we must establish whether change is desirable and feasible. People will not readily see change as desirable. We are often all too ready to ignore the question of what is feasible in a given time. Circumstances sometimes demand that changes be made dramatically and quickly. If so, we should be aware of the tensions so caused, recognize them explicitly and seek to manage them. If you do not measure them you cannot manage them!

CASE STUDY

Health Service Trust (HST)

This case study sets out extracts from documents drawn from an organizational review of a National Health Service (NHS) Trust in the UK. Since recent reforms health service 'providers' are organized as trusts which are managed by a board but remain part of the UK NHS.

Brief

1. This diagnostic study was undertaken to provide an input to the trust board. The objective was to present a summary of views of managers and professional staff about the effectiveness of the existing corporate structure and management arrangements of HST. The purpose of the review was to aid the board in ensuring that HST has in place a structure and management which aid the achievement of the objectives of the trust. Specifically, the

▶▶

terms of reference were as follows:

(a) Review the management arrangements of HST and make recommendations for change aimed at increasing the efficiency and effectiveness of HST.
(b) The review should consider and take into account the recommendations and suggestions made in a number of recent reports, including:
   ● Hospital Manager – Consultant – Nurse Study Report, June 1992 (completed by a consultant);
   ● Audit Commission's Nurse Management Review, August 1992;
   ● King's Fund Organizational Audit Visit, September 1992 (both national organizations concerned with public service management and health service management).
(c) The study will be wide ranging and cover all aspects of HST's management.
(d) Any recommendations must fully support HST's philosophy of clinical management and devolving authority and responsibility as near to the point of delivery of care as possible.
(e) The review should aim to streamline channels of authority and accountability at all levels in the organization.
(f) The review should encompass management support.
(g) The proposed structures must not increase and preferably should reduce management costs of HST.

Approach to the study

2. A working group of managers was established who would work with the consultant in carrying out this diagnosis. This allowed a large number of interviews to be carried out quickly and ensured the relevance of the review. The consultant and the working group designed the interview schedule and identified the target group to be interviewed. A total of 121 interviews were carried out across HST from board level down to ward sisters. (Three people refused to be interviewed.) The consultant and the working group have been involved in summarizing the results and in drafting this report. In addition a number of individuals wrote to the consultant expressing views relevant to the management review.

3. The following information is included as appendices:
Appendix 1: the interview schedule.
Appendix 2: a list of specific comments drawn from the interview notes.
(Neither is included here.)

Arrangement review of HST

4. A number of points were held in common by the majority of those interviewed. HST was seen as a well-regarded organization comprising many capable people. It was seen as innovative and as having many specialties which were known nationally for various developments. Almost all respondents thought that the team of which they were a member is effective, cohesive and friendly. Individuals and teams were seen to possess the necessary technical, professional and other skills and were seen to work together well.

5. Communication was seen to need improvement but recent improvements were also acknowledged. Nevertheless an examination of Appendix 2 will quickly reveal many expressed concerns in this area. Linked to this, people expressed concern about management style and change. There has been a lot of change recently. Many feel that changes have been neither handled sensitively nor communicated effectively. Some suggest that there is too little co-operation and too defensive an approach; others feel that there are too many committees, working parties and that it is difficult to identify a decision-making forum. The UMT (Unit Management Team) is seen as too large and too diverse (regarding the interests represented on it) to be a source of effective decisions.

6. Many of those interviewed put the case for greater devolvement. Some called for devolvement of finance and for personnel to directorates, some called for greater devolvement *within* directorates, some called for devolvement of hotel services, some called for devolvement of other services. Linked to this, some referred to the importance of service agreements between directorates and directorates providing services.

7. Many of those interviewed held strong views about the impact of split sites on effectiveness; however, varying views are held. Some felt that certain smaller units are effective because they can be managed as small cohesive units and would not wish to lose this advantage; however, most recognized that split-site working brings duplication, higher costs, frustration and problems of communications, management and control. The infrastructure generally was seen as a source of constraint and all would prefer major new capital development whilst recognizing that this is an issue outside this management review.

8. There is a widely recognized lack of accountability of a range of issues. Beds are not managed as a whole – some of those interviewed indicated that HST needs to get to grips with this soon. Linked to this, admissions and discharge policies were seen as ill defined by some. Purchasing and stock control were seen as in need of further improvement. The whole business-getting process was seen as needing organizing. As more and more of the workload comes from GP fund-holders, people health purchasing is carried out by health authorities and GP fund-holders – general practitioners to whom budget has been devolved are questioning how to find the time to obtain this business, manage the expectations of fund-holders, engage in service development and relate to other purchasers. The role of clinicians was perceived to be central *but* no one could see how they were to find time to play it effectively. Most, if not all, clinicians involved in management were already devoting all of their available management time. How more was to be made available was perceived to be an important dilemma.

9. Linked to this, there is a widely held view that whilst the principle of clinical directorates and the involvement of clinicians in management is sound, the individual clinician often finds the demands of managing the directorate cannot be met within the existing sessional allowance. Conversely the need to, and their own preference to, maintain their clinical work makes providing more time not a valid option. This is clearly recognized as a big dilemma. Many clinicians also felt they had received little or no relevant training in

▶▶

management, some pointing out, however, that clinical and other demands had meant that they had been unable to attend what was provided.

10. There is complete agreement that much more needs to be achieved on information and on budgeting. Too many people either are unclear about budgets, costs and related matters (e.g. what budget is available, what things cost) or believe the available information (whether budget reports or other information) is too 'global', does not provide the right information, *or is wrong*. It is widely recognized that much improvement is already underway but there is a wide measure of cynicism about the present situation. All recognize this as a key constraint to further devolvement and to a flatter corporate structure.

11. It is important to recognize the strong feelings expressed regarding the need for a flatter structure and for a greater clarity of structure, accountability and of roles, job descriptions and so on. Some say HST is overmanaged. Some say it is impossible to find out who to go to in the event of problems affecting patient care. Widely held is the view that people have insufficient resources to deliver patient care. More consultants, more junior doctors, more space were constant comments from many, but this is not the whole of it. Many wish to see quicker decisions, more decisive management, more visible management, more access to top management. All of this is seen as requiring a flatter structure, greater clarity of accountabilities, much improved budgeting and information, improved communication, job descriptions and the like. In particular decision making and professional representation needed review. The UMT was not an effective decision-making body and other medical consultative arrangements would need to be reconstituted. Many recognized that the roles of business development managers and nurse managers were not clearly distinguished in practice and also varied across the clinical directorates. This created unnecessary confusion for some and needed to be resolved. Linked to this are a number of career issues, not least for nursing staff.

12. Turning to corporate structure and management, there was both a measure of agreement and significant controversy. These varying views are therefore set out more fully, as follows:

(a) Of the 118 people interviewed 67 made specific comments regarding the corporate structure. Of the 51 who did not so comment, all had indicated that other changes would lead to improvements at HST, and more than 90 per cent of them were clear that *management changes* were needed, most commonly to clarify roles and accountabilities, to improve communication and to devolve authority throughout the organization.

(b) Of the 67 who made clear comments on the structure 45 argued that the number of *clinical directorates should be rationalized*, most commonly to between four and six. These views we expected alongside other views. Each of the 45 wished to see at least one of the following:
   ● greater clarity of roles and job descriptions starting at board level and throughout the organization;
   ● improved decision making, particularly at the UMT;

- improved professional representation;
- improvement of support to directorates;
- more authority to business managers and/or specialty managers.

Many were clearly concerned, however, that fewer, larger directorates implied changes in the workload of the clinical director which they, as individuals, would not welcome. Some made the point that they did not know whether clinicians would wish to take on the larger management roles implied by a rationalized structure.

(c) The remaining 22 interviewees wished to see *no change to the existing clinical directorate structure*; however, all of these people wished also to see one or more of the changes listed under (b) above. In addition, two stated explicitly that they felt there were too many directorates. Clearly, therefore, whilst there is controversy over whether or not to rationalize the clinical directorate structure there is a strong measure of agreement that significant management and other changes are necessary. It is difficult, therefore, to accept at face value the views expressed by a number of people that a period of stability is needed after so much change and that this is a reason not to rationalize the clinical directorate structure because the people saying this are calling for other changes in any event. It is important, however, to take note of this desire for a period of stability (see below). One commented that he believed in smaller directorates but he noted that the existing directorates were not all working effectively and that there was a need to build up the role of specialty managers. Another indicated that the real constraint to a rationalized directorate structure was split-site working.

(d) Fifty-one of 67, commenting on the structure, proposed that the roles of clinical managers, business managers and nurse managers should be defined and/or standardized across the structure.

(e) Fifteen of those commenting on structure argued that *professional representation should be strengthened*. Most commonly this point was made in relation to medical representation; however, some made it with respect to nurses.

(f) Many interviewees argued either that support services should be devolved, or that greater continuity be achieved (e.g. by nominating finance staff to take responsibility for particular directorates) and/or that service agreements be established.

Conclusions and recommendations

13. The first point to make is that the expressed need for a period of stability is accepted. This will allow consolidation of achievements to date and concentration on the development of the trust and its services/businesses. It follows that to be credible any recommendations must be seen to deal with the relevant issues. Moreover, it must be clear that any changes are fundamental enough to deliver significant improvements along the lines of the management review. Finally any changes should be consistent with, and preferably supportive of, the patient-centred care initiative currently being planned.

14. Secondly, it is clear that any changes should deliver both a clearer, simpler and flatter organizational structure and one which creates career possibilities for employees. In addition it should engage clinicians in the priority work of management in ways which are

▶▶

consistent with the limited time they have available *and* which make the best use of their management time. The two priorities which this review points to are the development of service so as to grow the business over time *and* the achievement of the business plan in any particular year.

15. There seemed to be a clear view that any changes include attention to arrangements for professional representation. It is self-evident that not all professionals can be involved in management and that there are many and often complex professional issues to be dealt with in HST. Professional representation with inputs at board level and operational management level were therefore needed.

16. There was clear agreement that quality assurance and effective information provision were essential whatever changes to management arrangements were to be made. Much progress has been made and is in hand. Any changes need to be carefully and thoroughly planned alongside the planning of change in these two key areas.

17. Overall it is recommended that HST consider, in detail, a rationalized clinical directorate structure which does the following:
(a) Organizes clinical care around four clinical areas each with a clinical chair and an experienced general manager.
(b) Devolves budget responsibility to specialty level.
(c) It is essential that responsibilities be so organized that clinical chairs along with specialty managers can devote sufficient time to managing budgets and developing the business of specialties and the clinical area (requiring attention to clinical/service development and working with clients/potential clients such as GP fundholders).
(d) As part of this the positioning of diagnostic services, theatres and ITU should be considered carefully. Basically these departments provide services to the various specialties. To manage and resource them properly it is essential that the specialties be properly charged for the use of these services.
(e) Any proposal for change needs to be integrated with plans to develop quality assurance and information systems. Responsibilities for operational management quality assurance, information and business management must be clarified at board level. In particular there seems to be a powerful case for a well-defined bed management procedure.
(f) Finally, professional materials management should be considered. Moreover, wage payment arrangements should be integrated within the personnel department to avoid duplication of information. The key here from experience elsewhere is to ensure that the payroll is managed by an experienced and capable payroll manager.

18. The purpose of this report is to present the views of managers and professionals. These are to be worked up into specific proposals to be presented to the board in a separate document. This work is now underway by the executive members of the board supported by the author of this report. The objective is to complete this work by 3 February for presentation to the trust board on 10 February.

Options for change

These options for change were considered by the trust board in the light of the above and in order to achieve the following:

Support a move toward a more devolved patient-focused care organization.
Involve clinicians in priority management tasks.
Simplify the reporting arrangements and structure.
Create effective cost centres.

The five options were as follows:

1. No change.
2. Fine tuning.
3. Create internal market.
4. Create a facilities directorate.
5. Reduce the functional directorates.

Option 3 was the most radical change involving reducing clinical directorates from 11 to four and requires the clinical chairs to contract with an operational services directorate for services (staff, facilities, beds, etc.) allowing them to focus on clinical outputs. However, this required extensive and sophisticated information systems not yet available and assumed a degree of attitude change and contracting skills not likely to be widely available.

Under option 4 the clinical chairs retain control over service inputs except beds which would be controlled by the director of facilities. Under option 5 functional directorates are reduced by merging operational services under the director of operation services, clinical directorates are reduced to five, the fifth being clinical support services. Briefly, a version of option 4 was selected as the basis for change on the grounds that the capabilities for option 3 were not available and could not readily be obtained, whereas options 1, 2 and 5 brought insignificant operational benefits and made no progress toward a more devolved approach to patient-focused care.

Conclusions

There are three main conclusions to draw here:

1. The case deals with changes to a professional service organization in which issues of professional autonomy, public service and managerial/operational effectiveness must be balanced.
2. Given that point, the systematic approach to diagnosis created learning because attitudes were clearly changing as a consequence of the impetus created by the review; thus people who had opposed the streamlining of clinical directorates now came to accept the arguments for such a change, and the inevitability of it. Conversely the board was seen as being prepared to listen to contrary views.
3. Risk analysis always represents a key issue in change decisions. The two key issues in risk analysis are impact and capabilities. What impact will be created where and on whom (which groups) and how will they respond? What capabilities are required either immediately or as a consequence of the impact, and can they be acquired? Is the change feasible, and over what time scale?

Concluding comment

In this chapter we have examined a number of checklists and questionnaires which readers may well find of use in assessing their own organizations. One thing is certain: no single measure of effectiveness is available. We need to adopt a broad-based approach. Readers may also find that they need to add some more specific questions to the various checklists provided here before using them. The next step is to try!

Exercises

1. To what extent could International Engineering be said to be efficient?
2. What are the three or four most important issues which International Engineering must focus on if it is to increase its effectiveness?
3. Critically evaluate the five options presented to Health Service Trust.

CHAPTER 10

Managing major changes

Introduction

So far we have examined how to assess organizational performance and how to design organizations that are structured and managed effectively. We have considered individual, group and organizational issues and problems, and also ways and means of responding to these issues/problems. Various skills have been examined. In this chapter we consider how to manage the process of changing an organization. Here we will find that this demands that we consider the impact of changes on the people affected by them in order to understand how people (managers and employees at all levels!) cope with changes. Moreover, it will be clear that major changes create highly complex 'managing' problems, particularly if the people involved are to learn from the process. Achieving change is one thing – learning from the process of change is an entirely different thing. Yet only if we do so can we sustain effective performance for the long term.

Analyzed simply, we could divide the concern over the management of major changes into two main questions: 'What changes should we implement?' and 'How may we implement them successfully?' To develop answers to these questions requires specific skills: to diagnose the need for change; to audit performance; to develop a vision of improvement; to describe or define new strategy. Achieving change also requires the skill to get things done, to achieve action. It is often disturbing and disruptive. By definition, change upsets the 'status quo'. Leadership is central because to achieve effective organizational change requires us to elevate analysis over consensus. Easy options are in short supply! The consensus view may reflect the lowest common denominator, the view that no one will oppose. It may not be an appropriate view for the future. Implementing major organizational change demands the combination of action and analysis into a new managerial synthesis.

In this and the next two chapters we propose to discuss this new managerial synthesis necessary for effective change. We propose to develop two main themes as follows:

1. What are the managerial skills required for effective organizational change? We will examine a number of key managerial skills.
2. Change is disruptive and disturbing. How do people experience change and how may they be helped to cope with the pressure of major changes?

Managers in all organizations deploy these managerial and coping skills to lesser or greater extents. Our purpose is to identify these two sets of skills so that managers can more effectively identify strengths and weaknesses and, thereby, further develop their capacities to achieve effective organizational change.

In SmithKline Beecham it is clear that 'the simply better way' approach is carefully thought through and relevant. Part of the early learning from the programme has been the role of leadership in energizing a sufficient critical mass of change and commitment to further change that prevents a reversion to past ways of doing things, which contributes to a change in the 'mind-set'. In common with other major corporates, SmithKline Beecham has developed a leadership behavioural role model as a means of defining how it wishes leadership to be displayed and as a development tool and process for the managers involved.

Managerial skills for effective organizational change

To manage change effectively involves the ability to create a new synthesis of people, resources, ideas, opportunities and demands. The manager needs skills rather like those of an orchestral conductor. Vision is essential and creativity paramount. Yet the capacity to create systematic plans to provide for the logistics of resources, support, training and people is central to any change programme. People must be influenced, departmental boundaries crossed or even 'swallowed up', new ideas accepted, new ways of working embraced and new standards of performance and quality achieved. The politics of the organization are crucial. Support must be mobilized, coalitions built and supported, opposition identified and considered. People need help to cope with the stress, anxiety and uncertainties of change. Continuity and tradition must be overturned, in part, as the old is replaced by the new. Yet, continuity and tradition provide people with stability, support and meaning and should not needlessly be destroyed. The effective management of organizational change demands attention to all these somewhat conflicting issues and challenges. So in a period of change, synthesis is the key. In this section we shall deal with the three following skill areas:

1. Managing transitions.
2. Dealing with organizational cultures.
3. The politics of organizational change.

Managing transitions

Company A manufactures a range of engines. It is a wholly owned subsidiary of a US-based multinational corporation. It supplies engines to a small number of end-user companies, each of which incorporates them into its own products. By the 1980s the company was experiencing severe external and internal pressures (see Table 10.1). This is a familiar enough pattern: a cycle of decline creating major challenge for management to find ways of achieving a transition to effectiveness. *The first and most important challenge was to develop an open attitude towards change at all levels.* The company had experienced little or no change in 30 years. Employees were accustomed to stability and managers possessed little or no skill in the management of change. New management at group level, recognizing this company as declining economically, brought in a new top management team, a managing director, engineering director and finance director. The new team moved quickly. The strategy adopted is shown schematically in Table 10.2.

The first step was to test the reality faced by the company and to draw people into this testing process. Employees at all levels needed to understand the problems the

Table 10.1 ● Internal and external pressures in an engine manufacturer

External pressures	Internal pressures
Recession High interest rate Falling orders	Inadequate organizational structures
High energy and material costs	Lack of confidence and fear of change, including the fear of redundancy
New products/materials technology being adopted in engine design and manufacture	Accustomed to slow change (or paralysis)
Increased competition both from abroad and because some end-users were beginning to switch to building their own engines	Limited managerial competence in managing change
	Lack of experience with new technology
Changes at group as a consequence of a change in ownership	Low productivity and quality
	Ageing plant with attendant maintenance problems
	Low morale, high absenteeism and industrial disputes
	Cash flow problems

Table 10.2 ● A strategy for change

Testing reality	New attitudes and structures	Achievements
Threat of closure and redundancy		New technology introduced in manufacturing technology and in materials
Encouraging understanding of the problems	Developing new attitudes to work and to change	
Developing new ideas for the future – new products		
Search for new markets and business (including subcontracting)	Training for new technology and to deal with change	Quality control system introduced
Open negotiation communication	Reorganization and contraction	New products
Full involvement of employees and unions	Investment in new technology	Labour flexibility

company was facing. Beyond this it was essential that people be given the chance to seek out and develop solutions. Thus on the one hand, openness in negotiations and communications with employees meant that the problems were better understood. On the other hand, through involvement of employees and by bringing in new skills (particularly marketing), new ways of doing things were sought. Employees were drawn into solving problems such as quality, absenteeism, factory layout and so on. Project groups from the design, marketing and production departments became involved in seeking new products. People were given the opportunity to try out new ideas, to experiment, to seek solutions. This, then, initiated a process of attitude change. Recognizing the problems and becoming involved in processes aimed at developing solutions led to a more open approach to the idea of change. Initially seeing it as unavoidable, employees began to recognize the possibility that constructive, albeit not painless, action was feasible. In these ways management and employees were facing the challenge identified in Table 10.3 (based upon Argyris and Schon, 1974).

Important in the above was the recognition that involvement of people in examining the problems and seeking to develop solutions was only one part of the approach. Top management involved themselves actively in that process. Moreover, all manner of developments and improvements were discussed in the context of the strategy that management had agreed upon in order to turn the company around. By showing

Table 10.3 ● **Learning from changing: implementing strategic change testing (the problem-solving process)**

	Decision making	
	Restricted (within the management team)	Extensive (involvement of those affected)
Negative	Little learning or change	Anxiety-creating behaviour
Attitudes to change (particularly within top management)		
Positive	Learning and change can occur only if *not* dependent on other people	Learning and change possible

people that new products were being developed, that new markets were being actively sought, that new materials were available, a 'vision of the future' was being established. Within such a context, project groups worked effectively and energetically. Thus began a process which led to some quick and some longer-term results. Attitudes changed over time as part of a process of trial and error, experimentation and success. Only when this process developed was training introduced. This process clearly involved personal and management development. More specific programmes of product, technical and skills training were deployed in support.

Opening up the reality-testing process through involvement merely creates uncertainty and anxiety unless those same people really believe that there is a positive attitude to change among those who will make the final decisions. I well remember discussing a proposed involvement scheme planned by a company which faced declining sales in the middle 1970s. A strategy for change and improvement had been articulated. There seemed no future other than decline unless this strategy was implemented. One employee rejected involvement on the grounds that it meant he would be 'conspiring in his own redundancy' – he could see no point to it. Where managers are clearly determined on change and have good ideas, the implementation of change is obviously feasible. People can also learn from changes implemented without extensive involvement as long as there is general agreement over such changes, and care devoted to training and communication. People will then learn new skills and new systems. But what if an important and influential group of those involved is opposed to the changes? Much will depend on the nature of that group, its power and the nature of its opposition. Its members may be capable of persuasion. Other opportunities might be created for them. However, to the extent that this is not so, to the extent that its members feel coerced, then an outcome combining effective implementation and learning becomes more difficult. But we should not see this as a single event; it is a process. Over a period of time some or all of the members of such a group may come to change their mind. We will turn to how this may be achieved in subsequent chapters; for the moment we merely note the problem.

Significant change involves learning. If reality is tested openly, and if open or constructive attitudes to change prevail, then we are most likely to achieve significant changes. Change is possible without open reality testing but only where people who are excluded from this testing process are not fully engaged in the changes to be implemented. If they are not involved in testing reality, they can neither understand the need for change nor feel committed to the changes, let alone learn from them. Public or extensive testing of reality in a declining situation merely creates anxiety unless a constructive attitude to change prevails, particularly within management. Thus to argue that effective communication is enough, without giving people the opportunity and support to seek solutions to problems, will merely sustain the spiral of decline. In this company the reality-testing process led to new attitudes which themselves both facilitated, and were in turn sustained by, training programmes for new technology, improved maintenance, quality control, by the emergence of new investment and new equipment, and by reorganization (including the formation of a marketing department and the introduction of quality control systems). The spiral of decline was being reversed.

Managing this transition to effectiveness, then, demanded both learning and change, as indicated by the following five criteria:

1. Learning is produced by *exploring dilemmas* or *contradictions* (e.g. improved quality was essential and end-users had to be convinced that they should continue to use company A's product, *but* ageing plant, managerial problems and low morale made this difficult to achieve).

2. Learning is based *upon personal experience and experimentation*. People will only learn if they understand the problems and are brought into the process of seeking solutions.

3. Learning can be encouraged in a climate which *encourages risk taking*, doing things and trying out new ideas.

4. Learning requires the *expression of deeply held beliefs* and will involve conflict. Only then can ideas emerge and be properly assessed before being incorporated into new systems, products, strategies, etc.

5. *Learning can be helped by recognizing the value of people and ideas*, developing learning styles which encourage individuals rather than close off discussion (see Argyris and Schon, 1974).

By 1983, company A had reduced staffing, improved the organizational structure, introduced a quality control system for the first time, achieved labour flexibility and developed new products. The leadership challenge faced successfully in this case was that of achieving change in the ways described, while maintaining the business through very difficult times. 'Selling' the solution to the group and 'buying' time were central to this and part of the politics of change, a matter to which we turn below.

Dealing with organizational culture: a major financial institution

Company B is a large financial institution with hundreds of branches in major towns and cities in its home country. It operates internationally. In recent years it has been very successful, with growth in profitability and turnover. Yet it faces major challenges. Deregulation, new technology, competition and growing complexity of the services it provides, to both private and corporate customers, are among the challenges that it faces. The company is involved in a major programme of branch rationalization. Some branches are being closed, others remodelled to provide either private or corporate services, others are being expanded as key branches. Early on in this programme of change it became clear that the company's property management department needed attention. Its property management performance was poor and outmoded. Its capacity to plan and carry through the branch rationalization programme seemed doubtful.

Property management was the responsibility of a central department employing 250 professional staff, mainly architects and surveyors, managed by a general manager. The general manager was drawn from the senior management team on a 2 year posting. All general managers at that time had mainstream finance backgrounds. Indeed, the culture of company B powerfully sustained the belief that the *only* important work was finance. All other work, whether property, computing or marketing, was secondary. Career paths for non-finance people were limited, departments being managed by people with finance backgrounds. The extent to which non-finance staff were undervalued may be seen by noting that in the property management department no one could remember anyone having any training and development since the day of their appointment. The morale of the property management department was low and the level of interdepartmental conflict (between the surveyors' group and the architects' group) was very high.

The company was organized into 12 regions, each managed by a regional director. Property management at regional level was uncoordinated. Regional directors took many of the decisions without being properly or formally accountable. Refurbishment decisions were under regional directors' control yet the costs of refurbishment were a charge on a head office account, and were not on the region's books. Moreover, the lack of co-operation between architects and surveyors diffused any professional input into property decisions taken at regional level.

The organizational culture

Company B typifies the *role culture*[1] under significant external and internal pressures. Often stereotyped as bureaucracy, this culture is characterized by stability, prescription, rules and standards. Functional departments are clearly specified. This can be a very efficient culture in stable environments. Role cultures emphasize high levels of commitment by individuals, either to a department or, in a professional role culture, to a particular profession. In this culture, position power is a predominant form of power. But in this case, the stability of the 1960s and 1970s had been replaced by the

---

[1] The terms role culture, task culture and power culture are taken from Charles Handy (see Handy, 1984).

turbulence of the 1980s. Property management expertise was now essential if the branch rationalization programme was to proceed.

To detail briefly the organizational changes decided upon, a property management professional was brought in to take charge and develop a modern property management strategy. This was only the second time in the history of company B that a non-finance manager had been appointed to this level and the first time such an appointment had been made from outside. Under his control property management was decentralized to regional teams, managed by regional managers. Small teams, closer to the regions, would be more likely to develop improved working relationships both within teams and between the property management team and region. Training and development was initiated for the professional staff. A career path was now opening up for them. All this was moving property management towards a *task culture*. Here, influence is based on expertise, i.e. the expertise needed to carry out the task. Teams of people work together to achieve objectives and tasks. This culture places demands upon people but it also provides for the merging of individual and organizational objectives in changing circumstances. It is an adaptable culture in which the needs of the task, rather than systems and procedures, predominate. In this case, architects and surveyors now work together more closely and manage the regional teams. For professional purposes there is a professional development role played by a deputy general manager in the now small head office property management function. Arguably, company B has moved towards a culture that is more appropriate to the challenge that it faces.

Organizational issues which must be faced if more adaptable organizational cultures are to be achieved are outlined by the following criteria:

1. *Management autonomy*, particularly with regard to reward systems: to what extent should local management have the ability to make decisions about gradings and salary dependent on market conditions and personal performance?

2. *Interchangeability*: movement across specialist/professional boundaries by internal promotions, fixed-term secondments, or short training periods would help to develop broader knowledge and experience. To what extent should promotion depend upon diversity of experience? Moves of this kind can sustain task forces or project teams. It can also reinforce individual autonomy, creativity and knowledge.

3. *Openness or public testing* of issues and problems would also be aided by interchangeability.

4. *Recent developments in management information systems* seem likely to bring about systems which managers can interrogate! This will aid *communication* partly through the *access* so provided, partly by the prospect of simplification of procedures and paperwork that such developments promise.

5. *Functional and professional advice* can be provided to a more local level utilizing task-team approaches such as that described briefly in the case where professional development, planning and control are centrally organized. The focus should be on *business needs* rather than on professional demands.

Other organizational cultures have been identified. The *power culture* is worth a moment's thought. It is frequently found in small, growing companies, including property and finance. These organizations are highly dependent on one or more strong leaders. Control is exercised from the centre and decisions are largely made on the outcome of a balance of influence rather than on rational grounds (which the uncertainties of our changing world will rarely allow in any event). An organization with this culture can react well to change but the quality of its top people is crucial. Individuals who are power orientated, risk taking and politically skilled will do well in this culture wherein accountability is personal and direct.

Managing in different cultures

One final thought on culture: we have discussed the links between organizational culture, the tasks to be performed and the rate of environmental change, but culture is a broader part of our affairs. At home and abroad we often find ourselves working with people from different occupational, local and national cultures. Effective management thus demands the capacity to deal with cross-cultural issues and influences. The important skill here is that of *empathy*. Managing change involves the need to influence people. Empathy, sensitivity to cultural differences, and the struggle to understand them and to communicate in an intelligible fashion are essential.

The property management professional brought this skill to bear in his work with the professional staff involved in the change process described above. While these boundaries cannot easily be crossed, people responded to the attempt, and change programmes were all the more feasible and relevant for a leavening of the cultural sensitivity. This skill will be discussed further in Chapter 10, which deals with coping with change.

The key issue of organizational culture emerges clearly. To achieve a more effective, professional, yet adaptable, property management department it is necessary to move towards a task culture. This demands openness, learning, good communication and the recognition of people's needs. Relating this to business needs is also important in order to give a clear sense of objectives and contribution.

Implementation

The important thing about the implementation of the above change is that it was carried out in two phases. Full consultation was undertaken over the issue of assigning people to regional teams. No one was given any guarantees, but all were asked to indicate preferences. For most people relocation was involved. Various factors had to be considered in creating teams: the correct mix of skills and people, regional team managers designate, as well as people's preferences for particular teams (and, therefore, particular parts of the country) were all relevant. What this consultation phase allowed was a careful explanation of the proposed changes such that people understood what was involved. The second phase was actually to form the regional teams. Originally, this was to be done gradually when office space was available in the various regions.

In the event, the teams were formed at head office, overnight! Doing it quickly had the advantage of creating a clear break with the past. Also, it meant that the teams could form and settle down in the secure head office environment. Relocation could then be more effectively handled by the regional team. The process took 3 to 5 weeks to settle down. Over the year the regional teams were all well established in the regions. Regional directors who originally had said that no space would be available for 2 years now seemed to jump at the chance of getting the new cohesive and more effective regional property management teams in their regions. The management of change is often a matter of the management of image. Create the image of success and it is surprising how quickly stereotyped attitudes can be changed.

The politics of organizational change

To understand how organizations are managed, experienced and changed we need to understand the politics of organization. This has become a widely accepted view. (Pettigrew, 1973, 1985; Pfeffer, 1981; Lawler and Bachrach, 1986 – all develop this view.) Moreover, the work of Child (1984) and Hickson *et al.* (1986) elaborates the importance of politics within a contingency theory framework. Organizational structures, technologies, decisions and outcomes are not given but rather are contingent on factors such as the environment (whether or not it is complex and changing, for example). Strategic choice is available. The contingencies limit or constrain; they do not determine. Thus it is that managers may *choose* how to operate, and choice creates the conditions for politics because people will support different views regarding these choices.

One fairly straightforward approach is to focus on the so-called 'dominant coalition'. Senior executives of an organization within such a group may have considerable influence over decisions, the use of resources and other changes. They create rules, policies, standards of performance and procedures which 'channel' employee behaviour. Major decisions on growth products, redundancy and restructuring are made at this level. But we must beware the assumption that 'dominant coalitions' provide a structure to an organization's political process. Coalitions are shifting. Membership varies over time. The concerns which people deem important also vary. To suggest that 'dominant coalitions' are formed and sustained, and then dominate decision making and action, trivializes the problem of understanding organizational politics.

Lee and Lawrence (1985) suggest that over and above '"dominant coalitions" and "strategic choice" we must study … the political situation and political activity, and accept that there will be many interest groups influencing structure … as they push towards their own goals'. Whether they prefer a pluralist view (seeing interest groups of equivalent power) is not clear. They suggest the adoption of a 'radical' view. Such a 'radical' view involves making no assumptions that organizations have goals, over which that management have the right to decide. Moreover, no interest group has any a priori rights, although Lee and Lawrence accept that interest groups might be assumed to have such rights, either by themselves, or by others. No set of values is judged as either 'right' or 'wrong'. One is tempted to add that if we suggest that people assume that organizations do have goals, and act accordingly, then the confusion created by these definitions becomes almost complete!

Individual behaviour is viewed as the impetus to all organized activity and emerges from the pursuit of personal interests and goals. Individual behaviour, they say, is essentially active and rational rather than passive, irrational or emotional. Conflict is the very stuff of organizational life. This seems overly simplistic. The distinction between the rational and the irrational has been replaced by the notion of 'multiple rationalities' (see Weick, 1969). Rationality is in the eye of the beholder. While there is much conflict in organizations, all have experienced situations where the absence of conflict is even more worthy of attention. As Lukes (1974) has made clear, one form of power is that of limiting the 'political' agenda such that particular issues or choices are not recognized as being important and are therefore precluded from consideration.

The world of organizational politics is characterized by structures of interests, goals, power and status which are inherently unstable. This does not mean that a given political order (e.g. the power of a dominant coalition) will be overturned. Rather, it seems likely that in a world of changing markets, technology, social ties, population, values and beliefs and politics, the political order in an organization will be necessarily unstable. To understand behaviour in organizations we must understand how that order is sustained or overturned. This may have less to do with the ebb and flow of individual goals and interests at the microlevel and more to do with how a particular organization's problems (say, in a declining market) are conceived, discussed and assessed. This means trying to understand how such a problem is approached through analysis, discussion, the production of reports and papers, and so on. Accountants, engineers, marketing and production personnel will be involved. Thus, different professional perspectives will be employed. The emergence of an approach, whether to develop new markets, disinvest, launch new products, seek a higher market share, or whatever, does not flow solely from the 'facts' but, rather, from a process in which professional, departmental and individual perspectives, attitudes and interests are involved. Pettigrew (1985) argues for just such an approach. Interest groups have different goals, time scales, values and problem-solving styles. Different interest groups have different rationalities. Change processes in organizations may be understood in part as the outcome of processes of competition between these rationalities expressed through the language, priorities and values of technologists, of accounting and finance, or from the perspectives of groups such as operational research, organizational development or personnel.

Proper study of organizational politics involves the examination of political process, activity and skill, and the study of what we refer to as 'professional rationality'. There we depart somewhat from Pettigrew. For us the interest is on professional rationality, being the language which represents the professional technique (whether engineering, accounting, personnel or operational research). It is somewhat simplistic to equate interest groups with professional groups. In our view the professional can be compelled to support one view of a problem through use of the rationality into which he or she has been professionally socialized and yet, individually, may experience feelings which impel him or her to a different view. As we shall argue later, changes in professional technique emerge when the tensions so created lead individual professionals to question their roles. An accountant can thus be aligned with engineers, personnel specialists and others who form an interest group supporting a particular project. Rationality emerges from professional technique, not simply from the emergence of interest groups; the latter are altogether too unstable. Interest groups form around specific interests regarding policies, practices, power, status and authority. Rationality comprises a means of dealing with the circumstances of a particular professional practice and ways of articulating and legitimizing that practice.

Managing change

To understand how organizations are managed, experienced and changed we need to understand their politics. In turn, this involves the examination of political process, activity and skill. Why is the use of power and politics a necessary part of managing change? Partly this is because of the departures from accepted norms:

> Innovative accomplishments stretch beyond the established definition of a 'job' to bring new learning or capacity to the organisation. They involve change, a disruption of existing activities, a redirection of organisational energies.
>
> (Kanter, 1983, p. 21)

Of course this is right, but the impetus to the use of power runs deeper. Any significant organizational change demands that existing ways of thinking about and talking about what we do can be overturned. Dominant views must be usurped. Experience tells us that the first attempt to articulate an alternative view, a novel concept, will frequently fall on barren ground. It will probably meet opposition and even outright rejection. To overcome such opposition or rejection, neither logic nor evidence, nor the participation of all concerned, appears to be enough. New ideas can seem unorthodox and even risky. A manager seeking support for new ideas must be sensitive to political processes.

Kodak, once the dominant player in photographic film, saw competitors take significant market share and through the late 1980s and early 1990s the company went through repeated restructuring, losing 40,000 jobs. Whilst substantial refocusing has been achieved, much turns on the success of digital imaging. A crucial issue is how to achieve the ability to adapt continuously in rapidly changing circumstances. Part of this has been about the realignment of resources away from functions towards customers. Cross-functional teams are seen as a vital building block of change strategy and the teams (some of which include customers) become the focus for organizational learning. Not least Kodak uses bench-marking to build unit goals which it uses to seek improvements within which cross-functional teams operate. This is based on the need for flat structures, more capable people, enhanced collaboration, evidence-based management, customer focus and increased energy and commitment.

Coping with organizational change

Thus far we have considered some of the managerial skills associated with the effective management of change. We now proceed to consider the impact of change upon the people directly affected, which will often include many middle and senior managers. We are concerned here with the people who must take on new tasks, develop new skills, be transferred, regraded or retrained. Once changes emerge, people must learn to cope as individuals. We will describe a simple model of how people experience change and, below, we will consider the model in more detail and examine how they can cope with the pressures created by change. Understanding this can enable senior managers to provide practical support to people undergoing change and may better enable them to avoid creating constraints on people, which makes their personal task of coping all the harder.

Coping with the process of change places demands on the individuals involved. Various issues need to be faced either by the individuals or by managers. Note, however, that these issues are of concern to all those who are affected by an organizational change, including managers. We will set down a practical framework for coping with change below, based upon ideas from various workers in the field, including Cooper (1981), Argyris (1982), Kirkpatrick (1985), Kanter (1983), and my own experience. Many managers I know arrange 2 hour workshops in groups of 10 to 12 people in which the participants are asked to discuss and then report back on those issues that they feel are important in a period of change. This can be a powerful method, facilitating a more knowledgeable and constructive approach to a major change, and it can lead to useful ideas. I also remember talking these ideas over with a senior manager in a diversified group who had introduced computerized photocomposition for a newspaper company in the early 1970s. The company had allowed the typesetters to try out the visual display units in a test room but *not* in a training environment. Providing support, they avoided any sense of formal training and were surprised to find that, allowed to learn at their own pace, the typesetters embraced the technology enthusiastically and quickly. This is important; giving people the chance, the time and the support to try things out for themselves is a way of allowing them to build their self-esteem under their own control *and* to solve the problem of change along the way. Only then does formal training have a really effective role as a means of ensuring consistent performance, disseminating best practices and so on. While it is often said that not enough training is done, it is too easy to be beguiled into introducing formal training programmes too early.

Rebuilding self-esteem

The ground covered in this section is summarized in Figure 10.1. Simplifying somewhat, we suggest that individuals have four main categories of need if they are to rebuild their self-esteem amidst a programme of organizational change. They need *intelligible information*. They will probably need to develop *new skills*, if only the skills of dealing with new people as colleagues or supervisors. They will need *support* to help them to deal with the problems. Encouragement to try out new systems is important. Provision of short workshops planned to achieve part or all of the work discussed in the preceding section can help. Technical support to aid solution of problems is often

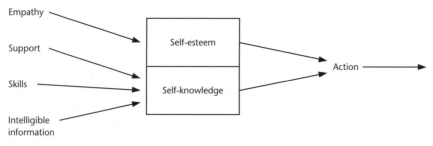

Figure 10.1 Rebuilding self-esteem

needed. Access to people who can help is useful. Control over the rate of personal learning should be possible. All these things can help. First and foremost, *empathy* (understanding) is a key issue, and Kirkpatrick (1985) rightly sees it as one of the key skills for managing change. Pierre Casse (1979) defines empathy as follows:

> Empathy is the ability to see and understand how other people construct reality, or more specifically how they perceive, discover and invest the inner and outer worlds. We all use empathy all the time. We constantly guess what people think and feel. The problem is that in most cases we guess wrongly. We assume that what is going on in somebody else's mind is somewhat identical to our own psychic processes. We tend to forget that we are different. Sometimes, drastically different. To practice empathy is to recognize and take full advantage of those differences.
>
> (Pierre Casse, 1979)

We see the skill of empathy as the struggle to understand. We can never fully see a situation as others see it. But we can struggle to try and individuals will respond to that struggle. They will also respond to someone who clearly does not try. Generally their response will be to ignore them if possible, to resist them and certainly to approach dealings with them cynically. Making information intelligible to its recipient requires these skills. We need to try to see things as the recipient will see them, in order to communicate. Often we do not try; we pass on the information we have. Usually we do so without attempting to make it intelligible, if we pass it on at all!

Thus far in this chapter we have discussed ways and means of introducing major changes effectively. Here we wish to stress one crucial point. Effective organizations are those which introduce change quickly and in which people – employees and managers – learn about the business or organization as this process proceeds. Achieving change without learning is possible, but sometimes not without struggle, if powerful groups oppose. Introducing change in ways which do not encourage learning is likely in the future to entrench negative attitudes to change. Only if people and organizations change, by learning from the experience of change, can effectiveness be achieved and sustained. We have attempted to draw together a range of ideas and practical steps to help people manage change effectively.

All these ideas and steps need to be integrated for effectiveness. Only if we manage transitions effectively can learning and change occur. This also acts as a constructive constraint on the politics of change which can so easily run out of control. Moreover, managing change effectively reduces anxiety and helps those individuals who find change stressful to cope with it. This in turn leads to a more positive attitude to change. Thus it is that we come full circle. If these ideas are synthesized in a managerial approach to organizational change, then there would seem to be a better prospect of success and effectiveness. Difficult and demanding in practice, we offer these ideas as the basis of how managers are able to see changes through. In Figure 10.2 we summarize the ideas presented here. The key point is that only by synthesizing the management of transition, dealing with organizational cultures and handling organizational politics constructively, can we create the environment in which creativity, risk taking, learning and the rebuilding of self-esteem and performance can be achieved. If we can sustain such a synthesis, then learning and change can follow. More important, because people have learned about the business through the process

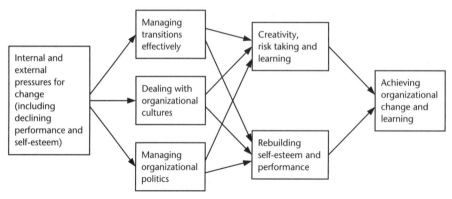

Figure 10.2 Managing major changes

of changing, the organization probably becomes more effective. By creating the conditions for extensive problem solving and positive attitudes to change, future effectiveness is created.

Coping with change

So far we have reviewed some of the processes by which people come to decide upon a new strategy, a new product, a new organizational structure, to close down a factory, and so on. What then? The easy answer is to say that the changes must be implemented; the resources must be obtained, the constraints considered and dealt with in one way or another. To say this is really to see the problem of organizational change from the perspective of those concerned in its introduction.

Now we consider the process of implementation of change from the perspective of those who are directly affected: the people who must take on new tasks, develop new skills, be transferred, regraded and retrained. Here, then, we refer to middle managers and other employees. Whether or not they participated in the planning, once the changes take concrete form they must learn to cope with them. Our concern is to describe a simple model of how people experience change as a precursor to considering how people come to cope with the pressures created by change. Better understanding of these processes will enable senior managers who implement change to develop a richer understanding of the issues they must face. Thus they will be better able to provide help and support for the people concerned and, perhaps more importantly, avoid creating constraints on the people involved which makes their personal task of coping with change more difficult. We start from the assumption that the individual concerned must be the prime mover if change is to be assimilated and if adaptation is to occur.

Often, the problems of implementing change are discussed largely as if 'resistance to change' is the main concern. In this chapter we see that the situation is, firstly, more complex than this and, secondly, is capable of much more positive or optimistic construction. Indeed, it is often possible to encourage 'resistance to change' by dealing with people as if that is the only response one expects! We have discussed various responses to change in an earlier chapter when our focus was upon planning and implementation of change. Now we pick up the threads of this argument in order to consider the practical and positive steps which can be taken to support people as *they* cope with change.

Change creates anxiety, uncertainty and stress, even for those managing change, and even if they are fully committed to change. Seldom are there any guarantees that the new approach will work, will deliver the goods! Those who wish the change to be successful often find themselves working long hours, dealing with problems, trying to overcome the doubts of others and doing everything needed to see the changes through. In working life, change and role strain are two important sources of stress. Role strain can be caused by not being involved in decisions, having inadequate managerial support, having to cope with technological or other changes, having to maintain standards of performance even under difficult circumstances, having responsibility for people who are uncooperative – all likely in a period of change! In non-working life 'moving home' is a key source of stress and this sometimes flows from change. Thus we should not be surprised by the links between change and stress.

One simple and helpful idea for managers dealing with change involves looking at the relationship between self-esteem, performance and stress. This is shown in Figure 10.3. The relationship turns out to apply to both performance *and* self-esteem. The problem is that people are different!

We do not all fit neatly onto the one curve. However, the general nature of the relationship seems to hold. In any event, if change causes stress we cannot be at the left-hand end of the diagram. We must be moving in the direction shown in Figure 10.4 and therefore down the curve. Is there a threshold beyond which behaviour becomes volatile and unpredictable? In fact, people respond differently. Some stress motivates people by providing challenge. But we need to avoid stressing ourselves and others overmuch; it can lead to people feeling 'swamped'.

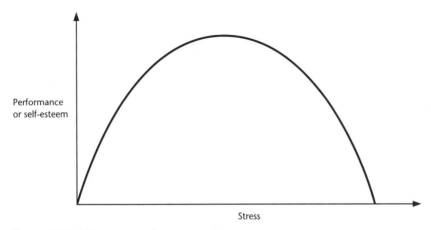

Figure 10.3 Self-esteem, performance and stress

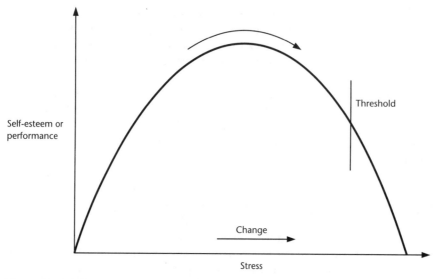

Figure 10.4 Self-esteem, performance, stress and change

The coping cycle

Changes which have a significant impact on the work that people do will have a significant impact on their self-esteem. So much is well established (see Cooper, 1981; de Vries and Miller, 1984; Kirkpatrick, 1985). Linked to this impact on self-esteem will be an impact on performance. We suggest that performance will be affected in three ways, as follows.

The new systems, processes, structures, etc., will have to be learned. This takes time. There is a *learning-curve effect* as people build their performance up through learning. There is also a *progress effect* as the new system is commissioned, the snags ironed out and modifications introduced to enable performance to be improved. I remember being invited to a large new factory in Scandinavia 'to see our new robots'. There were 27 of them and on the day of the visit only six were working. In some cases this was because the staff involved had not yet learned to program or maintain them; in others it was because the robot had proved incapable of meeting the task requirements without modification. Thus, while learning-curve and progress effects are interrelated they are, however, quite different in origin. New systems never work 100 per cent to specification first time! And if the specification is wrong … !

In addition to these performance effects there is also the *self-esteem effect*. We suggest the significant organizational changes create a decline in self-esteem for many of those who are directly affected. This decline has an impact on performance. The link between satisfaction, feelings of well-being, self-esteem and performance has been the subject of much research. Lawler (1978) and Steers and Porter (1979) present excellent reviews of much of this work. Whatever the causal mechanisms involved and whatever the direction of the relationship there does seem to be a clear link, albeit a small one.

Combine the suggested self-esteem effect with the learning-curve effect and the progress effect and we get a significant potential effect on performance. All the effects are interrelated. We propose that the driving force for rebuilding performance subsequent to a major change will be the rebuilding of self-esteem. However, as we shall see, this can be helped by action on the learning-curve and progress fronts. We summarize this discussion with a simple model based upon the work of de Vries and Miller (1984) and Adams *et al.* (1976). In the model we propose five main stages. These are capable of more detailed analysis but for both practical and pedagogic purposes we have presented a simplified model. The model is shown in Figure 10.5.

Stage 1: denial

When significant changes are first mooted the initial response may be to deny the need for change: 'We have always done things this way.' 'Why change, we are making a profit, aren't we?' 'Don't change a winning team.' 'We tried that before but it did not work.' 'You will never make it work.' Faced with the possibility of changes, people will often find value in their present circumstances, often in work situations which they would bitterly complain about at other times. That this is paradoxical should not surprise us. Our actions are impelled by complex and often contradictory motivations. Thus miners threatened with the closure of their pit can defend their pit and jobs with vigour, yet still believe fervently that working conditions are dangerous or arduous. If major organizational changes come suddenly and dramatically, then paralysis can often result. Adams *et al.* (1976) refer to a kind of immobilization or a sense of being overwhelmed, of being unable to reason, to plan, or even to understand what is going on. For the individual, a suddenly announced redundancy can have such an impact, but there is often a longish period of gestation as ideas are discussed and the changes

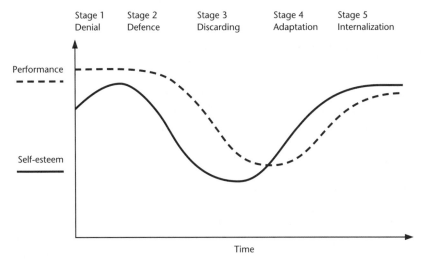

Figure 10.5 The coping cycle

are planned. If the changes are not particularly new or dramatic and if there are obvious opportunities for people, then this paralysis is felt less intensely. The tendency to deny the validity of new ideas, at least initially, does seem to be a general reaction, however. Built into this is the likelihood that self-esteem actually increases in this first stage. The advantages of the present job are emphasized, attachments to the job, the work group and valued skills are recognized. The sense of being a member of a group subject to external threat can lead to increased group cohesiveness. All this may lead to increased self-esteem. A sense of euphoria can develop. We have shown performance to be stable, however. If self-esteem does increase we would guess that performance would not improve, either because the discussion of impending change can absorb energy or because often there are systems in place which may hold back performance improvement (payment systems, for example). If the change is dramatic, novel and traumatic (say, involving a sudden job change or redundancy), then this stage can involve an immediate decline in performance. Generally, however, there is a warning period and performance will not decline immediately. One way of handling the stage is to minimize the immediate impact of the change. This allows people time to face up to a new reality.

Stage 2: defence

Reality obtrudes, however. The early discussion of changes leads to concrete plans and programmes of change. Now the realities of change become clearer and people must begin to face new tasks, working for a new boss or with a different group of people, perhaps in a different department or a new location. Thus they become aware that they must come to terms with the way in which they work, and perhaps with more general changes in life (if, for example, relocation involving a house move is required). This can lead to feelings of depression and frustration because it can be difficult to decide how to deal with these changes. This stage is often characterized by defensive behaviour. People may attempt to defend their own job, their own territory. Often this will be articulated as ritualistic behaviour. I can remember the introduction of computer-aided learning in business schools many years ago. Many embraced these ideas enthusiastically; many simply rejected them: 'My subject is unsuitable.' One colleague provided an impressive show of activity on the computer, finally concluding that after much effort he had failed to make computer-aided learning work for that subject. Years later, computer-aided learning in that subject is commonplace. Was this a ritual? Again, this defensive behaviour seems to have the effect of creating time and 'space' to allow people to come to terms with the changes.

Stage 3: discarding

There now emerges a process of discarding. The preceding stages have focused powerfully on the past. Now people begin to let go of the past and look forward to the future. We do not know how this happens. We know that support can be helpful, as can providing people with the opportunity to experiment with new systems without the pressure of formal training programmes, and so on. Now it is possible for optimistic feelings to emerge. It may well be that the discarding process is impelled by an awakening sense that the present anxieties are just too much to bear, or that perhaps the future is not as forbidding as it first seemed. Now we may observe behaviour which appears to identify the individual with the changes involved, who will start to talk openly and constructively about the new system, who will ask questions about it, who in a sense will say: 'Well here it is – we are committed to it – here's how I see it.' People may begin to solve problems, take the initiative and even demonstrate some leadership. Thus it is that self-esteem improves.

Discarding is initially a process of perception. People come to see that the change is both inevitable and/or necessary. It becomes apparent to them. Adaptation starts with recognition. Here we see human courage amidst difficult circumstances as the individual accepts new 'realities'. This can be exciting for individuals and groups. Taking the risks of publicly facing a new reality there is a sense in which they re-establish their own identity, the identity which may have seemed threatened by the changes being introduced. Thus it is that self-esteem begins to flow back like the returning tide.

The crisis of change creates great tensions for those involved; this much we have seen. It creates a plethora of reasons for people to feel upset and disorientated. The new job we have been assigned to appears to be of lesser status, valued skills seem unnecessary, the new work appears to be frustrating. The new system or machine appears to be unusual, even frightening, although with practice it becomes commonplace. The crucial point is that this process needs time. Discarding involves experimenting and risk. Time is needed for individuals to recreate their own sense of identity and self-esteem as they 'grow' into the new situation.

Stage 4: adaptation

Now a process of mutual adaptation emerges. Rarely do new systems, procedures, structures or machines work effectively first time. Individuals begin to test the new situation and themselves, trying out new behaviours, working to different standards, working out ways of coping with the changes. Thus the individual learns. Other individuals also adapt. Fellow workers, supervisors and managers all learn as the new system is tried out. Finally, technical and operational problems are identified and modifications made to deal with them; thus progress is made.

Significant amounts of energy are involved here. The process of trial and error, of effort and setback, and the slow building of performance, can often be a source of real frustration. In these circumstances people can evince anger. This is not resistance to change; rather, it is the natural consequence of trying to make a new system work, experiencing partial (or complete) failure which may or may not be under the control of the individuals concerned. This anger does not result in attempts to oppose but, rather, articulates the feelings of those trying to make the new system work. While managers should ensure that the right training and support is available, we argue that they should generally remain in the background, allowing the people who are directly involved to make it work. By doing so, these people will develop the skills, understanding and attachments needed for the system to be run effectively in the longer term.

Stage 5: internalization

Now the people involved have created a new system, process and organization. New relationships between people and processes have been tried, modified and accepted. These now become incorporated into an understanding of the new work situation. This is a cognitive process through which people make sense of what has happened. Now the new behaviour becomes part of 'normal' behaviour.

It appears that people experience change in these ways, initially as disturbance, perhaps even as a shock, then coming to accept its reality – testing it out and engaging in a process of mutual adaptation and finally coming to terms with the change. Self-esteem and performance vary, initially declining and then growing again. The variation of performance flows from mutually reinforcing individual and operational causes, as we have seen. The 'engine' for rebuilding performance is the self-esteem of the people involved. (Note here that we talk of relative levels – notional performance might be improved tenfold as a consequence of new technology – the problems we have discussed may mean that in the early stages following the introduction of the new technology only 60 per cent of notional performance is achieved. While this means that 40 per cent is being lost, it does represent a sixfold improvement!) Finally, we do not suggest that people go through these stages neatly, or that all go through them at the same time or at the same rate. Some may not go beyond the denial of change.

The important point is that people do seem to experience significant changes in these ways *and* that this leads to a number of practical ways in which the problems of coping can be handled.

Coping with the process of change

Coping with the process of change places demands on the individuals involved; various issues need to be faced either by these individuals or by their managers. Note, however, that these issues are of concern to all affected by an organizational change, including managers. In the following pages we will set down a simple framework of coping with change, identifying issues to be faced.

Coping with change: issues to be faced

Know yourself

Issues

Would I have chosen this to have happened? Do I accept it? Can I benefit from the changes? What is the worst that can happen to me?

Discussion

Here we are concerned with feelings about the changes to be introduced. In particular, we are concerned with the question of the worst that can happen to the individual. This might be the loss of a job. Alternatively, it might be a transfer to a new job or new department. Or it might mean taking on new skills. It is often difficult for managers to provide this kind of detailed information (see the section on information below). However, it is often possible to provide some level of guarantee at an early stage. Doing so sets boundaries on the problems for the individuals concerned. It provides them with vital data as they try to make sense of how the changes will affect them *and* how they feel about it.

Issues

Do I know what I want? Do I know what I don't want?

Discussion

These are difficult questions to face. How many of us have clear answers to them? Yet answering them (even if only in a tentative way) is essential if we are to come to terms with changes. In essence, individuals can be encouraged to think about these questions through using diagnostic techniques of various kinds. A good example would be the job diagnostic survey (see Hackman and Oldham, 1976), which aims to obtain information about how people react to different jobs, including their present jobs and jobs they might prefer. The approach involves examining responses in terms of issues such as various job characteristics (skill variety, task identity, task significance, autonomy, feedback, dealing with others), experienced psychological states (experienced meaningfulness of work, experienced responsibility for work, knowledge of results) and affective outcomes (satisfaction, internal work motivation and growth satisfaction). An approach of this kind can be used, perhaps as part of a workshop activity (see below), to encourage people to think about their present job and the demands it places on them, their own preferences and the jobs likely to result from the changes. This could allow them to examine work design problems, and could both provide solutions of value and be a process through which individuals begin to think about the new situation in a constructive fashion.

Issues

What skills and abilities do I possess? How might I develop new skills?

Discussion

This issue emerges directly from the preceding one. If we can begin to answer questions about the kind of job we want, then we can go on to consider the skills and abilities we possess and view them in the light of the changes to be introduced. How relevant will they be? What new skills are needed? Can I develop such skills? Can such development be seen as an evolution from my present skills? For example, if we consider the case of a typist being introduced to word processors it is clear that some of the existing skills (keyboard skills, layout skills, language usage) will be transferable and some new skills will be needed. Again these issues can be examined by utilizing an instrument such as the job diagnostic survey and approaches more directly concerned with skills analysis (see Carnall, 1976).

Issues

Have I experienced similar changes? How did I cope? Can I take the initiative?

Discussion

Many people have undergone many changes either at work or in their personal lives. What can they learn from those past experiences? What ways did they use to cope with the changes? How long did it take them to resolve issues and make the personal adaptations necessary? Facing questions like these helps us set the present changes in a broader life context. It also enables us to develop ideas about coping with those present changes or of where we need help to do so.

Issues

Can I cope with stress? Am I able to handle conflict? Can I avoid conflict? How well do I manage my time? Do I blame myself?

Discussion

We have already seen that stress is a necessary part of organizational change. Similarly in the chapter on the politics of change we saw that conflict was a necessary part of change. We need to develop means of dealing with these linked phenomena. In particular, we need to examine how we respond to conflict and whether we are able to minimize or deal with it. Conflict is likely to increase the level of stress that we experience. Can we limit its impact? Perhaps more important, we must face the issue of self-blame. Individuals undergoing changes which appear to make their skills or experience unnecessary will often blame themselves: 'This proves that I am no use.' 'I have been put on the scrap heap.' People say these sorts of things when blaming themselves. If change undermines self-esteem, self-blame merely reinforces that situation. People should be encouraged to face this issue. Do I blame myself? Do I feel useless, paralyzed, confused? Can I begin to deal with those feelings? What can I do to overcome them? Will working out a new role in the new situation allow me to do so? Self-blame in these circumstances seems to be unavoidable; making it explicit can be helpful.

Issues

Do I take stock of my situation? Am I prepared to reflect on myself and how I feel about change? Do I expect others (perhaps managers or union representatives) to deal with these issues?

Discussion

Do I respond to change as an independent person or do I allow myself to be dependent upon others? What do I define as my responsibilities? We noted earlier that discarding the past had an important element of risk and personal growth attached to it. People handle crises in their non-working lives (divorce, bereavement, and so on). There is no reason to suppose that they cannot do so in their working lives.

Know your situation

Issues

Can I describe the situation? Can I explain the new system? For my own work area? For the department as a whole? Can I explain why the changes are necessary?

Discussion

If one does not understand the changes to be introduced, one is in no position to come to terms with them as an individual. There is no better test of understanding than the task of explaining to another. If people cannot understand the changes, then this implies a failure to communicate them effectively. While managers often say that they have described the changes to their employees it may be that they have not done so in a manner which those people find intelligible. This means describing it in the listener's own terms, which does not necessarily mean describing it in a lower or simplified form; rather, it means in a relevant form. Kirkpatrick (1985) provides us with a useful approach to this problem focusing upon barriers to communication created by the sender and through the receiver emphasizing that feedback is important if effectiveness in communication is to be ensured. In fact, using these coping with change ideas as the basis for short workshops can provide for more effective communication about changes.

Issues

Do I know how I am expected to behave? What standards of performance will be required? Who will I work with? Who will I report to? Who will I be responsible for?

Discussion

If I do not understand the new situation, I am unlikely to be able to deal with these questions. Yet if people are to adapt they need to be able to answer them. These questions are really the behavioural element of the questions raised under the last section. They also begin the process of establishing precisely what others expect of us in the new situation.

Issues

Can I try out the new system in advance? Is it possible for me to experiment with the new system? To learn by trial and error?

Discussion

Coming to terms with new systems takes time, requires experiment and risk and involves learning. Very often, the first time that many people face a new system is either on a training course or when the system is installed. Both situations create expectations which can mitigate against risk. Often, training programmes, unless sensitively handled, involve comparisons between people. No one welcomes feeling stupid or ineffective in front of others. If we are trained to handle a new system we may feel that we cannot control our own learning because we are holding back the group, or because the trainer has so much ground to cover and we feel we cannot or should not hold things up. Trying out new systems for ourselves and by ourselves allows us to familiarize ourselves with the system at our own rate. We can begin to come to terms with new systems if our first attempts are not organized in such a way as to make us feel that we are being evaluated. I (the author) once discussed this point with a senior manager from a newspaper group which had introduced computerized printing technology. In doing so the company had bought a number of workstations long before they were needed for production purposes.

These workstations were placed in a room which operators were allowed to use at any time and unsupervised. Instruction was available but was delivered at the rate that the operator wished and not to a predetermined training plan. Thus the operators controlled their own learning. The company found that people made rapid progress, including many who had been considered unlikely to take on the new technology.

Know others who can help

Issues

Is there benefit in talking things over with family, friends or colleagues? With my manager? With strangers!?

Discussion

There is some evidence to suggest that many people do not discuss work 'in their own time'. If change creates uncertainty and stress, this can mean that they lose important opportunities. Simply talking through a problem can be helpful – this of course requires that we understand the changes well enough to be able to describe them to others. It seems to make sense to encourage people to discuss their problems. Discussion with colleagues can be facilitated by running workshops. Much the same applies to talking things over with the manager involved. Sometimes there is benefit to be had from talking things over with a complete stranger!

Working on self-esteem

Issues

Test out ideas and beliefs.

Discussion

Working with our ideas and beliefs about a change can usefully form the basis for building our self-esteem. Consider the case of a department in which computers are being introduced. The people involved might believe that computers create unemployment and that they will thus lose their jobs. Is this true? In all circumstances? In these circumstances? What has management said about the issue? Is it the subject of negotiations? Have guarantees been given? People might also think that they are too old to get to grips with the computer. Is that true? What help can be obtained? Can I try it out now? Work on the issues discussed above will feed into this and help people to make progress. Perhaps the important point is for us to recognize that we need to build our self-esteem as part of dealing with a programmed change. We need to recognize that this is an essential, unavoidable part of this process.

Issues

Talk out issues with yourself!

Discussion

On the face of it this may sound rather silly. Discussing the point recently on a senior management programme one manager said that he always got his people to write out those issues that they felt were important in a change situation. Talking or writing involves thinking through systematically. Writing creates a publicly available record. To deal with our feelings about changes we need to understand them better. Thus talking them out (or writing them down) is an important facilitating process, and something which could form part of a workshop programme.

Issues

Let go of the past. Accept that this will create a sense of loss.

Discussion

We have already discussed the need, and the processes through which people will discard the past. It is important to recognize that this will create a sense of loss and will cause anger. It is inevitable, and it is important for all of us to recognize that it is inevitable. Managers must ensure that time and space are allowed for people to experience these feelings and that this is legitimate. The temptation to calm people down, to soothe their fears and anger, may be compelling but must be treated with caution. If we are not careful, we deny feelings which must be experienced if change is to be accepted. Most important, we should recognize that this process of letting go of the past, while painful, does involve learning and is really part of the process through which individuals choose the future.

Issues

Set goals, act, look for gains.

Discussion

The discussion presented examines issues and questions which must be faced, and ways of doing so. It seems clear that they could form the basis of a series of workshop activities for people who are involved in significant change programmes. While not a 'blueprint' for success, they do provide a basis for constructive work and progress. Problems of layout, work design and work organization often abound with new systems. Problem-solving activities to deal with these matters provide an excellent opportunity for people to get to grips with a new system.

Rebuilding self-esteem

Simplifying somewhat, we suggest that individuals have four main categories of need if they are to rebuild their self-esteem amidst a programme of organizational change. They need to understand the changes and thus need intelligible information. They will probably need to develop new skills, if only the skills of dealing with new people as colleagues or supervisors. They will need support to help them to deal with the problems. Encouragement to try out new systems is important. Provision of short workshops planned to achieve part or all of the work discussed in the preceding section can help, as can technical support to solve problems, access to people who can help, and allowing people to control their own learning. First and foremost, empathy, under-standing, is a key issue. Kirkpatrick (1985) rightly sees this as one of the key skills for managing change. We have discussed empathy earlier. In this chapter we have dis-cussed a range of ideas which can be used as a way of developing or practising empathy – of trying to see changes the way others see them and using that as a 'basis for build-ing self-esteem'. If these four needs can be met by appropriate resources, then it is pos-sible for people to carry through the personal work needed for them to rebuild their self-esteem and to act. Thus they can adapt to changes and develop new skills, abilities and roles with which to face the future.

However, two problems must be faced immediately. The issues we have discussed are difficult for individuals and groups, whether employees or managers, to face and discuss. The first relates to the provision of information by individuals. Is that as straightforward a matter as it seems on the face of it or are there problems here? What processes can hinder coping activities? The second problem relates to the problem of ineffective behaviour.

Providing information

At a practical level much of what we have said has been concerned with information. People need to understand the new system if they are to understand their own part in it. Information must be shared if people are to judge the impact of changes upon them-selves and upon 'their' jobs. Does this mean that openness and sharing information is a good thing, and the more the better? Some will say that this is so. We can only make mature judgements if we have the relevant information.

Others will point to the uncertainty surrounding many changes. What if the manager you exhort to pass on information does not have it to share? Then the question of confidentiality is often raised.

In fact, there is a dual problem which must be faced when significant changes are underway. For the individuals concerned, the demands of a change situation can be revealing to themselves and to others. We often respond emotionally because we feel that the new demands, the new situation, strip away barriers and reveal parts of our-selves which we have kept private. One's recent performance, the good and the less so, are now examined as the planners gather data to justify the change. One's skills are examined and explored. One's work behaviour comes under observation and analysis. The individual is asked what he or she feels about the present system, process, job, machine or structure. How well does it work? What are its problems? How might it be improved? What are the best things about it? What are the worst things about it? Thus the individual provides information.

As Bok (1984) makes clear, this is not without problems. To the extent that this probing enters the individual's personal domain (or territory), then it is an invasion of the self. That human beings will use ingenious means to protect their privacy has long been understood (see Roy (1954) for fascinating case material based upon well-known observational studies in industrial settings). Should we be concerned about it? Yes, if it is our concern to see these same people actively supporting and committed to the changes. What does this mean? We would suggest that it tells us how important it is to collect information from people *on their own terms*. Only then will we minimize the chances of invading their personal domains. Information is needed, of course, but the more we can get the people involved to collect and interpret their own information, feeding it into the broader analysis of the section, department or organization, the better. Empathy becomes a crucial skill (see above). Do we mean that people should be free to keep poor performance secret, or problems? We do not, but we must accept that there is a need for secrecy; the question is one of balance. Secrecy may be indispensable to individuals, to groups and to organizations.

> Secrecy for plans is needed, not only to protect their formulation but also to develop them, perhaps to change them, at times to excuse them, even if to give them up. ... Secrecy guards projects that require creativity and prolonged work: the tentative and the fragile, unfinished tasks, probes and bargaining of all kinds. ... Lack of secrecy would, for instance, thwart many negotiations, in which all plans cannot be revealed at the outset. Once projects are under way however, large portions of secrecy are often given up voluntarily, or dispelled with a flourish.
>
> (Bok, 1984, p. 181)

Some degree of control over information provided may be justified at the individual level to protect identity, plans and action, or choices for the individual. Thus it applies as much to the senior manager as it does to the employee. This, then, is the dual nature of the question.

Openness and sharing of information is valuable as a means of facilitating change. Yet other pressures apply. There are counteracting pressures which create limits for the individual whose job may be changed, for the people who have taken the initiative, planned and gained support for change, and who are now seeing it through to implementation. Our concern, then, should not simply be to provide information but, rather, to establish the means by which people involved can control the information to be provided – not a purist answer because there is no guarantee here against abuse. But no such guarantee exists short of domination and coercion. Making the issue explicit seems likely to create conditions under which valid and relevant information can be established without undermining the identity of those involved. To do otherwise is to be careless of the people involved in a change situation and careless of the quality of information to be obtained.

Give people time

People need time to get through a major change. This is especially true if the change requires them to solve problems. Spend time with people. It is important to listen to their views. They may well know better than you do about the details of a particular job, system or work area. Always reinforce the new situation in your discussion. Empathy is important (see Chapter 10) but remember that the concern should be to help them build energy for change. Encourage people to put off those decisions which are not needed immediately. Recognize that everyone needs to feel their way forward in a period of change. Help them to see personal milestones, jobs to train for, objectives to achieve, systems to get working. Routines and milestones provide stability and structure. People need time to get through change but they also need to structure that time. Do not impose this structure. Encourage it to emerge.

Involving people

Whether, when, to what extent and how people are involved in a change situation needs careful thought because there are both advantages and disadvantages, as discussed in the following.

Advantages and disadvantages of involving people

Advantages

1. Improved decisions because people have better detailed knowledge of jobs and systems.
2. People will better understand the aims of the change, and the working of new systems.
3. Creates a feeling of ownership.
4. Redirects energy in support of change rather than against change.
5. Allows us to experiment.
6. Builds a better understanding of change and how to achieve it.

Disadvantages

1. Takes longer, particularly at the planning stage.
2. Therefore requires more time and effort in the early stages.

In addition, involving people may lead to greater uncertainty and instability as individuals or groups use the involvement process as a means of opposing change. However, if the objective is the effective implementation of change, this latter is less of an issue. These same people are likely to oppose the change, whether or not they were involved. If they are not involved the opposition will come out in different ways. Below, we list some useful criteria in planning how people are to be involved in change.

Involving people

This may depend on the following:

1. The complexity of the changes and the strength of linkage between different parts of the changes.
2. The expected opposition and the level of dissatisfaction with the present situation.
3. The level of credibility of the people promoting change.
4. Impact of change on people, both positive and negative – how many 'winners', how many 'losers'?

5. Where the quality of the decisions is more important than their acceptability alone.

6. Where rumour is likely, whatever happens.

These factors need to be considered. Sometimes changes are probably best imposed by top management. There is no easy answer but, just as important, involvement of top management is not always the way forward. However, there are two further points to add. Because there are real advantages in involvement, some level is always worth considering. Usually, there are many details to be resolved in which people can and should be involved. The point here is to make clear precisely how and to what extent involvement is planned. Just as important is involving key power-holders and opinion-leaders. They will influence the attitudes and behaviour of others and therefore their open support is worth seeking.

Concluding comment

The quote at the start of Chapter 8 says it all. The above will take a little time. But if we do it well it will release energy in support of change. We often underestimate the time and energy needed to introduce change. Paying attention to the issues dealt with here will save time in the longer run. The current changes will be implemented more quickly. The organization will become more receptive to overall change.

Exercises

1. Can you identify any means by which the method for implementing change in Company B took account of the coping cycle model?

2. How important is the corporate culture? To what extent does corporate culture effect innovation?

3. Can you apply the coping cycle model to any change you have experienced?

CHAPTER 11

Programmes of change

Introduction

Many people often ask me whether or not a total quality management programme is an example of what this book talks about. Similarly people refer to business process re-engineering. When I say yes they then ask me what is different about such programmes of change. To this I answer nothing except that the 'packaging' is different. Thus far in this book we have been concerned to analyze change and the problems of change. Through such analysis comes better understanding and thus we are able to handle change more effectively.

But is that enough? In the real world change must be defined and 'sold'. It 'must be controlled (at some level). It must be managed to achieve and sustain momentum. Managers need to attract attention. In this chapter therefore we are concerned with programmes of change. We shall examine some of the important design parameters facing those taking overall responsibility for a major change effort. Our concern will be on how to create a programme of change.

What we deal with here is relevant to generic organization-wide change and to multi-organizational change. Total quality management programmes and business process re-engineering programmes are currently good examples of how to achieve change. A joint venture would be a classic multi-organizational example.

One of the problems we each of us experience when we attempt to relate models of change with our real-world experience of change is that formal models of change generally give an impression of change as a neat, orderly sequence of activities or stages. Conversely, our experience is usually altogether more 'messy'. Activities are often going on in parallel. We often recycle through different stages as we pilot a new organizational design on new marketing policy only to find that in some respects it does not work. As we shall see, our response is to see change as a spiral process and to view it as comprising three essential characteristics (each of which comprises many detailed ingredients, programme elements, etc., to make it up).

Cycles of change

Figure 11.1 identifies these three characteristics as necessary conditions for effective change. These conditions are awareness, capability and inclusion. For change to be successful those involved must understand the change, its objectives, their role and so on. Understanding *and* credibility are vital. Only then will they feel confidence in the likelihood of success and only then is there the prospect of energizing them to act appropriately. Given that, they must have or be helped to acquire the necessary capabilities to handle the new tasks and new work situations. As we sketched out in Chapter 10, people must feel that they can cope with the new situation. Finally, they must feel 'included' in the change process. To be successful those involved need to feel that they value the new objectives (individual and/or corporate) and that they both choose and feel able to choose.

Judson (1990) sketches an outline of five key issues, each of which can be related to one of these three necessary conditions:

Awareness

1. How thoroughly does everyone affected … understand the needs of customers, objectives, strategy and timetable, resources required and new behaviour, techniques, systems, etc.?

2. How systematic a process has been instituted for tracking implementation and for making corrections whilst change is in process?

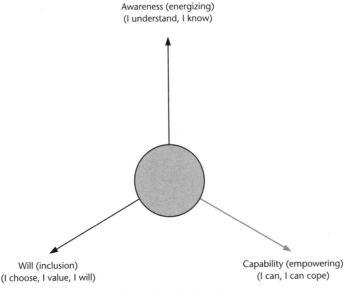

Figure 11.1 Necessary conditions for effective change

Capability

3. How completely have the resources required been identified and provided, including financial resources, skills and time?

Inclusion

4. How strong is the commitment of relevant managers and employees to implementing the change including how credible do they view the change as being, to what extent do they 'own' the approach, how can commitment be sustained, etc.?

5. How consistent and credible is the climate of accountability for the implementation period including to what extent will those involved live up to their commitments, what are the consequences of failure, will reward systems differentiate between success and failure and how visible and consistent is leadership behaviour?

Turning now to Figure 11.2, we can see how to put some 'flesh' on these ideas. At its simplest the figure defines three stages of change as follows:

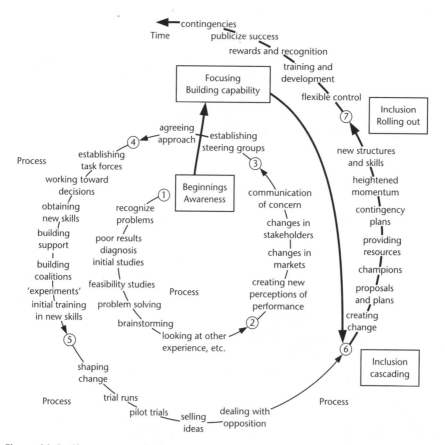

Figure 11.2 Change as a cyclical process

Stage 1: beginnings

Here the problems are recognized, awareness raising begins, diagnostic studies are undertaken, feasibility studies are begun, we look at the experience of other organizations and so on. This begins to create a new perception of achievable performance in what may be rapidly changing markets, technologies and so on. The main focus of this stage therefore is that of creating awareness but, as we shall see, awareness building continues long into the next stage.

Stage 2: focusing

We show the first stage as including the establishment of a steering group taking responsibility for the 'problem' and even agreeing the basic approach. The next stage we call focusing. Here effort at building awareness continues but also people are moving towards decision and action. Task forces may be established. If new skills are needed then the first attempts to seek them or to attempt to create them internally will begin. Effort will be directed at building coalitions in support of the changes, both through work with opinion-leaders and through other means. Pilot trials and experiments often will be undertaken. Visits will be organized to sites and organizations which have already implemented the changes. Early results will be used to further 'shape' and modify the change programme. Much attention will be devoted to 'selling' the new ideas and dealing with likely opposition.

Stage 3: inclusion

Now the focus of the change activity broadens. We both cascade and roll out. Cascading is about creating and implementing a communication plan. Rolling out is about implementing the change throughout the organization as a whole. The two are often linked. Thus if two organizations are merged the initial announcement is often followed by a process of senior management appointments. This is followed by a process to decide the corporate structure for the merged entity. In turn this is followed by a series of lower-level appointments. Then may follow detailed examination of work organization, information systems, procedures, etc., in which small task forces (for example) are charged with the job of picking the best ideas from the two original organizations to implement in the new. Here we see a process of decision and action both cascading down the organization and rolling out at each level across the organization. This cyclical process is illustrated in Table 11.1.

Learning and change

We have already noted that learning is a characteristic of effective organizational change possibly best viewed as a consequence of change. This raises the question of whether we can identify any meaningful equivalence between individual learning and the processes of organizational change identified in the above. Juch (1983) has identified what has become a very influential model of learning which sees the learner at the centre possessing levels of sensory, cognitive, contractual (communication) and operational skills. The process of learning comprises a cycle of four stages: namely, thinking, addressing, doing and sensing, with four barriers. He characterizes the four as

Table 11.1 ● Cycles of management (from Juch, 1983)

Stage	Task/activity	Process
1. Thinking	Objectives Policies Forecasts Proposals Projects	Preliminary discussion
2. Addressing	Budgets Targets Commitments Organizing Scheduling	Decision making
3. Doing	Controlling Training Reporting Progress chasing	Monitoring
4. Sensing	Analysis Evaluation Problem solving	Evaluation

follows:

1. 'Gate', through which ideas are converted to intentions and declared to others.

2. 'Rubicon', through which some proposals are considered as attracting commitment.

3. 'Window', through which attention to certain outcomes is raised.

4. 'Skin', through which new perceptions about, say, possible performance, are accepted, leading to a repeat of the cycle.

Clearly it is not difficult to relate these ideas to the processes of change which we have identified. Juch (1983) presents a 'cycle of management' which does. So the four stages being linked to typical management tasks or activities are as shown in Table 11.1. Derived from this revision of Juch's presentation and linking the change model with his learning model we get Table 11.2. Juch explicitly includes an evaluation stage which we have omitted – largely because formal evaluation is rarely practised and also because the learning appears to take place throughout the process. There is an equivalence between our beginnings stage and the Argyris concept of action maps (see Chapter 5). Argyris contends that, faced with contractions in behaviour, the process of mapping can lead to changes towards more effective behaviour, implying a much

Table 11.2 ● Cycles of change

Stage		Task/activity	Process
1. Thinking	Beginnings	Diagnosis Feasibility studies Brainstorming Communication of concerns Problem recognition Establish steering group	Getting started
2. Addressing	Focusing	Task forces Training Buying in new skills Building support Building coalitions 'Pilot' trials	Building capability
3. Doing	Inclusion Cascading Rolling out	Creating change Champions Proposals for change New structures and skills Team building Rewards and recognition Sell change Publicize success	Building and sustaining change

more natural process of learning than Juch's model suggests – although in making this point I do not mean that Juch adopted a static view of learning (i.e. that it did not take place until all thinking, addressing and doing were complete). The view offered here is that life, work and managing change were never so simple!

Again one can see how 'personal learning cycles', 'change coping cycles' (see Chapter 10) and the organizational change cycle may fit together. Learning cycles may be 'nested' within the 'change coping cycles' which in turn are nested within the organization's change cycle. Add to that the concept of adoption of innovation, which suggests that people vary in the pace of adoption of new ideas from innovators, early adopters to laggards, and it is possible to suggest some interesting lines of thought both for the practice of organizational change and for research.

Can we, for example, pick out the most likely innovators? Many observers suggest that they are venturesome and prepared to accept risks. De Vries (1980) would probably add that they are prepared to take calculated risks. Kirton (1988), the originator of the Kirton adoption–innovation test or KAI, identifies various differences between innovators and adopters suggesting that both are essential to success. Amabile (1988) identifies components of individual creativity (e.g. product and technical skills and knowledge, cognitive style, work styles, attitudes and motivation) which she sees as emerging from cognitive abilities, perceptual and motor skills, education, training, experience in developing new ideas, the ability to minimize extrinsic constraints, which certainly suggest lines for further research but which *might* allow us to identify potential 'change champions' and 'change agents'. The champion might be the risk taker, strongly achievement orientated, with the capability of ignoring or at least settling for one-side constraints until ideas are shaped through the process of early trials. Amabile (1983) suggests that the appropriate cognitive–perceptual style includes the following:

- The ability to break the existing mind-set.
- The ability to hold open options for a long time.
- The ability to suspend judgement.
- Excellent memory.
- The ability to break out of 'performance scripts'.

All of this appears very similar to the 'block-busting' capabilities we discussed in Chapter 5 above.

Grundy (1994) adds important insight into strategic learning to the Juch model. For him strategic learning and strategic action are two linked cycles. Set out in Figure 11.3 is a modified version of his idea. Thus strategic learning is a dual process of action and learning. Both loops operate simultaneously but are not often well synchronized. In much the same way the learning loop is often not completed and the learning maximized because formal evaluation is not encouraged. In effect, Grundy supports our original view of this: that it does not require a separate stage but rather a linked process

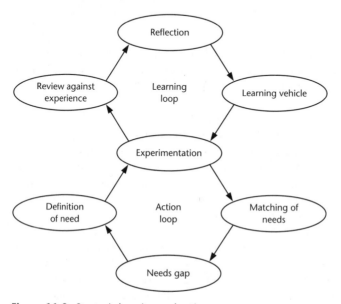

Figure 11.3 Strategic learning and action

aimed at achieving the learning. Thus not least there could be a management development programme used both to roll out and to cascade major changes throughout an organization. Grundy also argues that a key feature of success is the ability to block out distractions (see our discussion of 'champions' above).

How do we block out distractions? Well, as we have already implied, this is partly an issue of cognitive style at the individual level. There are things we can do at the team and organizational levels, however. Following Grundy (1994), we include the following:

- Manage personal and corporate agendas in order to meet the needs of stakeholders, your board or other influential people along the way.
- Define some 'givens' to stabilize the process.
- Flexible control to spread learning beyond the top team.
- Build learning into the organization through regular customer surveys, staff surveys, quality assurance, performance improvement, etc.
- Keep task forces etc. involved until implementation is complete.
- Involve top managers at the centre of the process.
- Use communication as a vehicle for learning.

All of this has implications for what and how we manage, which we have touched on at various points in this book.

Programmes of change

Given that major strategic change creates tensions and conflicts, not least within an organization, *and* that many fairly rigidly structured organizations already experience such tensions, how can we encourage at one and the same time integration and learning? Set out below are a series of steps:

1. *Building relationships*: company conferences; cross-functional management; development and functional training; job rotation; building *networks*.
2. *Creating project groups*: solving problems via project groups and task forces; creating *centres of excellence* throughout the organization.
3. *Focused training and development*: total quality management programmes; action-learning-based management development; company-tailored development; business process re-engineering programmes.
4. *Career management*: defining and developing *managerial competence*; performance appraisal; career counselling and planning.

Each of these steps is designed either to link or interface individuals in problem-orientated settings or to link the individual to the organization in an output-orientated way, focusing upon achievement of objectives. Thus managing change appropriately can and should create and sustain both learning within the organization and also its integration.

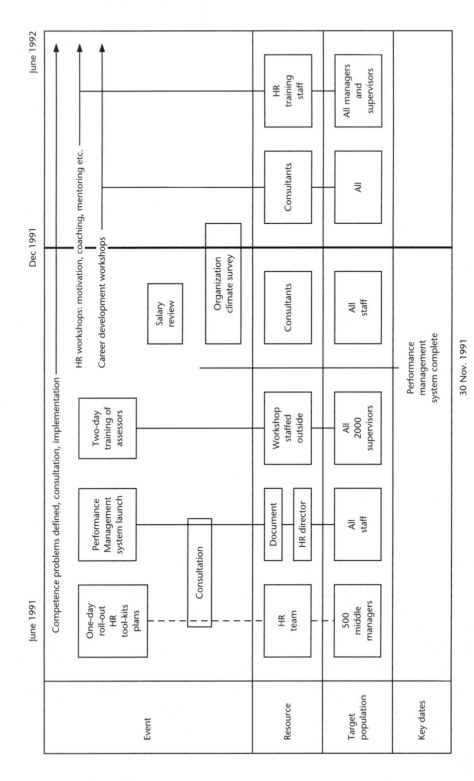

Figure 11.4 Implementation programme

If these are the issues which we must consider in creating a programme of change and if there are various stages to include, what will a programme look like in practice? Normally it is possible to create a project plan which sets out the key events, including time scales, resources and inputs, target population and key dates/milestones. Set out in Figure 11.4 is such an implementation programme detailing the development of a human resources (HR) strategy within an oil industry 'major' over the period 1991–2.

CASE STUDY

Wilkinson Sword

Wilkinson Sword is a well-known f.m.c.g. (fast-moving consumer good) and manufacturing group trading throughout Europe and North America. It manufactures razors and other personal care products. With headquarters in Germany, it was valued at US$600 million in 1990. During the period of the change to be described the group was experiencing major operational problems: the owners were moving towards divestment and a wide and complex set of financial arrangements was being refinanced and/or restructured.

Beginnings

The chief executive's initial problem was that in difficult circumstances he was trying to manage the group 'blind'. The most successful product had been launched in too many markets. Demand far outstripped supply. Retail customers are threatening to withdraw business. The group is only profitable in Europe, and there mostly in Germany. The 'star' produce needs specialist equipment to expand manufacturing with an 8 month lead time. Inventory levels are high and on a worsening trend. The monthly report was 60 pages long and unintelligible.

A project was defined, designed to help the board understand the following:

● How the group had been managed to date using the existing management information.

● What the perception was of the three factories and regional sales organizations as to their financial reporting responsibility.

● What 'culture' was predominant in the various financial departments.

The initial conclusions were as follows:

● Local general managers were dissatisfied with management information.

● Financial controllers reported reliably and promptly to the German head office but received no feedback of any kind.

● Each business unit had proceeded independently to develop local internal reporting systems and software.

● Rarely did financial controllers meet each other or visit head office.

● Local computer managers knew nothing of developments elsewhere in the group.

▶▶

● There was little understanding by group management of local activities, traditions, cultures, etc.

Rethinking the problem the chief executive recognized the above as consistent with a review he had undertaken of strategy as a whole, and management style in group finance was part of the problem.

Too much emphasis on the detail, overmuch concern with involvement and a concern not to 'upset' others suggest some of the problems Argyris refers to – see above. The appointment of a new chief financial officer (CFO) delayed progress because the immediate priority was a series of pressing financial problems.

The next major step was for the CFO to visit group operations in Germany, Italy, France, Spain, the UK, the USA and Canada to evaluate local hardware and software and to identify aspects of local software which might be used more widely. From these visits and subsequent discussion a brief for a common integrated system was agreed, including features such as modular design, European upgrades in facilities, tailored to unit level, capable of being networked to local PCs and of remote access and supplied on the basis of support and training available in local languages.

Focusing

Project groups were created to work toward solutions. Each was international in make-up and each would have a make-up of people appropriate to the study tasks. The tasks ranged from a review of the information needs of the sales organizations, the adaptability of local systems to wider use, to a review of local area networks and DOS applications. A senior manager was identified as project manager for the programme of change now unfolding, with the study groups reporting directly, in turn reporting to the CFO.

All of this effort was creating a new recognition of the reality for information systems design in the group including the following:

● Each territory needed to be seen and see itself as part of an international group.

● Needs were essentially *local*.

● Recognition that skills and inputs came from *throughout* the group.

Subsequently the study groups reported to the next of the quarterly 'global conferences' organized by the group with all managing directors in attendance. Also examined were problems of liquidity, profitability, marketing and supply.

In response to the financial problems it was agreed that the group would not impose the budget that year, but rather that local budgets were to be set with quantified 'stretch' beyond the previous year. A new reporting format, with monthly reports and a budget package, was now emerging and sent to local management for consultation. Local management were allowed extra time to complete the budget pack and parallel running of the new pack was organized for the last 3 months of the current financial year.

▶▶

Inclusion

As the study groups completed their work, from one group had come proposals for particular hardware/software combinations. Each study group was now briefed to examine this option in detail. This set up a process of local presentations by the supplier, with site visits to see the system operating elsewhere in order to assess customer/user views. A detailed technical evaluation was also undertaken and provided to the study groups. In parallel the CFO and project manager were making local visits reviewing existing infrastructure. A crash programme of PC replacement, upgrades, laser and desktop colour printers, etc., was implemented. Local choices were encouraged where compatibility was broadly available. Training plans and budgets were emerging from the study groups. Again a sense that local views mattered began to emerge.

Now a systems proposal was made to the group board. The plan set a date for installation, progressive roll-out, existing systems in place for a period but with a 12 month plan to install, pilot, test, train, etc., and bring the new system on-line.

Learning

The main lessons were as follows:

- An effective change project brings together the people who need to be involved in a well-structured way, with clear reporting and accountability but with sufficient freedom to encourage the sharing of skills, experience, needs, etc.
- It is vital to avoid preconceived ideas on options.
- It is important to minimize 'fear of change' by having those affected by change involved in the process of change.
- It makes sense to allow *time* for learning to develop to allow people to select the right solution for local needs. It was more important to get the right solutions than to get quick solutions.

Exercises

1. Can you see how Wilkinson seeks to build learning into the process of change?
2. Focus on a change which you have experienced. Can you identify the cyclical processes of change described in this chapter?
3. Identify a change which you have been involved in at work or in college. Have you sought to learn from the experience? How?

CHAPTER 12

Learning from change

Introduction

What, then, can be learnt from the process of introducing major organizational changes? How can we ensure that we do learn from our experience? Throughout this book the answers to these two questions have been consistent. Developing a more open process for managing change will create the conditions for learning. Planning, implementing and monitoring change more systematically will allow us to consolidate that learning. Let us repeat an earlier point. This is not a prescription for an ideal approach; rather, we would argue for pragmatism combined with the capacity to learn rather than pragmatism driven by an *ad hoc* approach.

CASE STUDY

ABF Ltd

Let us return to the case study outlined in Chapter 8. The reader will recall from the detail provided that there was considerable evidence of both managerial ineffectiveness and the need for specific changes. Top management did not understand the causes of this managerial ineffectiveness, nor how to tackle it. The managing director, who had held the post for some years, adopted an autocratic management style. After an early period of profit growth the company had stagnated, profits remaining stable despite growth in sales. Consultants had been used to review systems and procedures and to help

▶▶

with the introduction of techniques such as materials requirements planning (MRP) systems.

As we saw, the finance director had played a major role in the changes. Let us look at what was learned from the changes, using his own assessment, made subsequently (Keeley, 1988). He reviews the approach he had adopted with individual managers, linking this to the specific changes made and to how he has used approaches such as those discussed in this book to learn from the experience. For our purposes two examples will suffice; many such assessments have been made.

Tony, the company accountant

Tony is the Company Accountant and reports directly to me. He is a qualified accountant who joined the Company late in 1986 and is an experienced man. He is very competent, particularly in the field of computers where his knowledge exceeds mine, and is also highly self-motivated. I have therefore used a delegating style with him and have gone out of my way to let him do things his way. Consequently, he has been able to make a substantial number of changes and introduce many new systems. In many cases replacing systems which I installed when I was doing his job. This leadership style appears to have been effective with him and he has achieved a great deal in terms of systems development.

Despite a high level of achievement on Tony's part, problems do occur. Deadlines are frequently missed. On several occasions he has got into a problem by devoting a substantial amount of time to new work, such as developing the computer system, whilst being over-optimistic regarding the amount of time necessary to set aside to accurately produce the routine work. It appears that he has not placed a high enough priority upon current work such as getting the monthly accounts prepared on time. He tends to work very hard towards those goals which he perceives as his own (e.g. new systems) whilst assigning the Company goals a slightly lower priority.

Missing these goals has been very personal, very difficult for Tony. He has been embarrassed by people such as the auditors, the Group Chief Accountant, Mike and myself waiting upon his promises and he has had to explain on many occasions that he is unable to deliver. I have therefore reverted as quickly as possible to a participating style. In as low key manner as possible, I have discussed with him future priorities such as accounting deadlines. I have shown as much sympathy as possible with his problems and avoided criticism but have not in any way avoided the subject of missed deadlines. I have initiated a two-way discussion on how we can meet deadlines in the future 'now that you have developed a computer system that is so much better than before'. I try to emphasise 'our' difficulties and 'our' failures whilst referring to 'your' successes. I have made particular efforts to engage in active listening and to try to accept all of his suggestions whilst avoiding my own suggestions except when he has not had any of his own. My general objective is to motivate him to organise things in his own way but to slightly increase the emphasis upon the Company's objectives so that the Company's objectives and his own are as closely matched as possible.

Recently I have noticed some improvement which seems to be sustained. I am

▶▶

gradually reducing my involvement but keeping some pressure on him, requiring regular up-dates on progress and future plans.

John, the production director

One of the major constraints was what I perceived to be the problem with John, the Production Director. Following an investigation by consultants a number of significant changes were to be introduced in the production department. These changes included the introduction of Just-in-Time techniques, MRP systems, total quality concepts and changes in the method of organising technicians and production managers. John had shown continued opposition to these measures although they eventually proved to be popular with the rest of the management. In view of John's intransigence towards change, the consultants had recommended that he be dismissed but at the last moment he voluntarily agreed to support the changes. At the suggestion of the consultants he agreed to use me as a supporter/counsellor. I was unavoidably absent from this meeting. Shortly afterwards I was away for two months for business reasons.

In view of the long delay and the fact that I was not present at the original meeting, I thought it inappropriate to broach the question of ongoing collaboration between John and me. I felt that John was suffering from the dilemma of having problems in his department which he was unable to solve, particularly those that required some degree of interpersonal skills. In the long term I think that John needs training to help him improve his interpersonal skills but in the short term I thought that it would be helpful if I were to try to alleviate some problem areas for him.

Improving the performance of John's production managers in dealing with disciplinary problems seemed to be the most obviously profitable area. I therefore asked him if he would be happy with me trying to sort out some ongoing personnel problems by direct contact with his staff. As I am Personnel Director and closely involved in general management, this could be done in a reasonably natural way. For some while there had clearly been disciplinary problems with the shop floor and these had not been properly addressed by management. Absenteeism was running at a very high rate and a number of people were taking 20–40 days off per annum on a regular basis; there were complaints from the production managers that some people, notably on the nightshift, were very difficult to supervise.

Somehow, the production managers had been unable to get to grips with discipline on the shop floor. A fair amount of aggression had been used by them but no improvement had been seen and shop floor morale was low. There had been claims from them in the past that these problems would be sorted out 'if the managers got enough support from the directors'. It was never entirely clear what was meant by this statement. However, I agreed with John that I would try to sort out whatever personnel problems there were and keep him generally informed about what I was doing. We agreed that he would let me know if he thought that I was interfering over much. I determined to talk to each relevant manager and to discuss their problems with them.

Initially their reaction was as it had been in the past. They said that if they were left to get on with their jobs, take whatever decisions were necessary and dismiss

▶▶

whichever people they felt fit, there would be no problems. They said that the personnel department had restricted management action on discipline in the past. I said that what I wanted to do was to examine each individual case and follow it through to its conclusion – hopefully an improved performance on the part of the employee.

My initial approach was to examine each employee file to see which had been issued with Written Warnings that could be followed up. When I produced a list of which employees needed to be spoken or written to again, two of the production managers admitted that they had each had a number of Written Warnings for their department on such things as unexplained absence, excessive sickness and bad discipline and that they had failed to hand them out. They each said that they had forgotten to do so. This seemed extremely unlikely and on further discussion it transpired that none of the production managers was sure what to do in any given disciplinary situation.

One of them had developed an extremely aggressive personal style over the years and tended to shout at people when they did something wrong. He did not really know how to follow up this approach, especially when the employee concerned seemed willing to enter into a reasoned discussion. The other two confessed that they found it very difficult to enforce discipline and were not sure how to go about it. With these admissions in the open, it was a relatively straightforward business from then on to tackle the situation.

We decided to start from scratch. I saw each of the worst offenders personally with one of the production managers present and explained the situation and said that their performance had to improve. Some employees said that a large contributory factor was the attitude of management and that they did not respect them. My response was to say that we were aware of our shortcomings throughout the Company, that all managers, including directors, would be receiving training, but that I expected an immediately improved performance from the employees as well. Also, the Company was looking for a situation in which genuine problems could be discussed between management and employee. However, failure to meet a satisfactory standard would not be tolerated in future. In other words, we wanted a frank and open atmosphere in which problems were discussable but we did not intend to be soft.

Most employees seemed to warm to this attitude although over the course of the months it was necessary to dismiss several that did not improve. After a fairly short while I found that the production managers were becoming enthusiastic and coming to me with progress reports. They also seem to be happier in what they are doing now that they have some direction.

During those months I re-wrote and substantially expanded the Company Handbook, a publication which I only introduced last year. I took the opportunity to call a meeting of all production managers and supervisors so as to ask their opinion of the section relating to disciplinary procedures. This was an excuse to discuss how to act in different situations and quite a lengthy and lively discussion ensued. It was surprising how many people were pleased that they had the opportunity to ask how to act in various situations. Having a set of rules to discuss removed some of the embarrassment of their admitting that they did not know how to act – they were able to ask what was expected of them in enforcing each rule.

All this indicates that frank and open discussion of problems helps to motivate staff. The managers and supervisors referred to above were very grateful to be treated in the 'telling' and 'selling' styles and had previously found themselves uncomfortable with John's delegating style because they lacked the maturity to deal with the situation in which they found themselves. It must be remembered of course that John had delegated by default, not because of a conscious opinion of the proper way to react to his subordinates. Although I do not envisage a situation in which I will continue to instruct managers and supervisors in this manner, I believe that they have been given more confidence to work under John with his delegation style.

A further example of increasing motivation by increased communication is the training course which many of our managers and supervisors attended several months ago. This was agreed with the consultants although Mike, who is very cynical about training, agreed that it could be run partly because the consultants supported it and partly because it was included in their original fee. It was a fairly short course at a local hotel and covered basic aspects of supervision and work planning but I felt that the biggest benefit was the opportunity it created for managers and supervisors to talk together about their work. Whilst there was little discussion afterwards regarding the individual topics dealt with on the course, there was a noticeable increase in *ésprit de corps* upon their return. It also created an expectation of further change and support and there has been substantial agitation from them for the Board to attend a fairly similar course – this has now been agreed.

Simultaneously, there was a change in the work pattern of the production managers. There was previously one nightshift manager with two dayshift managers splitting their duties but without the two shifts overlapping. Problems occurred in both areas on days and there had been severe disciplinary problems on the nightshift for years. With the three managers working rotating shifts and covering the whole 24 hours, there was substantial opportunity for improvement. For example, whereas the nightshift manager could previously hide from his problems at night, it was now necessary for him to discuss them openly with the manager that was about to take over from him and problems had to be faced because they would be noticed by the next person working on that shift. This enhanced the atmosphere of having to address problems frankly and openly. It was interesting to note that whereas previously they had failed to hand out warnings, there have recently been instances where they have gained such confidence and enthusiasm that they have been competing to be the one to hand out the warning. One manager even insisted upon coming in from holiday in order to see a particularly difficult employee who had worked exclusively for him before the rotating shift system had been introduced.

By working hard to create an atmosphere in which managers could take the task of changing their approach without fear of reprimand, it was possible to encourage behavioural change. This was enhanced by ensuring that frank admissions (e.g. regarding the written warnings) were not 'punished' but at the same time it was necessary to ensure that the proper approach was discussed.

Managing change for management development

It was clear from Chapter 8 that significant changes were introduced and important performance improvements achieved at ABF Ltd. The two examples given above demonstrate how important management style and management development can be in a period of change. Developing a more open and positive management style was seen in Chapter 8 as a precursor of other much needed changes. Here it becomes clear how important this is for development and learning by these managers during the process of change. Turning back to Table 10.3, it is now all too obvious that learning and change will only be possible given a positive attitude to change (from top management) and an open approach to developing changes, ideas and solving the problems along the way. Without both we have some combination of stagnation, anxiety and resistance to change.

It is important for us to recognize that significant change programmes are not discrete events. The objective is not simply profitability or increased effectiveness, crucial as these are to all of us; rather, it is about increased adaptability and effectiveness. We assess these latter qualitatively (Chapter 5). But do not leave this book with the view that this is about increased satisfaction as such; rather, it is about increased openness, a greater willingness to face and deal with problems, more openly handled conflict. The net result may, superficially, seem less happy. There will be more analysis, more debate and greater effort directed at improving performance and cost-effectiveness.

All this needs patient and sustained effort. There is plenty of room for misunderstanding along the way. Many people's assessments may appear to be contradictory. Take an example I know of change in a social services organization. Specifically, the changes were aimed at alleviating the problems so often associated with the institutionalized care of the elderly mentally disturbed. Among many changes introduced was a residents' council for each 'home'. A comment from the minutes showed one patient saying: 'There's been a fall in the discipline. I don't like it.' The changes included movement towards giving residents influence over their own care, including the right of access to their own files. Unless handled sensitively, such changes can create anxiety and uncertainty. This is partly a direct consequence of the 'fear of freedom' (Chapter 7).

Thus leadership, sensitivity and empathy, along with involvement, openness and the rest, are the order of the day in a period of change. We need to recognize that people do need time to go through stages in the experience of change identified in the 'coping cycle' (Chapter 10), that people go through change at different rates. The coping cycle then becomes a reasonable basis against which to monitor change. Where are people on the 'coping cycle'? Does this explain their attitudes and behaviour?

The resident quoted above may well have been somewhere in the second or third stages of the coping cycle. That would make the resident's assessment entirely predictable. Once people are coming through the coping cycle, then we can seek evidence of improvement, both quantitatively and qualitatively.

How can we decide that people are coming through the experience of change? We look for two main things: firstly, we look for motivated and enthusiastic attempts to make the changes work well; secondly, we look for people who no longer talk only about the past. If people talk about changes in terms of the future and how they (and the organization) can benefit, then it is a reasonable guess that they are through the 'discarding' process that we described in Chapter 10. Now we can monitor improvements and *feedback, feedback, feedback*, to build self-esteem, to build success through improved self-esteem. Effectively managed change turns out to be more a matter of ongoing process, of building the capacity to improve into the organization.

Developing the facilitative management style *as part of manager development* is important in this process. We can identify a typical 'role model' of the manager, using this style, drawing again on Argyris (1982) and Argyris and Shon (1974, 1978). The manager concerned to facilitate the process of change adopts the following methods:

- Seeks 'clients' with problems, demonstrating the intention of helping people to resolve the problems that they recognize as such.

- Views problems broadly and seeks both organizational and technical means of dealing with them.

- Adopts changing, broad-based criteria for success.

- Develops solutions drawing upon information, knowledge, experience and views from the people involved in the system, department or organization under consideration.

- Recognizes that some technically sound solutions may well have to be rejected on interpersonal or organizational grounds.

- Recognizes that the application of professional technique can remove control from people (see Chapter 6). This can often impede commitment to change and lead to poor solutions. Joint control between the specialists, line managers and others involved (e.g. unions and professional associations, group managers in a multi-divisional organization) will build a greater willingness to collaborate.

- Clients/line managers/staff/users are becoming more willing to accept professional, specialist advice *but* they increasingly *expect* to be more active and involved in the processes of diagnosis and implementation of change.

- Expects challenge and criticism from line managers/users and others involved. Recognizes that people will employ a range of criteria in evaluating choices. Sets out to develop informed choice and internal commitment for everyone involved.

- Recognizes that planning, implementing and establishing change is a corporate activity and responsibility.

All this is fine if there is the time, energy and money to allow for it, but what if the organization is in, or close to, crisis? It is to looking at recent experience of managing in the crisis situation that we now turn to see whether this situation demands different management styles.

The management of crisis and turnaround

We often say that we learn more from our failures than from our successes. Our understanding of organizational effectiveness can be enriched by examining the causes of failures. Whether a failure is associated with the use of technology, or the collapse of a business, a close examination of the events leading up to the failure will identify opportunities which might have been used to forestall the failure. The lack of prior intervention is clearly 'ineffectual' behaviour. Failures may appear to be caused by changes of environmental conditions that organizations cannot control; events may cause severe difficulties for any organization, and nothing can change that. However, in so far as failures are caused by problems within organizations, these causes are both deep rooted and important. Environmental change raises questions of how to respond. Competitive pressures may require innovation in product design or production processes. Managers are not simply subject to environments but can also respond to them to ensure continued effectiveness.

Increasingly, the study of failures is becoming a part of organization studies. Much credit for this development must go to Hall (1980) and to Bignell *et al.* (1977). Both Child and Bignell *et al.* identify some of the indicators or conditions of failure.

Child (1984) identifies a number of 'warning signs of a structural problem'. These include overloads of work, poor integration between departments, a reducing capacity for innovation and weakening control. Bignell *et al.* in their introduction also develop a number of 'conditions of failure'. Typically, the background to a failure will be characterized by the following five factors:

1. A situation or a project in which members of several organizations are involved.

2. A complex, ill-defined and prolonged task which gives rise to information difficulties.

3. Ambiguities associated with the way to handle the situation or project (relevant regulations being out of date or not enforced).

4. Members of the organizations concerned operate with stereotyped attitudes with respect to the behaviour of other people and treat complaints from the general public or members of other organizations in a fairly cursory manner, believing them to come from non-experts who do not fully understand the issues involved.

5. Where signs of possible hazards emerge, some will be recognized and planned for but others will be neglected because:
   (a) they are not recognized by those working within a particular occupational or organizational stereotype;
   (b) of pressure of work;
   (c) recognizing them and taking action would require the investment of time, money and energy;
   (d) few of the individuals concerned feel that quite probably it will not happen anyway.

Thus, in general 'failures' are characterized by problems of communication, problems of perception and attitudes, problems of uncertainty, inadequacy of procedures for handling the situation and therefore of training. While there is some overlap with Child's list, important additional factors are identified here. We should note, however, that Child was concerned to identify signs of problems stemming from the structure of an organization, whereas Bignell *et al.*'s list deals with conditions for failures generally. We should also note that not every failure will be caused by all the problems previously identified. Lorange and Nelson (1987) identify the following four signs of organizational decline:

1. *Entrapment*: blinded by their own previous success, people can demonstrate a powerful tendency to self-deception. Upturns can follow downturns and we can delude ourselves into not recognizing the message that more and longer-lasting downturns indicate: that of being out of date.

2. *Hierarchy orientation*: where decisions are made more on issues of internal politics than in terms of market and competitive goals.

3. *Desire for acceptance, conformity*: already discussed as 'group think' in Chapter 5.

4. *Too much concern for consensus and compromise*: all decisions being turned over to teams, working parties and the like.

Lorange and Nelson also identify a number of early warning signals of decline, as follows:

1. Excess personnel, particularly of staff and line management.

2. Tolerance of incompetence.

3. Inflexible and time-consuming administrative procedures.

4. Process dominates substance; for example, where the process of corporate planning leads to the production of thick binders full of numbers and strategic options which do not get implemented.

5. Lack of clear goals.

6. Absence of and fear of conflict.

7. Poor communication.

8. Outdated organization structure.

There are similarities between the signs of organizational decline given above and the syndrome of ineffective leadership and change management discussed in Chapter 6 (see Table 6.1) and the various organizational syndromes identified in Table 12.1.

If we can identify some of the origins of and signs of crisis and decline, how can such situations be managed? The need to turn an organization around creates pressure to achieve sustainable changes quickly but without the resources that are often available in periods of growth. The organization must reorganize and rationalize either at the level of the firm or, sometimes, at the level of the industry in order to cut overcapacity. Difficult decisions must be taken and implemented. Pulling out of traditional areas of activity is easier said than done. Building up new areas of activity may require new skills and new people. Redesigning products, updating processes and revitalizing services takes massive effort. Taking advantage of new technologies quickly enough to capitalize on them is often a key issue. It must be done quickly enough to turn them to advantage but not so quickly that the firm becomes overexposed with an ill-developed technology. For Taylor (1983) these challenges require a new style of management, incorporating the following eight features:

1. *Decisiveness*: the situation calls for a speed of decision and ruthlessness in decision making: a willingness to take unpleasant decisions and to face public criticism in order to ensure the continuation and recovery of the overall business.

Table 12.1 ● Organizational syndromes (from Miller and de Vries, 1985)

Syndrome	Characteristics	Symptoms	Strengths	Weaknesses	Examples
Tight control	Distrust Analytical Centralized Reactive Sophisticated Information systems	Incremental change 'Muddling through' Too much consultation Too many meetings Poor innovation	Good knowledge of threats and opportunities Diversification	Lack of clear strategy Insecurity	Dramatic loss of market or market share
Systems focus	Tight, formal controls Standardization Hierarchical structures Conformity	Lack of innovation Ritual Low involvement Inflexibility Fixation Distinctive competence	Efficient operations Well-integrated product–market strategy	Traditional structures predominate Managers dissatisfied over lack of influence and discretion	Achievement of dominance from relatively weak position Frequent loss of control during history
Personal style	Highly centralized Inadequate structures Poor information systems	Unbridled growth Inconsistent strategy into and out of markets Decisions without analysis Little consultation	Change	Wasted resources Problems of control Inadequate role of second-level managers Rash expansion policies	Rapid growth Chief executive wishing to 'prove' him- or herself
Paralysis	Lack of confidence Leadership vacuum Bureaucratic Hierarchical	Insular Decisions avoided Change difficult	Efficient operations Focused strategy	Limited to traditional markets Apathetic managers Weak competitive position	Well-established, same technology, customers and competition for many years
Leaderlessness	Leadership vacuum Power struggles	No involvement Incremental change Poor information flows Effective power in shifting coalitions of second-level managers	Creativity	Inconsistent strategy Lack of leadership Climate of distrust Poor co-operation	'Withdrawn' chief executive

2. *Direct communication*: management must rely more on personal face-to-face meetings and telephone conversations, rather than on formal committees and paperwork systems.

3. *Personal responsibility and accountability*: there must be a greater emphasis at all levels on personal responsibility and accountability for meeting the targets and deadlines which are necessary if the business is to survive.

4. *Central control of funds*: this accountability is accompanied by a tighter central control of cash and an assumption by top management of the right to reallocate cash among divisions.

5. *Investment and disinvestment*: there is a need to rethink the future prospects for each product and market segment – in terms of the growth and profit potential and how to stay competitive in price, quality and service often on a lower level of business, and take radical decisions to invest or disinvest.

6. *Expansion internationally*: as growth slows down in traditional markets, it is necessary to expand internationally, sometimes into politically risky areas.

7. *Personal negotiation*: the restructuring and rationalization that is taking place demands political skills of a high order and the ability to negotiate with employee representatives, with pressure groups, and with government bodies both at home and abroad.

8. *Innovation and risk taking*: there is a recognition that firms must adopt and develop the new technologies, or 'go under' – introducing new products and processes and pioneering new businesses. With the above this also forms part of the management of turnaround.

The key problem is to manage the contraction of traditional activities while at the same time expanding new activities. This must be achieved quickly and with limited resources, often under significant pressure from curious, demotivated staff and problems with the media. Turnaround strategies often include the following:

● Mergers and co-operative supply, design or manufacturing/assembly agreements.

● Sales of assets.

● Programmes aimed at reducing overheads.

● Improved systems of cost and budgetary control.

● Value-for-money programmes.

● Productivity improvement programmes including closing old-fashioned plant, concentrating on few facilities, automation, quality improvement, new technology.

● Developing new corporate strategies.

While 'turnaround' is often discussed in connection with private sector companies, it is worth noting that similar pressures have been faced in the public sector. Strategies for change in the public sector may include the following:

● New systems of management (e.g. the introduction of general management in the health service in the UK).

- New strategies and approaches (e.g. the development of commercialization programmes and marketing in higher education).

- New systems for human resource development (e.g. appraisal systems in education).

- Rationalization, simplification, automation and reorganization (across organizations, both public and private).

From what we have said thus far it is clear that crisis situations are likely to have had a long and identifiable history, with clear signals of decline along the way. It is also clear that decisive action is needed and that turnaround strategies include a characteristic range of techniques, systems and approaches. Does the time and resources pressure created by crisis mean that the 'role model' for facilitative management is not relevant?

There are two points to make in dealing with this question: firstly, throughout this book we have made very clear the point that managing change demands a complex set of skills and styles within which both effective leadership and facilitative management styles are equally important; secondly, turnaround management still requires commitment. As Taylor (1983) makes very clear, it demands a high level of interpersonal skills. If the organization wishes to avoid the present crisis and the next one, managers and employees need to learn from the changes being made. The very fact of the crisis if clearly communicated can impel support. If so, the learning we are talking about can follow. We re-emphasize: managing change effectively is not about being 'soft' with people – it is about making demands of them.

Turnaround situations bring the prospect of sudden and dramatic changes. The impact of these changes can create the stresses referred to in Chapter 10. But if managers are seen to be dealing with the long-ignored fundamentals (the fact they have been ignored leading to crisis) then this can motivate commitment and energy for change. Even so, the lessons of Chapter 10 need to be considered along the way. Under pressure, people can achieve a lot, but the quality of decisions and actions can also flag and fail. Thus a careful watch for the signs of stress should be a part of senior management's 'agenda'. In summary, then, even in crisis situations attention needs to be given to longer-term effectiveness by being careful over the process of managing change.

Exercises

1. What now is your assessment of the approach to change adopted by ABF? To what extent is ABF really focused upon mind-set change?

2. To what extent do crisis and turnaround generate special change characteristics and demands?

3. What is the role of the leader in change as far as promoting learning and development is concerned?

CHAPTER 13

A strategy for effectiveness

Introduction

Throughout this book we have dealt with a range of concepts and techniques dealing with organizational structures, diagnosis, effectiveness and the management of change. Throughout, we have identified guidelines, techniques and 'role models' for more effective management practice. This chapter sets out two practical ways of organizing your own application of the ideas covered in the book in *your own organization*. We go on to summarize the practical ideas considered in other chapters.

A project approach is something that organizations adopt more and more often when major changes are in preparation, or are being implemented. Whether or not one adopts a 'full-blown' project management approach, it makes sense to prepare for, and manage, change in the more professional ways we have identified here, always taking full note of the concluding comment to Chapter 8: pragmatism above theory, but never 'adhocracy'!

We now present three exercises which can be used by yourself, your management team, colleagues and employees as part of the planning and management of change. One of these is force field analysis, which we introduced in Chapter 9. Here we will set out how force field analysis can be used more fully. The second is a simple implementation exercise. Finally, we present a self-assessment exercise to help you to review your own personal strengths and weaknesses in this area.

Force field analysis

Force field analysis provides a technique for analyzing complex problems. It 'is based on the idea that any situation can be analyzed as a balance between two sets of forces, one set opposing change, one set prompting or supporting change (see Chapter 9). The analysis proceeds in a number of stages, as follows:

Stage 1: define the problem in terms of the present situation, with its strengths and weaknesses and the situation you would wish to achieve. For example, in International Engineering, management may wish to achieve contracts with high staff-hour rates and a more commercially focused approach at all levels of the organization.

Stage 2: identify the forces working for and against your desired changes. They can be based on people, resources, time, external factors, corporate culture. Draw a force field diagram.

Stage 3: underline the forces that you believe to be most important. For each force opposing change list the actions you could take to reduce the strength of this force. For each prompting force list the actions you could take to exploit or build upon this force.

Stage 4: agree on those actions which appear most likely to help solve the problem of achieving change. Identify the resources you will need. Identify how those resources can be obtained.

Again, taking International Engineering as an example, designing and implementing a new performance appraisal system will help to support moves to a more commercially orientated culture, but it will take time. The first set of action required involves restructuring the organization to achieve a more effective input of marketing, engineering and project engineering into the organization's top management. This can then be supported by a new appraisal system.

The implementation exercise

This exercise comprises two checklists (Tables 13.1 and 13.2), which are designed to help you think about aspects of the organization which might help or hinder the implementation of change. Please complete the two checklists by focusing on a significant organizational change in which you have been or are now involved.

In the exercise above the two checklists each deal with five areas. For each area there are potential problems dealt with by the checklist. Below are set out these problems and *some* possible solutions.

Problems and solutions

Checklist 1: readiness for change

Company 'track record' of changes (questions 1–3)

The potential problems are:

1. Have past changes met with resistance?

2. Were past changes poorly understood?

3. Are employees too cautious?

Table 13.I ● Questionnaire 1

Checklist 1: Readiness for change

Please tick the appropriate statement.

1. In the past, new policies or systems introduced by management have been:

   Seen as meeting employee's needs

2. Employees may be best described as:

   Innovative

3. The most recent and widely known change in the organization is viewed as:

   A success

4. Expectations of what change will lead to are:

   Consistent throughout the organization

5. What people directly affected by the changes can tell you about the organization's business or strategic plan:

   A full description

6. Outcomes of the change have been:

   Specified in detail

7. Present work procedures to be affected by the change are seen as needing:

   Major change

8. The problems to be dealt with by the changes were first raised by:

   The people directly involved

9. The proposed change is viewed by end-users as:

   Crucial to the organization's future

10. Top management support for the proposed change is:

    Enthusiastic

11. Top management have:

    Committed significant resources to the changes

12. The management performance appraisal and review process is:

    An important part of management development

13. The proposed change deals with issues of relevance to the business plan

    Directly

14. The proposed change:

    Makes jobs more rewarding financially and otherwise

15. The proposed change is technically:

    Similar to others already underway

Not well understood	Greeted with some resistance	Vigorously resisted
Independent	Apathetic	Conservative or resistant to change
Moderately successful	Had no obvious impact	Not successful
Consistent among senior management but not otherwise	Not at all consistent	Unclear
A description of where it affects their own department or activity	A general idea	Nothing
Outlined in general terms	Poorly defined	Not defined
Significant alteration	Minor improvement	No change
First-line management and supervision	Senior management	Outside consultants
Generally beneficial to the organization	Largely a matter of procedure	Beneficial only to part of the organization
Limited	Minimal	Unclear
Expect the change to be implemented from existing resources	Have withheld resources	Have not planned the resources needed
A helpful problem-solving process	Routine	An obstacle to improvement
Partly	Only indirectly	Not at all
Makes jobs easier and more satisfying	Replaces old tasks and skills with new ones	Makes jobs harder
Similar to others undertaken in the recent past	Novel	Technically unclear

Table 13.2 ● Questionnaire 2

Checklist 2: Managing change

Please tick the appropriate statement.

1.	The implementation plan provides:	Clear targets
2.	The likelihood of project deadlines being met is:	High
3.	Day-to-day control of implementation is being managed by:	One specific person
4.	Implementation begins in:	One small work area or department
5.	The plan is being introduced:	Almost 'overnight'
6.	Those involved initially were selected:	Because they were flexible and supportive
7.	Training is being carried forward with:	Outside training only
8.	Training is designed to:	Solve problems with the new system
9.	Training involves:	Only key end-users or those affected
10.	Implementation of the change will:	Allow people full control of the tasks they perform
11.	Managers discuss changes with users and others:	To develop the plans for change
12.	Implementation has:	Built-in incentives and rewards
13.	Benefits will occur:	Immediately
14.	Direct benefits will be:	Clearly apparent to users
15.	Effects will be:	Measurable in quantitative terms
16.	During change, people need to put in:	Very considerable effort, skill and extra work
17.	Management provide people with:	Excellent support
18.	People experience:	High levels of pressure or stress during change

Acceptable targets	Broad objectives	No targets
Moderate	Low	Non-existent
Several people involved	No specific individual	Not sure
A number of units	A major department or division	Throughout the organization
Rapidly	Gradually	Very slowly
Because they were very committed to the organization	Because they most needed change	No reason
Specially designed session in-house plus outside training	Technical or user manuals	Not at all
Involve the user's experience	Cater for a wide range of audiences	Take no account of users
Everyone affected	Does not involve end-users	No training provided
Help people better control the tasks they do	Mean that tasks are controlled by the 'system' or the technology	Control the people performing the tasks
To get ideas and feedback on implementation	To keep them informed	To control progress
Provision for some recognition of success	No specific incentives	Problems for the people using the system
Quickly	Within a year of implementation	Over a year following implementation
Apparent only to managers	Apparent only to top managers	Only indirect benefits
Measurable only as 'ratings'	Largely anecdotal	Not clear
Considerable effort, skill and extra work	Some extra effort, skill and work	No extra effort, skill or work
Good support	Limited support	No support
Considerable pressure or stress during change	Some pressure or stress during change	No pressure or stress

4. Did recently introduced changes have limited or little success?

The solutions are:

1. Keep everyone informed by making information available, explaining plans clearly and allowing access to management for questions and clarification.

2. Ensure that change is solid realistically by making a practical case for it. Explain change in terms which the employee will see as relevant and acceptable. Show how change fits business needs and plans. Spend time and effort on presentations.

3. Prepare carefully by making a full organizational diagnosis, spending time with people and groups, building trust, understanding and support.

4. Involve people by getting feedback on proposals, getting people to fill out the checklists, discussing the data from these checklists.

5. Start small and successful by piloting, with a receptive group of employees, in departments with a successful track record. Implement changes in clear phases.

6. Plan for success by starting with things that can give a quick and positive pay-off. Publicize early success. Provide positive feedback to those involved in success.

Expectations of change (questions 4–6)

The potential problems are:

1. Do different people hold different ideas about the change?

2. Do people know what to expect?

3. Are objectives clearly defined?

The solutions are:

1. Clarify benefits of changes by emphasizing benefits to those involved, i.e. to the company.

2. Minimize surprises by specifying all assumptions about the change. Focus on outcomes. Identify potential problems.

3. Communicate plans by being specific in *terms* that are familiar to the different groups of employees. Communicate periodically and through various media. Ask for feedback. Do not suppress negative views but listen to them carefully and deal with them openly.

Who 'owns' the problem or the idea for change? (questions 7–9)

The potential problems are:

1. Are the procedures, systems, departments, products, services involved seen to be a problem?

2. Was the change planned or introduced by top management or staff departments?

3. Is the change viewed as a matter of procedure?

The solutions are:

1. Specify plans in terms that people understand. Ensure that employees' problems are addressed explicitly as part of the change. Arrange for visible outcomes.

2. Clarify employees' views by exploring their concerns about the changes and examining impact on the day-to-day routines.

3. Present a clear case by specifying who wants change and why. Explain longer-term advantages. Identify common benefits. Present potential problems clearly. Listen to problems.

Top management support (questions 10–12)

The potential problems are:

1. Does top management support the change?
2. Will top management provide resources?
3. Is the management performance appraisal process an obstacle to change?

The solutions are:

1. Build a power base by becoming the expert in the problems involved. Understand top management concerns. Develop informational and formal support. Develop a strong and polished presentation in top management language.
2. Develop clear objectives and plans by establishing a clear timetable. Set up review processes to be supportive. Bring in top management and middle management to the review process. Focus meetings on specific outcomes and specific problems.

Acceptability of change (questions 13–15)

The potential problems are:

1. Does the planned change fit other plans?
2. Is there a clear sense of direction?
3. Does the proposed change place greater demands on people?
4. Does the change involve new technology, products/services, expertise?

The solutions are:

1. Identify relevance of change to plans by reviewing plans and specifying how change fits. Incorporate changes into on-going developments. If possible, frame changes in terms of the organization's style.
2. Clarify plans for change by communicating simply and openly.
3. Implement with flexible or adaptable people, people familiar with some or all of the change, in a part of the business where there are strong supporters for change. Recognize why people support change (career, rewards, company politics).
4. Do not oversell change by being adamant about conflicts with present practices. Encourage discussion of these conflicts.

Checklist 2: managing change

Clarifying plans (questions 1–3)

The potential problems are:

1. Does the plan identify clear phases and deadlines?
2. Is the timetable realistic?

3. Is responsibility for change clear?

The solutions are:

1. Assign one person to be accountable for change.
2. Define goals carefully by checking feasibility with people involved, experts, other companies, using measurable goals where possible but always looking at broader goals and outcomes.
3. Define specific goals by defining small, clear steps, identifying and publicizing critical milestones. Assign firm deadlines.
4. Translate plans into action by publishing plans. Build in rewards for performance. Give regular feedback.

Integrating new practices and procedures (questions 4–6)

The potential problems are:

1. On how wide a scale will the change be introduced?
2. Is the speed of implementation too fast?
3. Are people involved supportive, informed, prepared?

The solutions are:

1. Plan the rate of change carefully by piloting to learn from experience, implementing for success, small steps and specific milestones. Allow *more* time.
2. Enlist firm support. Ensure that new procedures, products, services are well understood.

Providing training and support (questions 7–9)

The potential problems are:

1. Are we providing specific training?
2. Is the training flexible and geared to people's needs?
3. Are we targeting the right people for training/education?

The solutions are:

1. Clarify objectives of training. Use existing skills and knowledge. Depend upon people as part of implementation. Use suggestions as part of the training.
2. Allow people to learn at their own pace. Provide opportunities for 'hands-on' experience. Make training relevant to the job. Have line managers 'project-manage' training.
3. Use different learning approaches. Respect and use people's experience. Allow people to solve problems and utilize their solutions.
4. Incorporate feedback into the training programmes.

'Ownership' and commitment (questions 10–12)

The potential problems are:

1. Does the change impose controls on people?
2. Does the change reduce managers' (or other's) discretion, initiative?

3. Are those people who are affected being consulted?

4. Are there incentives, benefits?

The solutions are:

1. Plan change to bring benefits by using it to increase personal control over the job (and accountability). Enhance people's jobs and status. Ensure quick, visible benefits. Provide incentives for people to opt for change.

2. Involve people by asking for suggestions. Specify milestones and ask for feedback. Publicize ways in which suggestions and feedback are utilized.

Providing feedback (questions 13–15)

The potential problems are:

1. Do visible benefits occur only over the long term (1 year)?

2. Are benefits visible to top management?

3. Is the impact on cost, productivity, resource utilization, market share (etc.) well documented?

4. Are benefits clear and direct for the people involved?

The solutions are:

1. Make sure that results are well documented, accessible, quickly available, positively described, relevant, achievement of 'milestones' recognized.

2. Arrange wide recognition of success of people involved throughout the organization. Specify how the change has helped the organization to achieve its goals.

Managing stress (questions 16–18)

The potential problems are:

1. Are people overstressed?

2. Is performance declining because of the level of stress?

3. Is there a higher incidence of 'people' problems, volatile behaviour problems between groups of people?

The solutions are:

1. Plan change to control the impact on people. Seek ways of controlling the pressure.

2. Allow more resources and time where the changes are novel.

3. Adopt a rapid implementation plan where people have been consulted *and agree to change.*

4. Empathy – constantly reinforce change – communicate and listen.

Self-assessment for change

Checklist 3 (Table 13.3) is designed to help you review your own skills in the area of planning and managing change. You should also consider the management-style

Table 13.3 ● Questionnaire 3

Checklist 3: Self-assessment – management skills for change

	Where I need to improve my performance	Where my performance is moderately good
A. *Preparing for change*		
1. Identifying problems and causes		
2. Remaining calm under pressure		
3. Involving others where appropriate		
4. Building an open climate		
5. Setting and agreeing objectives		
6. Drawing out the inputs and contributions of others		
7. Checking for agreement		
8. Reviewing objectives regularly		
9. Seeking new information		
10. Presenting ideas		
B. *Planning changes*		
11. Identifying opportunities and solutions		
12. Critically evaluating options		
13. Communicating information clearly		
14. Leading brainstorming meetings		
15. Identifying problems of implementation, resources needed and appropriate priorities		
C. *Implementing changes*		
16. Identifying what needs to be done		
17. Identifying priorities and deadlines		
18. Identifying impact of change on people		
19. Identifying and dealing with the impact of stress on myself		
20. On others		
21. Allocating tasks		
22. Co-ordinating plans and action		
D. *Monitoring changes*		
23. Making the time to review progress		
24. Discussing problems openly		
25. Giving feedback		
26. Identifying areas for improvement		
27. Building on success and keeping motivation high		
28. Building team spirit		
29. Improving the use of resources		
30. Allowing enough time for change		

Where my performance is good	Action plans to improve performance
	(i) (ii) (iii) (iv) (v)
	(i) (ii) (iii) (iv) (v)
	(i) (ii) (iii) (iv) (v)
	(i) (ii) (iii) (iv) (v)

exercise included in Chapter 6 and review your own management approach against the various guidelines, checklists and 'role models' provided in the book.

Having gone through the exercise, identify the main areas where you feel you need to improve your skills and performance. Then identify three or four priority areas for improvement. In doing so you may care to consider the typical problems of change that people in your organization experience, as identified in the implementation exercise. Finally, look for practical ways in which you can improve your approach and style.

Throughout this book we have discussed management skills for managing change in two contexts: firstly, we have looked at the context of a significant change being introduced within an organization; secondly, we have looked at the changing demands of the organization of the future. There is much in common between the skill sets needed in each context.

The future organization seems likely to require adaptive behaviour, will have fewer levels of management and therefore fewer managers, flexible and more open boundaries, will be customer focused, knowledge based, value added will be a key determinant of performance and learning a measure of longer-term effectiveness. Facilitating, team-building skills seem appropriate both to the new organizations and to change in organizations. In addition, however, the new organization demands more interfacing skills, negotiation skills and networking skills. All are needed within the organization when change is needed. Multi-organizational changes demand them. The future organization may make these skills a particular priority.

In Chapters 6, 9, 11 and 12 we examined management issues such as the need for 'productive reasoning', the need to bring 'human scale' to organizational leadership and change and to the characteristics of successful innovators. Central to this treatment is the thought that being an effective manager of change is not about being 'nice' to people. Whilst many of the skills needed are in the domain of so-called 'soft' management skills they are difficult to acquire and to deliver in practice. Ultimately, being 'nice' is a recipe for being ineffective!

Exercises

1. Consider a change situation with which you are familiar. Analyze it using force field analysis.

2. Complete the implementation exercise on that change situation. What key implementation issues emerge?

3. Complete the self-assessment exercise. What issues arise for your own development of change management skills?

CHAPTER 14

Strategies for corporate transformation

Introduction

Any book dealing with change needs to address the issue of transformation. The very nature of our organizations are being recreated. The command and control mind-set has been reformulated albeit not necessarily to empower people. Oddly enough, whilst we increasingly seek to empower people with sufficient information and flexibility to allow them to resolve issues locally, this combines with other pressures in the opposite direction.

Supply chain pressures push the need for predictability in the process. Even a small business can be affected. Thus a small firm supplying timber to a national do-it-yourself chain such as Sainsbury Homebase (in the UK) or to manufacturers of furniture for IKEA must deliver 'right on time' and 'right first time' – by which is meant the right quantities of various sizes between, say, 8 and 9 p.m. on a set delivery day later in the week in which the weekly order arrived electronically over the previous weekend. Similarly structures based around the value-added concepts explained in Chapter 3 are more 'transparent'. There is no place to hide in the value-added organization!

Alongside these new pressures has come a recognition that planned change does not always deliver and that, in pursuit of rapid change and achieving shorter time-to-market lead times, market mechanisms have a role to play in creating more innovative and adaptable organizations. For many of the changes we need it is more effective to achieve change through creating the conditions for adaptability up-front. Increasingly, therefore, organizations seek to utilize 'market-induced' change.

'Market-induced' change

In essence 'market-induced' change is an organizational change strategy relying on ensuring that market pressures and changes are recognized early and that those close to the marketplace are also influential over product–service decision making. Reuters is a good example.

CASE STUDY

Reuters

Reuters provides a broad range of information and news services for global markets. Formerly a TV news agency, it is part of a rapidly changing business sector experiencing rapid changes in technology, merging of formerly separable sectors (print, radio, video, information services), globalization of TV services including news in particular, new competitors and so on.

Clearly there is a need to manage creative people and creative *output*. Like many of its competitors it has sought to create a highly flexible and organic structure. It operates on the basis of 'front-line business units' supported by corporate control, dealing with finance, legal, tax, etc., and global supplies, offering marketing, development and operations support services.

In the business units rapidly changing demands have meant that teams must be built and reformed rapidly. Decision making is widely dispersed and there are few levels in the structure. The demands of the task in hand take priority; there are few organizational rules other than those related to schedules and the technology in use. The issue is that of balancing the need for creativity against the need for structure, schedules, etc. Thus two points emerge from this case study. In rapidly changing markets overly elaborate corporate structures can inhibit creativity and market responsiveness. Conversely, however, providers of information services must place high value on service reliability including availability. Thus *time*, from the client's perspective, is a key issue. Moreover, investment levels are often substantial and this latter point argues for planned change. One cannot justify and manage multi-million-dollar investments as market-induced changes! Thus balance between planned and market–induced models of change is very important.

However, this should not mislead us. We are talking about much more than structures and explicit planning models. The culture and style of the organizations are a much more important aspect for our purpose.

For example, McKinsey, the world-famous consultancy known as 'The Firm', is seen by some as the supreme example of networking. Access to key decision makers via interlocking networks of contacts and shared experiences is a pivotal resource. As an example of the value of discipline, reputation and access, it is a leading light. But still we must explore the point about discipline. What has been one of the oft-quoted models of change in the last 10 or 15 years – the McKinsey 7S Model, which comprises systems, structure, style, strategy, skills, staff and superordinate goals – reflects the influence of the company. The point is that McKinsey achieves much through its access but can only do so through the value it attaches to the intellectual power of its people and built into the consulting models it deploys. Not least therefore, 'The Firm' projects an image of success, access, being 'in the know', internationalism, but mainly value through the intellectual reputation it has acquired. The crucial point is to note the symbiotic nature of its approach. Access is vital and remains a necessary but not sufficient resource for success. McKinsey stays close to its market by networking with key decision makers through the way people move between it and key corporates globally. But its reputation flows from providing value through intellectual rigour. All of this is articulated through the style, culture and reputation of the organization.

As we have seen in Part I, all of the above turns upon two transformation strategies. The first demands that we reconfigure resources around value to the customer and that we put in place credible measures of value at all levels of the company. Transparency becomes a key attribute of transformation therefore, but focused upon improved performance. The second is to make the ability to learn a central resource for strategic change.

Learning as a transformational resource

It is obvious that learning and transformation are part of the same process. In both parts of this book we have shown how strategic or transformational change both involve and demand learning. As we saw above in Part I, the learning organization must find ways of 'capturing knowledge' and converting 'tacit' into 'explicit' knowledge. Whilst the organizational mind-set to create a learning organization needs to shift to one in which we assume that everyone thinks before they act, a key point is the ability to capture and convert knowledge. This point can readily be illustrated by looking at the retail sector.

Here, large out-of-town stores sell groceries and electronics. Stores like Toys "R" Us, PC World and Waterstones (Books) dominate particular niches. Growth in catalogue shopping increasingly focused 'up market' is a feature, as is direct selling of financial services (cutting out traditional players in the sales channel). Telephone banking becomes more important and who knows how huge Internet commerce will become.

All of the above has required increasingly sophisticated IT. This technology allows organizations to provide advanced logistics, real-time inventory control and just-in-time restocking. But it also allows a company like Toys "R" Us to analyze sales patterns in order to identify the toys likely to 'win' in the Christmas shopping period. Immense quantities of scanned data, matched with demographics, through store cards, give large retailers key information about the value chain. Thus it is that the design and deployment of IT infrastructure can serve a multiplicity of purposes including that of learning. In a similar way IT infrastructure can facilitate what is known as the 'whole-life' approach to asset management – wherein the full costs of capital assets, from acquisition to disposal, are looked at, measured and managed.

Strategy for corporate transformation

If we see strategic or transformational change as a learning process, then strategies based around Figure 14.1 appear to be relevant.

The figure seeks to show the relevant elements in the process of transformation. The change situation or context will certainly include an environment of radical changes impacting upon the organization concerned. Within the organization we need to be concerned with the management systems driving the organization towards greater adaptability. These will include performance management systems, for example. To what extent is performance management focused upon outputs? To what extent are those outputs linked to key result areas identified in the strategy and the budget process? To what extent does performance management present a framework for market-induced change?

Similarly value-added design represents a set of design principles and approaches using the balanced scorecard, activity-based costing, value chain principles and output models which focus on creating highly responsive organizational arrangements. Both approaches require an external focus and good change management skills.

These management systems can be complemented by diagnostic tools and techniques included in this book, not least because the use of these tools and techniques will help us to develop our management systems to cope better with the radical environmental changes to which we have referred. These elements taken together leave us with some capacity to implement transformation. In broad terms we look at this in terms of four main elements in an implementation index:

1. Critical mass of support.

2. Problem-solving orientation.

3. Programme management skills.

4. Clarity of strategic focus.

If these elements are positive, the conditions are more likely to be conducive to strategic change.

Figure 14.1 Building blocks for corporate transformation

In our view for too long the discussion of change has been hijacked by those arguing that it was a behavioural issue. If only we could deal with the people issue in change, all would be well. Our view is that this is dangerously misleading. If people need to see changes as relevant and critical before they commit themselves – and that appears to be a non-controversial point – then strategic or transformational change has an important cognitive component. If 'mind-set' change is a vital component then the same point holds.

'Mind-set' change implies paradigm change. A 'paradigm' is defined as a constellation of values, perceptions and practices held in common. Clearly there is a powerful cognitive component here. If we are to change the 'mind-set' by definition the task is cognitive. Thus we argue that whilst strategic change does have an important behavioural component, no less important is its cognitive component and thus it is that we place significant emphasis here on tools and techniques for analysis.

Anyone who objects that it is the way the tools are used which makes the difference is not arguing against this point at all. For us, however, the starting point of change is about vision – a cognitive process. Someone once said:

> If the rate of change outside the organization is faster than the rate of change inside, the end is nigh.

We see this as the enduring challenge to anyone seeking to understand and manage change. We hope that this book contains ideas, concepts, tools, techniques and case studies which will help you make sense of this changing world.

Exercises

1. Overall, what have you learned about major change through your work on this book?

2. How would you go about change given that learning?

3. Is radical transformation possible?

References

....

Adams, J., Hayes, J. and Hopson, B. (1976) *Transitions – Understanding and Managing Personal Change*, Oxford: Martin Robertson.

Adams, J. L. (1987) *Conceptual Blockbusting*, Harmondsworth: Penguin.

Alexander, L. D. (1988) 'Successfully implementing strategic decisions', *Long Range Planning*, **18** (3).

Amabile, T. M. (1983) *The Social Psychology of Creativity*, New York: Springer Verlag.

Amabile, T. M. (1988) 'Creativity to organizational innovation', in Gronhaug, K. and Kaufman, G. (eds), *Innovation: A cross-disciplinary perspective*, Oslo: Norwegian University.

Argyris, C. (1962) *Integrating the Individual and the Organization*, New York: Wiley.

Argyris, C. (1982) *Reasoning, Learning and Action*, San Francisco: Jossey-Bass.

Argyris, C. (1985) *Strategy, Change and Defensive Routines*, New York: Pitman.

Argyris, C. (1990) *Overcoming Organizational Defences*, Needham Hts, MA: Allyn and Bacon.

Argyris, C. and Schon, D. (1974) *Theory in Practice: Increasing professional effectiveness*, San Francisco: Jossey-Bass.

Argyris, C. and Schon, D. (1978) *Organizational Learning: A theory of action perspective*, Reading, MA: Addison-Wesley.

Bachrach, P. and Baratz, M. (1963) 'Decisions and nondecisions: an analytical framework', *American Political Science Review*, **57**, 532–42.

Barnatt, C. (1995) *Cyber Business*, New York: Wiley.

Barnett, J. H. and Wilstead, W. D. (1988) Management: concepts and cases, PWS-Kent.

Bartlett, C. A. and Ghoshal, S. (1989) *Managing Across Borders: The transnational solution*, Boston, MA: Harvard Business School Press.

Beer, M., Eisenstat, R. and Spector, B. (1988) *The Critical Path to Change*, Boston, MA: Harvard Business School Press.

Bennis, W. (1984) 'The 4 competencies of leadership', *Training and Development Journal*, **38**, 15.

Bennis, W. and Nanus, B. (1985) *Leadership: The strategies for taking charge*, New York: Harper and Row.

Bignell, A., Peters, G. and Pym, C. (1977) *Catastrophic Failures*, Milton Keynes: Open University Press.

Birchall, D. W. (1993) 'Information technology survey', Henley Management College Working Paper.

Bok, S. (1984) *Secrets*, New York: Random House.

Bones, C. (1994) *The Self Reliant Manager*, Henley-on-Thames: Routledge.

Bowers, J. L. (1970) *Managing the Resource Allocation Process*, Boston, MA: Harvard University Press.

Brooke, M. (1984) *Centralization and Autonomy*, London: Holt, Rinehart and Winston.

Bryman, A. (1983) 'Organization studies and the concept of rationality', *Journal of Management Studies*, October, 391–408.

Bryman, A. (1987) *Leadership*, London: Heinemann.

Burns, J. G. (1978) *Leadership*, New York: Harper and Row.

Burns, T. and Stalker, G. M. (1961) *The Management of Innovation*, London: Tavistock.

Capra, F. (1986) 'The concept of paradigm and paradigm shift', *Revision*, **9**, 11–12.

Carnall, C. A. (1976) *Diagnosis for Change*, Henley: The Management College.

Carnall, C. A. (1986) 'Toward a theory for the evaluation of organisational change', *Human Relaions*, **39**, 745–66.

Casse, P. (1979) *Training for the Cross Cultural Mind*, Washington, DC: Society for Intercultural Education.

Castells, M. (1996) *The Rise of the Network Society*, Oxford: Blackwell.

Chandler, A. (1962) *Strategy and Structure: Chapters in the history of the American industrial enterprise*, Cambridge, MA: MIT Press.

Child, J. (1984) *Organization*, London: Harper and Row.

Clark, K. B. and Fujimoto, T. (1991) *Product Development Performance*, Boston, MA: Harvard Business School Press.

Cooper, G. (1981) *Psychology and Managers*, London: Macmillan.

Cooper, G. and Hingley, P. (1985) *The Change Makers*, London: Harper and Row.

Dalton, M. (1959) *Men who Manage*, New York: Wiley.

Deal, T. E. and Kennedy, A. A. (1982) *Corporate Cultures*, Reading, MA: Addison-Wesley.

De Vries, K. and Miller, D. (1984) *The Neurotic Organization*, New York: Jossey-Bass.

De Vries, M. F. R. (1980) *Organizational Paradoxes*, London: Tavistock.

Doz, Y. L. and Prahalad, C. K. (1991) 'Managing DMNCs: a search for a new paradigm', *Strategic Management Journal*, **12**, 4.

Dubin, R. and Spray, S. L. (1964) 'Executive behaviour and interaction', *Industrial Relations*, **3**, 99–108.

Ernst, D. (1994) 'Inter-firm networks and market structure', University of California, Berkeley, BRIE Research Paper.

Fiedler, F. E. (1967) *A Theory of Leadership Effectiveness*, New York: McGraw-Hill.

Forrester, J. W. (1969) *Industrial Dynamics*, New York: Wiley.

Fromm, E. (1944) *The Fear of Freedom*, London: Routledge.

Fukuyama, F. (1995) *Trust: The social virtues and the creation of prosperity*, London: Hamish Hamilton.

Galbraith, J. W. (1977) *Organizational Design*, Reading, MA: Addison-Wesley.

Goffee, R. and Jones, G. (1996) 'What holds the modern company together?', *Harvard Business Review*, November–December.

Gordon, W. J. (1961) *Synectics*, London: Harper and Row.

Gouillart, F. J. and Kelly, J. N. (1995) *Transforming the Organization*, New York: McGraw-Hill.

Gould, M. and Campbell, A. (1987) *Strategies and Styles: The role of the centre in managing diversified corporations*, Oxford: Blackwell.

Greiner, L. (1972) 'Evolution and revolutions as organizations grow', *Harvard Business Review*, July–August.

Grundy, T. (1994) *Strategic Learning in Action*, London: McGraw-Hill.

Hackman, J. R. and Oldham, G. R. (1976) 'Motivation through the design of work', *Organizational Behaviour and Human Performance*, **3**, 12–35.

Hall, R. (1980) *Organization*, New York: Wiley.

Hamel, G. (1996) 'Strategy as revolution', *Harvard Business Review*, July–August.

Hamel, G. and Prahalad, C. K. (1994) *Competing for the Future*, Boston, MA: Harvard Business School Press.

Handy, C. (1983) *Taking Stock*, London: BBC.

Handy, C. (1984) *Organizations*, 2nd edn, Harmondsworth: Penguin.

Hastings, C. (1993) *The New Organization*, London: McGraw-Hill.

Hart, A. (1997) 'Team Midwifery', Brighton Health Care NHS Trust Research Report.

Hellreigel, D., Slocum, J. W. and Woodman, R. W. (1986) *Organizational Behaviour*, 4th edn, St Paul, MN: West.

Hersey, P. and Blanchard, K. (1977) *Management of Organizational Behaviour: Utilizing human resources*, 3rd edn, Englewood Cliffs, NJ: Prentice Hall.

Hersey, P. and Blanchard, K. (1988) *Organizational Behaviour*, New York: Prentice Hall.

Hickson, D. J., Butler, R. J., Cray, D., Mallory, G. R. and Wilson, D. C. (1986) *Top Decisions*, Oxford: Basil Blackwell.

Hofstede, G. (1968) *Cultures Consequences*, Harmondsworth: Penguin.

Horne, J. H. and Lupton, T. (1965) 'The work activities of middle managers', *Journal of Management Studies*, **12**, 14–33.

Hurst, D. K. (1995) *Crisis and Renewal*, Cambridge, MA: Harvard Business School Press.

Itami, H. (1987) *Mobilizing Invisible Assets*, Cambridge, MA: Harvard University Press.

Jameson, B. J. (1984) 'The reception of politics into management development', unpublished PhD thesis, Henley-Brunel University.

Janis, I. (1972) *Victims of Groupthink*, New York: Houghton Mifflin.

Janis, I. L. (1989) *Crucial Decisions*, New York: Free Press.

Janis, I. and Mann, F. (1976) *Decision-Making*, New York: Free Press.

Juch, B. (1983) *Personal Development*, Chichester: Wiley.

Judson, A. (1990) *Making Strategy Happen*, London: Blackwell.

Kanter, R. (1983) *The Change Masters*, London: Gorge Allen and Unwin.

Kay, J. (1995) *Foundations of Corporate Success*, Oxford: Oxford University Press.

Kingston, W. J. (1977) *Innovation*, London: John Calder.

Keeley, S. (1988) 'Managing change at ABF', unpublished MBA dissertation, Henley-Brunel University.

Kirkpatrick, D. (1985) *How to Manage Change Effectively*, New York: Jossey-Bass.

Kirton, M. J. (1988) 'Adaptors and innovators', in Gronhaug and Kaufman (eds), *Innovation: A cross-disciplinary perspective*, Oslo: Norwegian University.

Kissinger, H. (1979) *The White House Years*, London: Weidenfeld and Nicolson.

Kotter, P. (1978) *Organizational Dynamics*, Reading, MA: Addison-Wesley.

Kotter, P. (1988) *The Leadership Factor*, New York: Free Press.

Landes, D. (1967) *Unbound Prometheus*, Cambridge: Cambridge University Press.

Lawler, E. E. (1978) *Motivation and the Work Organization*, Monterey, CA: Brooks Cole.

Lawler, E. E. and Bachrach, S. B. (1986) *Power and Politics in Organizations*, New York: Jossey-Bass.

Lawrence, P. R. and Dyer, D. (1983) *Renewing American Industry*, New York: Free Press.

Lawrence, P. R. and Lorsch, J. (1967) *Organization and Environment*, New York: Richard D. Irwin.

Lee, R. and Lawrence, P. (1985) *Organizational Behaviour Politics at Work*, London: Hutchinson.

Lindblom, C. (1959) 'The science of muddling through', *Public Administration Review*, **19** (Spring), 82–8.

Lipniack, J. and Stamps, J. (1994) *The Age of the Network*, New York: Wiley.

Lorange, P. and Nelson, G. (1987) *Strategic Control*, San Francisco: West.

Lorsch, J. (1970) 'Introduction to the structural design of organization', in P. R. Lawrence and J. Lorsch (eds), *Organizational Structure and Design*, New York: Irwin-Dorsey.

Lukes, S. (1974) *Power, a Radical View*, London: Macmillan.

Macpherson, C. (1962) *The Political Theory of Possessive Individualism*, Oxford: Clarendon Press.

Mant, A. (1983) *Leaders We Deserve*, Oxford: Martin Robertson.

March, J. G. and Olsen, J. P. (1976) *Ambiguity and Choice in Organization*, Bergen: Universitets Forlaget.

March, J. G. and Simon, H. A. (1958) *Organizations*, New York: Wiley.

Merkle, J. (1980) *Management and Ideology*, San Francisco: University of California Press.

Merton, R. K. (1940) 'Bureaucratic structure and personality', *Social Forces*, **18**, 560–8.

Milborrow, G. (1993) 'Management development to the year 2000', paper presented to the Management Development Conference at Henley Management College, Henley, UK, 20 October.

Miller, D. (1990) *The Icarus Paradox*, New York: Harper Collins.

Mintzberg, H. (1973) *The Nature of Managerial Work*, New York: Harper and Row.

Mintzberg, H. (1994) *The Rise and Fall of Strategic Planning*, Englewood Cliffs, NJ: Prentice Hall.

Nonaka, I. and Takeuchi, H. (1995) *The Knowledge Creating Company*, Oxford: Oxford University Press.

Norburn, D. (1988) 'The chief executive: a breed apart', *Strategic Management Journal*, **10**, 1–15.

Orgland, M. Y. (1997) *Initiating, Managing and Sustaining Strategic Change*, London: Macmillan.

Ouchi, W. (1981) *Theory Z*, Reading, MA: Addison-Wesley.

Parry-Jones, R. (1996) 'A vision for the future', *European Business Journal*, Summer, 47–55.

Peters, T. and Austin, N. (1985) *A Passion for Excellence*, New York: Random House.

Peters, T. and Waterman, R. H. (1982) *In Search of Excellence*, New York: Harper and Row.

Pettigrew, A. (1973) *The Politics of Organizational Decision-Making*, London: Tavistock.

Pettigrew, A. (1985) *The Awakening Giant: Continuity and change in ICI*, Oxford: Basil Blackwell.

Pfeffer, J. (1981) *Power in Organizations*, New York: Pitman.

Porter, M. (1985) *Competitive Advantage: Creating and sustaining superior performance*, New York: Free Press.

Prahalad, C. K. and Hamel, G. (1990) 'The core competence of the corporation', *Harvard Business Review*, **68** (3), 79–91.

Pressman, J. L. and Wildavsky, A. (1973) *Implementation*, San Francisco: University of California Press.

Putnam, R. W. and Thomas, D. (1988) 'Organizational action map: pay and performance', in R. Putnam (ed.), 'Mapping organizational defence routines', mimeo, Harvard Graduate School of Education.

Quinn, J. B. (1992) *The Intelligent Enterprise*, New York: Free Press.

Quinn Mills, D. (1991) *The Cluster Organisation*, New York: Wiley.

Rickards, T. (1985) *Stimulating Innovation*, London: Frances Pinter.

Rifkin, J. (1995) *The End of Work*, New York: Putnams.

Rose, M. (1975) *Industrial Behaviour: Theoretical development since Taylor*, London: Allen Lane.

Roy, D. (1954) 'Efficiency and the fox', in 'Formal intergroup relations in a piece-work machine shop', *American Journal of Sociology*, **60** (33), 255–66.

Schein, E. (1965) *Organizational Psychology*, New York: Prentice Hall.

Schnattsneider, E. E. (1960) *The Semi-Sovereign People*, New York: Rinehart and Winston.

Scott, W. R. (1981) *Organizations: Rational, natural and open systems*, New York: Prentice Hall.

Senge, P. (1990) *The Fifth Discipline*, London: Random House.

Simon, H. A. (1957) *Administrative Behaviour*, New York: Free Press.

Stalk, G. and Hout, J. M. (1990) *Competing Against Time*, New York: Free Press.

Steers, R. M. and Porter, L. (1979) *Motivation and Work Behaviour*, New York: McGraw-Hill.

Stewart, R. (1977) *Managers and their Jobs*, London: Macmillan.

Stewart, R. (1982) *Choices for the Manager*, London: McGraw-Hill.

Stewart, V. and Chadwick, V. (1987) *Changing Trains: Messages for management from the Scot Rail Challenge*, Newton Abbot: David and Charles.

Strauss, G. (1963) 'Tactics of lateral relationships: the purchasing agent', *Administrative Science Quarterly*, 161–86.

Strauss, G. (1976) 'Organizational development', in R. Dubin (ed.), *Handbook of Work, Organization and Society*, New York: Rand McNally.

Taylor, B. (1983) 'Turnaround – recovery and growth', *Journal of General Management*, **8** (2), 32–8.

Trist, E., Higgin, C. Murray, H. and Pollack, A. (1963) *Organizational Choice*, London: Tavistock.

Van der Erve, M. (1994) *Evolution Management*, Oxford: Butterworth–Heinemann.

Vroom, V. and Yetton, P. W. (1973) *Leadership and Decision-Making*, Pittsburgh: University of Pittsburgh Press.

Walton, R. E. (1985) 'From control to commitment: transforming work-force management in the USA', in K. Clark, R. H. Hayes and C. Lorenz (eds), *The Uneasy Alliance: Managing the productivity–technology dilemma*, Boston, MA: Harvard Business School Press.

Watkin, J. W. N. (1970) 'Imperfect rationality', in R. Borger and F. Coffi (eds), *Explanation in the Behavioural Sciences*, Cambridge: Cambridge University Press.

Watson, G. H. (1993) *Bench-marking*, New York: Wiley.

Weick, K. E. (1969) *The Social Psychology of Organizing*, New York: Addison-Wesley.

Weick, K. E. (1991) *The Social Psychology of Organizing*, 2nd Edn, Reading, MA: Addison-Wesley.

Wilensky, H. (1967) *Organizational Intelligence*, New York: Basic Books.

Williamson, O. E. (1975) *Market and Hierarchies*, New York: Free Press.

Woodward, H. and Buchholz, S. (1987) *After Shock: Helping people through corporate change*, New York: Wiley.

Woodward, J. (1965) *Industrial Organization: Theory and practice*, London: Oxford University Press.

Index

....

Note: Page references in *italics* refer to Figures; those in **bold** refer to Tables